The Evolution of Retirement

NO LONGER
the property of
Whitaker Library

D1294249

NBER Series on Long-term Factors in Economic
Development
A National Bureau of Economic Research Series
Edited by Claudia Goldin

Also in the series

The Evolution of Retirement

An American Economic History, 1880–1990

Dora L. Costa

The University of Chicago Press

Chicago and London

DORA L. COSTA is the Ford Career Development Associate Professor of
Economics at the Massachusetts Institute of Technology and a faculty research fellow of the National Bureau of Economic Research.

The University of Chicago Press, Chicago 60637
The University of Chicago Press, Ltd., London
© 1998 by The University of Chicago
All rights reserved. Published 1998
Printed in the United States of America
07 06 05 04 03 02 01 00 99   2 3 4 5
ISBN: 0-226-11608-5 (cloth)

Library of Congress Cataloging-in-Publication Data

Costa, Dora L.
    The evolution of retirement : an American economic history,
1880–1990 / Dora L. Costa.
        p.   cm. — (NBER series on long-term factors in economic devel-
opment)
    Includes bibliographical references and index.
    ISBN 0-226-11608-5 (alk. paper)
    1. Retirement—United States—History.   2. Aged—United
States—Economic conditions.   3. Aged—United States—Social conditions.   4. Aging—Government policy—United States.   5. Social
security—United States.   6. Old age pensions—United States.
7. United States—Economic policy.   8. United States—Social policy.
I. Title. II. Series.
HQ1063.2.U6C7 1998
306.3'8'0973—DC21   97-29755
                                                             CIP

⊗ The paper used in this publication meets the minimum requirements of
the American National Standard for Information Sciences—Permanence
of Paper for Printed Library Materials, ANSI Z39.48-1992.

National Bureau of Economic Research

Officers

John H. Biggs, *Chairman*
Carl F. Christ, *Vice Chairman*
Martin Feldstein, *President and Chief Executive Officer*
Gerald A. Polansky, *Treasurer*

Sam Parker, *Director of Finance and Corporate Secretary*
Susan Colligan, *Assistant Corporate Secretary*
Deborah Mankiw, *Assistant Corporate Secretary*

Directors at Large

Peter C. Aldrich
Elizabeth E. Bailey
John H. Biggs
Andrew Brimmer
Carl F. Christ
Don R. Conlan
Kathleen B. Cooper
Jean A. Crockett

George C. Eads
Martin Feldstein
George Hatsopoulos
Karen N. Horn
Lawrence R. Klein
Leo Melamed
Merton H. Miller
Michael H. Moskow

Robert T. Parry
Peter G. Peterson
Richard N. Rosett
Bert Seidman
Kathleen P. Utgoff
Marina v. N. Whitman
John O. Wilson

Directors by University Appointment

George Akerlof, *California, Berkeley*
Jagdish Bhagwati, *Columbia*
William C. Brainard, *Yale*
Glen G. Cain, *Wisconsin*
Franklin Fisher, *Massachusetts Institute of Technology*
Saul H. Hymans, *Michigan*
Marjorie B. McElroy, *Duke*

Joel Mokyr, *Northwestern*
Andrew Postlewaite, *Pennsylvania*
Nathan Rosenberg, *Stanford*
Harold T. Shapiro, *Princeton*
Craig Swan, *Minnesota*
David B. Yoffie, *Harvard*
Arnold Zellner, *Chicago*

Directors by Appointment of Other Organizations

Marcel Boyer, *Canadian Economics Association*
Mark Drabenstott, *American Agricultural Economics Association*
William C. Dunkelberg, *National Association of Business Economists*
Richard A. Easterlin, *Economic History Association*
Gail D. Fosler, *The Conference Board*
A. Ronald Gallant, *American Statistical Association*

Robert S. Hamada, *American Finance Association*
Rudolph A. Oswald, *American Federation of Labor and Congress of Industrial Organizations*
Gerald A. Polansky, *American Institute of Certified Public Accountants*
John J. Siegfried, *American Economic Association*
Josh S. Weston, *Committee for Economic Development*

Directors Emeriti

Moses Abramovitz
George T. Conklin, Jr.
Thomas D. Flynn

Franklin A. Lindsay
Paul W. McCracken
Geoffrey H. Moore

James J. O'Leary
George B. Roberts
Eli Shapiro

Relation of the Directors to the
Work and Publications of the
National Bureau of Economic Research

1. The object of the National Bureau of Economic Research is to ascertain and to present to the public important economic facts and their interpretation in a scientific and impartial manner. The Board of Directors is charged with the responsibility of ensuring that the work of the National Bureau is carried on in strict conformity with this object.

2. The President of the National Bureau shall submit to the Board of Directors, or to its Executive Committee, for their formal adoption all specific proposals for research to be instituted.

3. No research report shall be published by the National Bureau until the President has sent each member of the Board a notice that a manuscript is recommended for publication and that in the President's opinion it is suitable for publication in accordance with the principles of the National Bureau. Such notification will include an abstract or summary of the manuscript's content and a response form for use by those Directors who desire a copy of the manuscript for review. Each manuscript shall contain a summary drawing attention to the nature and treatment of the problem studied, the character of the data and their utilization in the report, and the main conclusions reached.

4. For each manuscript so submitted, a special committee of the Directors (including Directors Emeriti) shall be appointed by majority agreement of the President and Vice Presidents (or by the Executive Committee in case of inability to decide on the part of the President and Vice Presidents), consisting of three Directors selected as nearly as may be one from each general division of the Board. The names of the special manuscript committee shall be stated to each Director when notice of the proposed publication is submitted to him. It shall be the duty of each member of the special manuscript committee to read the manuscript. If each member of the manuscript committee signifies his approval within thirty days of the transmittal of the manuscript, the report may be published. If at the end of that period any member of the manuscript committee withholds his approval, the President shall then notify each member of the Board, requesting approval or disapproval of publication, and thirty days additional shall be granted for this purpose. The manuscript shall then not be published unless at least a majority of the entire Board who shall have voted on the proposal within the time fixed for the receipt of votes shall have approved.

5. No manuscript may be published, though approved by each member of the special manuscript committee, until forty-five days have elapsed from the transmittal of the report in manuscript form. The interval is allowed for the receipt of any memorandum of dissent or reservation, together with a brief statement of his reasons, that any member may wish to express; and such memorandum of dissent or reservation shall be published with the manuscript if he so desires. Publication does not, however, imply that each member of the Board has read the manuscript, or that either members of the Board in general or the special committee have passed on its validity in every detail.

6. Publications of the National Bureau issued for informational purposes concerning the work of the Bureau and its staff, or issued to inform the public of activities of Bureau staff, and volumes issued as a result of various conferences involving the National Bureau shall contain a specific disclaimer noting that such publication has not passed through the normal review procedures required in this resolution. The Executive Committee of the Board is charged with review of all such publications from time to time to ensure that they do not take on the character of formal research reports of the National Bureau, requiring formal Board approval.

7. Unless otherwise determined by the Board or exempted by the terms of paragraph 6, a copy of this resolution shall be printed in each National Bureau publication.

(Resolution adopted October 25, 1926, as revised through September 30, 1974)

For my parents

Contents

Preface

Academics have recently shown a renewed interest in the problems of aging. Conferences have been organized to study the labor force participation, health and longevity, and savings and spending patterns of and policies and attitudes toward the aged. Scholarly articles are being written about the elderly. Large-scale surveys of the elderly population are in progress. Of course, for scholars and policy makers to take an interest in the elderly is nothing new. Many of the issues studied today were debated when states contemplated the introduction of old-age pensions in the 1910s and in the 1920s and when the Committee on Economic Security was set up to advise President Roosevelt on a system of social security. These debates, as do those today, took place when retirement rates were rising and when the share of the population that was older than sixty-four was increasing. They were not then, nor are the debates now, concerned solely with the welfare of the elderly. The behavior of the aged relates to several issues of economic interest, including the effect of aging on savings rates, investments in the next generation's human capital, and economic growth.

The debates on aging have acquired a new urgency. Although in the United States the share of the elderly population has been growing steadily for more than a century, the baby-boom generation, those children born during the fertility explosion of 1945–64, will swell the relative size of the elderly population once its members start to turn sixty-five. With relatively few working-age people in the population in proportion to the elderly, the state will find it harder to pay for the burgeoning costs of such old-age assistance programs as Social Security, Medicare, and Medicaid, which already account for more than a third of federal spending.

Rising retirement rates among men older than sixty-four are compounding the burden of caring for the elderly. When Social Security was first being considered, rising retirement was viewed as largely involuntary, attributable to the inability of the elderly to maintain the fast work pace required by modern machinery. Now that over 80 percent of men older than sixty-four are retired, most researchers attribute the rise of retirement to such voluntary factors as rising incomes and an increased demand for leisure. By examining the origins and evolution of retirement, I hope to uncover the factors underlying the rise of retirement and determine how the relative importance of these factors has changed over time.

The increased numbers of the elderly, their longer lives, and their longer periods of retirement have changed the nature of retirement. The elderly now live in separate residences. They are now healthy enough to spend some of their retirement years engaged in recreational activities and travel. The changing nature of retirement may have increased its attractiveness relative to work and thereby induced even more retirement. These issues, too, are addressed.

Analyzing the rise of retirement requires a thorough knowledge of the data and the numbers the researcher is working with, the use of economic modeling and of demographic and statistical techniques, and some familiarity with biology. But the final results should be readily accessible to nonspecialists. I therefore explain some of the economic, demographic, and statistical concepts that may be unfamiliar to nonspecialists and, wherever possible, use graphs rather than tables to convey the patterns in the data more clearly. Nevertheless, the reader uninterested in the technical details will still be able to follow the various arguments presented. My feelings toward this book, so replete with facts, figures, graphs, and tables, are like those of Thucydides toward his *History:* "The absence of romance in my history will, I fear, detract somewhat from its interest; but I shall be content if it is judged useful by those inquirers who desire an exact knowledge of the past as an aid to the interpretation of the future, which in the course of human things must resemble if it does not reflect it. My history has been composed to be an everlasting possession, not the showpiece of an hour."

Acknowledgments

Some of the ideas in these chapters originated as part of my Ph.D. dissertation written at the University of Chicago under Robert Fogel, Claudia Goldin, and Sherwin Rosen. Others originally appeared in published papers and unpublished manuscripts, including papers written with coauthors. I expand on these ideas here with new data and new methods, correct the occasional error, and polish the arguments.

The research that produced these papers and this book would not have been possible without the support of various institutions. The National Institute of Aging (NIA) and the National Science Foundation have generously funded the collection of the data used in this book under National Institutes of Health (NIH) grant AG10120 and National Science Foundation grant SES9114981, and Larry Wimmer supervised the collection of the data. I have also used data obtained from the Social History Research Laboratory at the University of Minnesota and from the Inter-University Consortium for Political and Social Science Research. The NIA funded analysis of the data under NIH grant AG12658. The Massachusetts Institute of Technology also funded analysis of the data from generous department support, the dean's fund, and the provost's fund. The actual manuscript was written while on leave from MIT at the National Bureau of Economic Research with the support of an NIA Aging Fellowship.

I would especially like to thank everyone who read and commented on either the entire manuscript or parts of it. Their efforts have improved it immeasurably. These include Susan Athey, K. Pat Burnett, Jean Crockett, David Cutler, Peter Diamond, Robert Fogel, Claudia Goldin, Matthew Kahn, Chulhee Lee, Peter Temin, Robert Willis, and an anonymous referee. I owe particularly large debts to Robert Fogel, Claudia Goldin, and Peter Temin, who have served as my mentors, pushing me to do better work, and to Matthew Kahn, who not only read the entire manuscript but also commented on the work in progress as he watched over its creation. The unpublished manuscripts that have been incorporated into the book have also benefited from the comments of colleagues. These include Richard Eckaus, Jerry Hausman, John Kim, James Poterba, and Sven Wilson. I also thank the members of the NBER Summer Institute for their comments on two chapters. I would also like to thank Anita Samen of the University of Chicago Press for guiding me through the publication process and Joseph H. Brown for an excellent copyediting job. I also need to thank Ruth Levitsky for dealing with many administrative details.

The study of the evolution of aging is not yet complete. This book summarizes the information available at the time of writing, but new data are being collected and are becoming available to the research community. These new data will further expand our understanding of the long-term causes underlying the rise in retirement.

1   The Problem of Old Age

> In 1930 there were 6,500,000 people over 65 years of age in this
> country, representing 5.4 percent of the entire population. This
> percentage has been increasing quite rapidly since the turn of
> the century and is expected to continue to increase for several
> decades.
>
> U.S. Committee on Economic Security (1935)

Not only are more men living past age sixty-five in America today than ever
before, but American men have also been abandoning the labor force at ever
younger ages. The retirement rate of American men older than sixty-four has
risen rapidly from a mere quarter at the end of the last century to over 80
percent today. At the same time the very nature of retirement has changed. For
most individuals retirement is no longer a time of withdrawal from all activities
and of dependence on family and friends; rather, it is a time of discovery, personal fulfillment, and relative independence. In the past, such an experience of
retirement was limited to the wealthy few who could afford it. Now it is an
option available to the majority of workers.

That most men can now look forward to a period of personal fulfillment at
the end of their working lives is one of the achievements of our century, but
such a retirement is expensive, and financing it poses budgetary dilemmas.
Most retirees today rely primarily on the Social Security system, and this system is facing a fiscal crisis. Because so many children were born during the
baby boom of the 1950s and 1960s and so few during the subsequent baby
bust, the number of retirees is expected to increase much more rapidly than
the number of workers. If men continue to abandon the labor force at ever
younger ages—and retirement rates have been rising for over a century—the
crisis posed by financing their retirement is likely to be even more acute. To
understand whether retirement rates will continue to rise we must examine the
origins of retirement.

At the beginning of this century few men retired—and certainly not early.
In 1880 over three-quarters of men older than sixty-four were in the labor force
and in 1900 65 percent. These were men who had begun their work lives when
the U.S. economy was predominantly agricultural. When they did retire, it was,
therefore, most likely to be from farming, and then from a nonagricultural
manual occupation, since relatively few white-collar jobs were available. The

availability of retirement income was a powerful inducement to leave the labor force, but, because wages were low, few men had such prospects. Many men left the labor force because of poor health or diminished employment prospects, becoming dependent on their children for support. But, poor health or not, most could not afford to retire. Instead, they continued to labor in pain. This pattern prevailed in the face of their high probability of becoming unemployed—on losing old jobs, they quickly found new ones.

On retiring, men who were well off continued to maintain households independent of those of their children. Farmers would often move from the farm to the local county seat, spending their time socializing with other retirees or reading newspapers. Those who were less well off or those few who were widowers and needed support would move into their children's households.

By mid-century rising incomes allowed many more men to retire. In 1950 only 47 percent of men older than sixty-four were still in the labor force. More of these men came from white-collar occupations than at the beginning of the century and fewer from farm occupations. The availability of retirement income was still an important factor in these men's decision to leave the labor force, but now retirement was no longer primarily self-financed. It was financed instead by Social Security Old Age Assistance and Insurance. However, most men still could not afford to retire because these programs were not very generous and because they had little in the way of other retirement income.

Men who retired at mid-century faced a much more enjoyable retirement than their predecessors. Fewer than 20 percent were dependent on their children for support, whereas close to 40 percent of their predecessors had been. Some of these men migrated to Florida or California to enjoy the warmer weather. Even without migrating they were able to enjoy many more recreational amenities than their predecessors. In addition to socializing with other retirees and reading, they could spend their time listening to the radio, at movie theaters, or touring in their own cars.

Today most men retire. Fewer than 20 percent of men older than sixty-four are in the labor force, and an increasing proportion of these men are working part-time. Most men who left the labor force worked in a white-collar job prior to retiring. A large fraction of retirees now state that they have retired to enjoy leisure. Health, unemployment, and income all have a smaller effect on the retirement decision of men older than sixty-four than they did at the beginning of the century. Income levels may now be high enough that incremental changes in income are no longer pushing men into or out of retirement. In addition, the institution of Social Security may have made age sixty-five, and later age sixty-two, the "normal" retirement age, thereby increasing men's desire to retire.

At the same time retirement may now be much more attractive relative to work than it was one hundred or even fifty years ago. The retired are now very unlikely to live in their children's households. Instead, they may have moved to a community with better recreational amenities, a better climate, and a lower cost of living. Their retirement can be spent in activities that include mass tourism, such low-impact sports as golf, and such mass entertainment as television.

In this book I present an economic history of retirement. My focus is on the evolution of retirement from 1880 to the present. Throughout this period retirement rates have been rising. In fact, much of the long-run rise in retirement rates occurred before the postwar growth of Social Security and private pension plans. I therefore investigate the factors that fostered rising retirement rates at the beginning of the century. Examining the origins of the decrease in the employment of older men will help us understand why retirement rates have risen in recent times and allow us to determine whether retirement rates are likely to continue to rise.

One possible explanation for the increase in retirement rates is rising household income. I study this in chapter 3 by estimating the income effect of a large government transfer—the Union army pension program, the first major pension program in the United States, covering Union army veterans of the American Civil War. Using a unique longitudinal data set that follows Union army recruits from youth to death, I find that pensions had a substantial effect on labor force participation rates. My findings suggest that the high labor force participation rates of men prevailing at the turn of the century arose because retirement incomes were too low to support older men fully and that, as retirement incomes have risen, so have retirement rates. I attribute much of the long-term increase in retirement rates to secularly rising incomes.

In chapters 4 and 5 I investigate several alternative explanations for increased retirement rates, including the shift from agriculture to manufacturing, reduced opportunities for part-time work and nonfarm self-employment, and the worsening average health of the population. Not only has the burden of chronic disease fallen tremendously, but health has also become less of a factor in the retirement decision. An increased proportion of the older workers who remain in the labor force are part-time workers. Low retirement rates among the self-employed relative to wage and salary workers and among farmers relative to nonfarmers are a recent phenomenon.

Increased income is not, however, the sole explanation for the rise of retirement. In fact, I show that, over time, men's retirement decision has become less sensitive to increases or decreases in income. Retirement has become much more attractive because the retired are no longer dependent on family and friends for support. They can now afford to maintain their autonomy even when no longer working. By examining data on the living arrangements of elderly men, I show in chapter 6 that, while at the beginning of the century men would have preferred to remain independent of their families, they simply could not afford to do so. Retirement has also become more attractive because men have more leisure-time activities among which to choose. I show in chapter 7 that rising income and technological change have made the complements of leisure, recreational goods, more affordable. The lower price of recreational goods and their increased variety have made retirement much more attractive than it was in the past. This, in turn, may have induced more retirement.

The elderly have in part financed retirement through public-sector resources. At the beginning of the century Union army pensions were the most widespread form of assistance to the elderly, serving about a quarter of the population older than sixty-four in 1900. In the late 1920s and early 1930s, many states provided pensions to the needy aged. These pensions were later replaced by Social Security Old Age Assistance and Social Insurance. As I discuss in chapter 8, the growth of these programs was made possible by the availability of revenue resources and was spurred in part by increasingly well-organized pressure groups. As the population ages, the elderly may become an even more powerful political force. But, as their numbers rise, it will become increasingly harder for the young to finance a lengthy retirement for the old.

We are not the first generation faced with an aging population and a rising number of retirees. The Committee on Economic Security, appointed by President Roosevelt to draft what later became the Social Security Act, used the 1930 population and trends to predict that, by 1990, 12.6 percent of the population would be older than sixty-four. Although the committee did not foresee the postwar fertility increase, declines in mortality at older ages were large enough that its predictions proved correct. The committee believed that the increasing size of the elderly population necessitated an old-age security program because modern industry had no need for older workers and, other than their labor, these workers had no other means with which to support themselves. It did not view the projected increase in the size of the elderly population as a cause for alarm because it was believed that only modest provisions were necessary to maintain the physical needs and health and comfort of the aged (e.g., Rubinow 1934, 223–24).

Aging had, however, emerged as a public issue even earlier. The first public commission on aging was instituted and the first major survey of the economic conditions conducted in Massachusetts around 1910. Other states soon followed suit. In the 1919 report of the Ohio Health and Old Age Insurance Commission, Dr. John O'Grady wrote, "Very few wage-earners can expect to be able to work until the end of their lives. They ordinarily look forward to a few years before death when they will no longer be able to earn wages. How are they to obtain a livelihood during those last years of life? This is the problem of old age as it affects the working-man" (p. 201). The elderly no longer face the problem of obtaining a livelihood. Social Security provides a safety net for even the poorest of the old, while pension wealth makes many elderly households relatively well off. In fact, many of the elderly now look forward to retirement. The new problem of old age is that the elderly population is likely to be so large that their pension and health care costs may impoverish the young. When D. W. Griffith titled his 1911 film *What Shall We Do with Our Old?* the common answer was to establish a system of social insurance to provide the old with pensions. Now that our system of social insurance faces a fiscal crisis, the common answer is to get the old back in the labor force. But is this likely to happen?

I seek to answer this question by examining the evolution of retirement since the end of the last century. My focus is, therefore, on the retirement of men. Until recently, relatively few women devoted their prime to market work. Women who entered the labor force early in their lives withdrew to work in the home on marrying, and, if they reentered once their children reached adulthood, they withdrew again in their late forties or early fifties. As late as the 1970s, interviews revealed that retirement was not a meaningful concept for most older, married women (Sherman 1974, 58). The majority of women continued working as homemakers. The important life event that they faced in old age was widowhood. At the end of the last century, 58 percent of women older than sixty-four were widowed, and many were dependent on their children for support. Although the fraction of women older than sixty-four who are widowed is still a high 50 percent, Social Security programs have reduced widows' dependence on their children. The experience of future cohorts—cohorts that have spent their entire careers in the labor force—is likely to be different. For them retirement will be a meaningful concept.

2   The Evolution of Retirement

> The past is but the beginning of a beginning, and all that is and
> has been is but the twilight of the dawn.
>
> H. G. Wells (1901)

The rise of retirement began, not with Medicare or the beginning of Social Security, but more than a century ago. In 1880 the majority of men older than sixty-four toiled in the labor force. That proportion fell steadily and continuously, and today men older than sixty-four in the labor force are in the minority. More recently, participation rates among younger men, those aged fifty-five to sixty-four, have been falling as well. At the same time that the age of retirement has fallen, life expectancy has risen, and the average number of years spent in retirement has increased. If present trends continue, those aged twenty today can expect to spend up to a third of their lives in retirement (Lee 1996).

The rise of retirement was already documented by the social reformers of the 1920s and 1930s (e.g., U.S. Committee on Economic Security 1935) and is familiar to many researchers. These researchers generally agree on the trend in retirement rates but disagree on explanations, citing both factors that have enticed men out of the labor force, such as the growth of Social Security, private pension plans, and income, and factors that have driven them out, such as sectoral shifts in the composition of the labor force, poor job opportunities, and ill health. In this chapter I first reexamine trends in the retirement of older men by individual characteristics (e.g., age, foreign birth, race, and residence) to provide insight into the rise of retirement. I then review explanations, ending with a discussion of how for many individuals retirement has evolved to become a recreation-filled life stage.

2.1   Retirement Trends

The term *retirement* generally connotes a complete and permanent withdrawal from paid labor, and entering retirement is often thought of as an abrupt change in the life of an elderly person. This conception of retirement accurately reflects the experience of most men today. Although some men do switch to part-time work at the end of their careers (Fuchs 1982; Ruhm 1990), about 75 percent of all retirement sequences today are transitions from a full-time job to being out of the labor force (Rust 1990). But we cannot be certain that defining *retirement* as a departure from paid labor, regardless of the number of hours worked, captures the meaning that the term had in the past. In the past men may have been more likely to phase work out of their lives slowly. Historians of New England colonial economies found that older property owners remained closely involved in farming or preindustrial enterprises, supervising the family members and others who provided the labor supply (e.g., Fischer 1977). The continued importance of farming and of artisanal enterprises to the American economy may have allowed owners to reduce hours of work and continue to operate their enterprises with the help of family members and hired labor. Nonetheless, the labor force participation rate is perhaps the best simple indicator of economic activity by the elderly.

Readily calculated from census data, the labor force participation rate states whether the elderly as a group are more likely to be consumers than producers. Although changing definitions of *labor force attachment* obscure its precise meaning, most historical work is based on the concept of "gainful" employment. This construct measures the proportion of individuals who claim to have had an occupation in the year before the census was taken. The current definition of *labor force,* initiated in 1940, depends, not on whether an individual had an occupation, but instead on whether an individual either worked for pay or sought employment during the survey week.

It is still possible to construct a consistent series of labor force participation rates on the basis of the construct *gainful employment* because one of the new questions that the census enumerators began to ask in 1940 was about employment and occupation in the past year. Participation rates can therefore be calculated for anyone who claimed to have had an occupation in the past year. Moen (1987) used this procedure to construct a labor force participation series for men aged sixty-five and over from 1860 to 1980, and I extend his series backward to 1850 and forward to 1990. I also calculate a labor force participation series for men aged fifty-five to sixty-four for every year in which machine-readable census samples are available. Figure 2.1 shows that, among men older than sixty-four, participation rates fell steadily, from 78 percent in 1880 to 65 percent in 1900. By 1930 the figure had dropped to 58 percent and'in 1990 to less than 20 percent. Among men aged fifty-five to sixty-four the decline from a peak of 95 percent in 1880 was somewhat less precipitous, falling to 82 percent in 1940 and 67 percent in 1990. Although the series based on the concept of gainful employment yields participation rates that are somewhat higher than those calculated under the current definition, both series exhibit the same patterns.

Questions have been raised about the estimation of labor force participation rates prior to 1940. Directions to the enumerators were often ambiguous and are open to different interpretations. Ransom and Sutch (1986) presented esti-

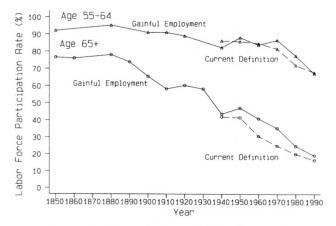

Fig. 2.1   Labor force participation rates of men aged sixty-five or over and of men aged fifty-five to sixty-four

Note: The series for men aged sixty-five or over calculated under the concept of gainful employment is Moen's (1987) series extended backward to 1850 and forward to 1990 using the integrated public-use census samples (Ruggles and Sobek 1995). The series for men aged sixty-five or over based on the current definition of the labor force is from Series D 29-41 in U.S. Bureau of the Census (1975, 132) and from table 622 in U.S. Bureau of the Census (1993). The series for men aged fifty-five to sixty-four were estimated from the integrated public-use census samples (Ruggles and Sobek 1995).

mates of labor force participation rates for men aged sixty or older for the period 1870–1900 that show no decline in male labor force participation rates until the institution of Social Security in 1935. Their estimates hinge on the argument that men who reported six or more months of unemployment in 1900 were retired and have been mistakenly classified as labor force participants. This view has been rejected by a statistical comparison of the characteristics of the retired with those of older men who reported six or more months of unemployment (Margo 1993), implying that the series presented in figure 2.1 accurately portray changes in the economic role of the elderly.

The United States was not the only country to experience declining labor force participation rates of men older than sixty-four since the end of the nineteenth century. Figure 2.2 shows that the U.S., British, French, and German series all follow the same long-term trend. Although the definition of the labor force also changed in Europe, the British series was compiled under a consistent definition because the British continued to collect data under both old and new definitions. The early participation rates in the French series were reestimated using the contemporary definition. The German series, estimated neither under a consistent definition nor for a consistent age group, provides a rougher indication of the true trend but nonetheless exhibits the same pattern. Among men aged fifty to sixty-four, the trends in the United States, Britain, France, and Germany are similar as well, evincing a marked decline after 1970 (see Johnson and Falkingham 1992, 90–91). The similarities in these series

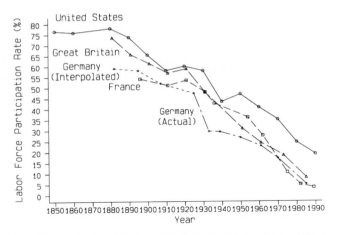

Fig. 2.2   Labor force participation rates of men aged sixty-five and over, 1850–1990, United States, Britain, France, and Germany
Note: Participation rates for the United States are from Moen (1987) extended backward to 1850 and forward to 1990 using the integrated public-use census samples (Ruggles and Sobek 1995). Participation rates for Great Britain are from Matthews, Feinstein, and Odling-Smee (1982), and those for France are from Marchand (1991). Those for Germany for 1925 and later are from Jacobs, Kohli, and Rein (1991). German participation rates for 1882, 1895, and 1907 are Conrad's (1990) estimates based on participation rates for men aged sixty to sixty-nine and seventy or older.

suggest that an analysis of the factors that fostered high retirement rates in the United States can explain, not just the rise of American retirement, but also that of European.

Labor force participation rates fell for Americans of all backgrounds. Although participation rates have always been higher among native-born whites compared to the foreign born, participation rates have fallen for both groups (see fig. 2.3). As seen in figure 2.4, black participation rates have fallen as well, with an especially sharp decline since 1920. Black men had much higher participation rates than white men from 1880 to 1950. The lifetime earnings of black men were much lower than those of whites, and they therefore would not have been able to save much money for their retirement. When the gap between white and black earnings began to narrow sharply after 1940, differences in participation rates at older ages narrowed as well. By 1960 white participation rates began to exceed those of black men, perhaps because the earnings opportunities of black men relative to Social Security retirement or disability payments were lower than those of whites.

2.2   The Timing of Retirement

Age sixty-five now marks the beginning of "old age." Participation rates of elderly males, for example, traditionally are given as those of men age sixty-five or over. This convention is largely due to the formulation of Social Security

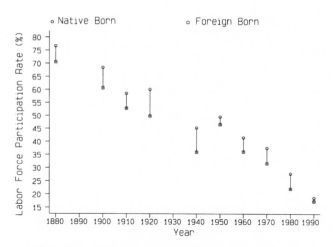

Fig. 2.3   Labor force participation rates of white men aged 65 and over by nativity, 1880–1990

Note: Participation rates were calculated using the concept of gainful employment.

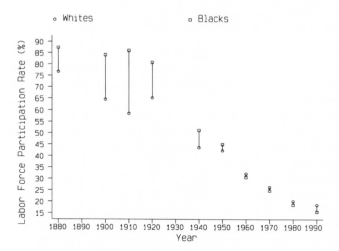

Fig. 2.4   Labor force participation rates of men aged 65 and over by race, 1880–1990

Note: Participation rates were calculated using the concept of gainful employment.

by the Commission on Economic Security. The Commission decided in 1934 that age sixty-five should be that of retirement, rejecting on financial grounds suggestions that the retirement age be below sixty-five and rejecting, as well, suggestions that it be above sixty-five to ensure congressional and public support for old-age pensions in a period of high unemployment. But the use of sixty-five as the age of retirement has a long history and was not an invention of the Commission on Economic Security. After becoming synonymous with work incapacity in Bismarck's Germany in 1883, it was adopted as a retirement age in the United States. In 1890, the Pension Bureau began to grant pensions to Union army veterans at least sixty-five years of age on the basis of age alone, unless the veteran was "unusually vigorous." The 1910 Massachusetts Commission on Old Age Pensions defined *the old* as those sixty-five or older because "the age of 65 is the one fixed as the pensionable age in most [pension] schemes" (p. 15). In 1920 post office letter carriers and clerks became eligible for civil service retirement benefits at age sixty-five. Many of the state old-age pension laws that had been established by 1933 had a pension age of sixty-five. Railroad retirements were also set at age sixty-five in 1934.

Calling all men sixty-five years of age or older *old* should not be taken as an indicator that, once a man reaches age sixty-five, he becomes useless in the labor force. Nonetheless, at the beginning of the twentieth century, aging was associated with a loss of productivity. Several early twentieth-century scientific studies found that people's mental capacities declined after age sixty, attributing the decline to the pathological disorders that accompanied old age (Achenbaum 1978, 46). William Ostler, a professor of medicine at Johns Hopkins, argued in 1905 that all men should retire at age sixty because by then they had lost all mental elasticity. He was not alone in his arguments. The English economist William Beveridge argued in 1909 that older workers lacked adaptability, a quality necessary in a time of rapid technological change. The statistician Frederick Hoffman wrote in a 1906 article that, given the relation between health and age, a nation could maximize its productive potential by having work begin at age fifteen and end at age sixty-five (see Graebner 1980, 29). At all other ages, productivity and therefore wages were low. In 1907 Congress declared Union army veterans who had reached age sixty-two to be half disabled and therefore entitled to pensions on the basis of age. Isaac Rubinow wrote in 1916, "Age 65 is generally set as the threshold of old age since it is at this period of life that the rates for sickness and death begin to show a marked increase over those of the earlier years" (p. 14). When the federal government argued for the constitutionality of the first Railroad Retirement Act before the Supreme Court, one of its arguments was, "It is a commonplace fact that physical ability, mental alertness, and cooperativeness tend to fail after a man is 65" (quoted in Graebner 1980, 160).

Both recent and past data show that productivity does decline with age. Average prices of male slaves in the American South peaked at age thirty-five, falling thereafter, suggesting that the difference between the income earned by a slave and the cost to the planter of maintaining him fell after age thirty-five (Fogel 1989, 69). The decline of earnings with age observed among working-class households after age thirty-nine in the early 1890s and the late 1910s suggests that there was a deterioration in productivity with age (Haber and Gratton 1994, 73). Among workers today productivity declines with age (Kotlikoff 1988). However, productivity has never declined sharply at any particular age. The decline has always been continuous. In fact, the net earnings of slaves were positive until they reached their late seventies, suggesting that the old were far from redundant in the labor force (Fogel 1989, 53). Thus, it is not that age sixty-five marks a discrete decrease in mental and physical abilities. But, because many policy makers believed that it did, it became codified in the Social Security Act and became a traditional age for retirement.

When labor force participation rates are calculated by single year of age, it is evident that work life is being increasingly compressed. Participation rates have fallen at younger ages because of the growth in schooling. They have also fallen at all older ages. The average decline in labor force participation rates of men older than sixty-four therefore does not arise from changes in the age composition of the population. Participation rates between ages sixty and sixty-five have fallen sharply since 1900 (see fig. 2.5). In 1880, 96 percent of all sixty-year-olds and 90 percent of all sixty-five-year-olds were still in the labor force, but, by 1940, the figures had fallen to 81 and 68 percent and, by 1990, to 66 and 39 percent, respectively. The decline in participation rates at older ages has been even greater. Eighty-one percent of all seventy-year-olds were still in the labor force in 1880, but only 22 percent were in 1990. Thus, it is not the aging of the population that has caused declines in labor force participation rates at older ages. Participation rates have been falling at all ages

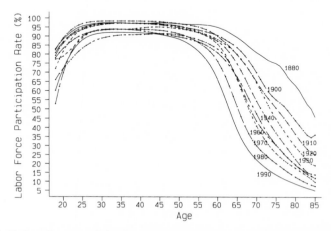

Fig. 2.5   Labor force participation rates of men aged eighteen to eighty-five by age, 1880–1990

Note: Participation rates were calculated using the concept of gainful employment. All years were smoothed using Cleveland's lowess running line smoother with a band width of 0.2.

above sixty-five. In fact, Bowen and Finegan (1969) estimated that the sharp rise in the elderly population above age seventy-five between 1948 and 1965 caused participation rates of those age sixty-five and older to decline by only 0.8 percent. More recently, participation rates have fallen for those age fifty to fifty-nine, with half the decline in participation rates at age fifty-five occurring between 1960 and 1990. In contrast, only one-third of the decline in labor force participation rates at age seventy occurred between 1960 and 1990.

Figure 2.5 does not give us the clearest picture of how the timing of retirement over the life cycle has changed. To determine changes in the timing of retirement, we must estimate the probability that a man retires at a particular age given that he has reached that age without having yet retired. This probability is often called the *hazard rate* and can be calculated from estimates of labor force participation rates at every single age. A high hazard rate at a given age indicates that a large fraction of men are likely to retire at that age.

Figure 2.6 plots hazard rates by age for the census years 1900–20, 1940–60,

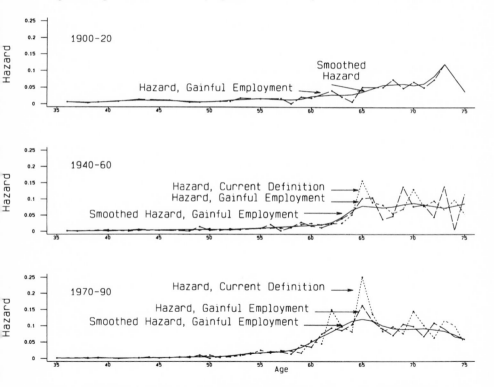

Fig. 2.6   Probability of retirement at single age given that have reached that age without having yet retired (hazard rate) under different labor force definitions, men aged thirty-five to seventy-five, 1900–1990

Note: Participation rates were averaged over the census years 1900–1920, 1940–60, and 1970–90. The smoothed hazard was estimated using Cleveland's lowess running line smoother with a band width of 0.2.

and 1970–90. Between 1900 and 1920, the probability of retirement at older ages rose fairly continuously, and no single age demarcated the shift to retirement. But, when Social Security was instituted in 1935, men became eligible for benefits at age sixty-five. The use of sixty-five as a retirement age for Social Security also led to its adoption as a retirement age, often mandatory, by many private pension plans. By 1940–60 there was a pronounced increase in the probability of age-sixty-five retirements, and this probability increased between 1940–60 and 1970–90. A spike in age-sixty-two retirements first becomes evident after 1960. In 1961 Congress amended the Social Security program to permit retirement at age sixty-two with reduced benefits. Age sixty-two is also a common early retirement age in private pension plans. When hazard rates are estimated by single census year, the spike at age sixty-two is much sharper in 1990 than in previous census years, overtaking that at age sixty-five. A small spike at age fifty-five, the age at which many private pension plans allow benefits for less than actuarial reductions, first becomes evident in 1990.

Thus, although the retirement age was always higher for men in their sixties, it was only after the introduction of Social Security that sixty-five (and later sixty-two) became the dominant retirement age. The existence of a dominant retirement age does not imply that health and productivity deteriorate rapidly after a fixed period. Rather, it suggests that the timing of retirement is determined by economic considerations and perhaps by custom as well.

2.3 Explanations

Retirement requires the individual to have accumulated assets to maintain consumption. By postponing the age of retirement, workers are able to enjoy a higher level of consumption both before and after retirement. The steady withdrawal of workers from the labor force at younger ages suggests either that the retirement income available to workers has increased or that workers are increasingly being forced out of the labor force only to face impoverishment in old age. The belief that the elderly were in need of assistance was propounded by the Social Security Board, which in 1935 argued that "the major part of the industrial population earns . . . scarcely enough to provide for its existence," leading industrial workers to "reach old age with few resources" (Shearon 1938, 3, 33). According to the Social Security Board, older workers were forced out of the labor force because modern industry had no use for them. Recent research has placed more emphasis on the increase in retirement income. This section examines both factors that have pulled workers out of the labor force and factors that have pushed them out.

2.3.1 Rising Retirement Income

Among the most popular explanations for the rise of retirement is that individuals can afford it. Rather than retiring because they are debilitated, they are retiring to enjoy leisure. If this explanation is true, then it is likely that more individuals are approaching old age with the wealth to support a comfortable retirement.

One way to assess trends in the economic well-being of the aged is to examine trends in home ownership. Information on home ownership is available from both early and recent censuses, whereas income information is available only in more recent censuses. Although information on home ownership is imperfect (because the census does not indicate which household member owned the home), attributing ownership to the household head is a reasonable assumption. Chapter 6 shows that the wealthier, who were more likely to own their own homes, were less likely to reside with family members. Figure 2.7 therefore plots the percentage of men age sixty-five or older owning their own homes by retirement status. Overall, the rate of home ownership declined from 1900 to 1920, largely because of movement out of agriculture, and rose from 1940 to 1990. But, among the retired, home ownership increased between 1900 and 1910, leveled off between 1910 and 1940, and then started to rise. The difference between home-ownership rates among the retired and those still in the labor force narrowed between 1900 and 1990 until, by 1990, there was virtually no difference. The narrowing of home-ownership differentials by retirement status suggests that the retired have increasingly been able to maintain the consumption levels enjoyed by those still in the labor force.

Although most early censuses did not provide wealth or income information, the censuses of 1850, 1860, and 1870 provided information on either real estate wealth, personal assets, or both. These censuses show that the old were much

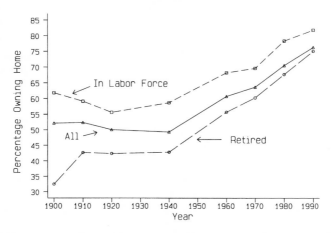

Fig. 2.7   Home ownership (percentage) among men aged sixty-five or older, by retirement status, 1900–1990
Note: Home ownership was imputed to the household head. Retirement status was calculated under the concept of gainful employment. The sample includes the institutionalized, who by definition are not home owners. Calculated from the integrated public-use census samples (Ruggles and Sobek 1995).

wealthier than the young and were becoming more so. Free males in 1850 older than sixty-nine were not as rich in real estate as men in their late fifties, but they still held real estate worth ten times that of men aged twenty to twenty-nine. Taking both real estate and personal wealth into account, men aged sixty-five and over in 1870 were much wealthier than any other age group (Haber and Gratton 1994, 71).

Additional evidence can be garnered from the early Consumer Expenditure Surveys of urban middle- and upper-working-class families still participating in the labor force. In both the Consumer Expenditure Surveys of 1889–90 and 1917–19, there is evidence that families were accumulating modest surpluses at all ages. Although the earnings of the male household head fell rapidly with age, the earnings of children allowed the family to maintain surpluses. Haber and Gratton (1994, 78) found that summing median savings between age twenty-five and age sixty-five yielded assets, in 1918 dollars, of $1,745 in 1888–90 and $3,015 in 1917–19. Mean surpluses yielded about $5,000 in each survey, suggesting that the typical household could expect to save between $2,500 and $5,000 in assets by the time the head of the household reached age sixty-five. The range in the general population is likely to be greater. The early Consumer Expenditure Surveys did not survey the unemployed, the retired, the young, and the dependent elderly. They surveyed very few professionals. The population mean may be greater and the median lower. Nonetheless, estimates from these surveys are upheld by studies of the wealth of older people in industrial states in the mid-1920s, in which about 40 percent of the elderly reported wealth of $4,245 or more.

By annuitizing wealth, Haber and Gratton (1994, 79) provide a rough assessment of trends in the economic well-being of elderly couples from 1870 to the mid-1920s. They find that mean wealth in 1870 implies that about 20 percent of men age sixty-five and over could have financed a ten-year annuity of $231 in 1917 dollars. The 1917–19 Consumer Expenditure Survey and studies from the 1920s therefore indicate that, by the late 1910s and early 1920s, 40–50 percent of men could finance a ten-year annuity of $616 in 1917 dollars.

Today, the median nonhousing wealth of households with heads aged sixty to sixty-five is $19,191 in 1917 dollars.[1] Since the median wealth of an elderly couple was about $3,000 in 1917, the assets of the elderly have risen over sixfold, an increase greater than that in GNP since 1917. Furthermore, the composition of these assets has changed. Among households with heads aged sixty-five to sixty-nine in 1991 the median of Social Security and pension wealth combined was $115,200, whereas the median of liquid financial assets was only $14,000 (Poterba, Venti, and Wise 1994). In the past retirees were largely dependent on their own savings and on their families for support. Private pensions were rare, and old-age assistance programs had not yet been instituted.

The first private pension plan was founded by American Express in 1875, but growth in pensions was slow. Only twelve private pensions existed in 1900.

The plans were typically noncontributory, paid out only very small sums of money, and could be withdrawn at any time at the discretion of the employer.[2] The federal government had no regular retirement or pension system for its employees until 1920. In the 1920s, changes in state laws led to the growth of contributory plans with mandatory deductions. By 1930, 2.7 million employees, about 10 percent of all private wage and salary workers, were covered by retirement plans. The tax incentives incorporated in the Revenue Act of 1942 assisted the expansion of pension plans after World War II, and 41 percent of all private wage and salary workers were covered by 1960, almost 50 percent by the mid-1980s (see fig. 2.8).

For the median elderly household today, Social Security, not pension payments, constitutes the major portion of income. The first state-provided old-age pensions were instituted in Arizona and Alaska in 1915.[3] Similar programs were enacted in Montana, Nevada, and Pennsylvania by 1923, and by 1929 pension programs were in place in Wisconsin, Kentucky, Washington, Colorado, Maryland, California, Utah, Minnesota, and New York. By the end of 1934 there were old-age pension laws in twenty-eight states, plus Alaska and Hawaii. These state programs were limited in scope. States did not necessarily make their programs mandatory. In many states, the pensionable age was seventy, and pensions were restricted to the very poor who did not have financially responsible relatives. In addition, pensions were given only to those who had resided within the state for a period of, generally, fifteen years, that is, a long time.

As first instituted in 1935, Social Security contained two programs providing assistance to the elderly. One was Old Age Insurance, which in 1939 be-

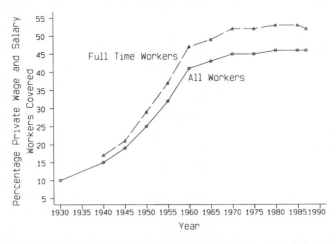

Fig. 2.8   Percentage of private wage and salary workers covered by pension plans, 1930–87

Note: Compiled from Series H 287-304 in U.S. Bureau of the Census (1975, 353) and table 4.1 in Beller and Lawrence (1992, 75).

came Old Age and Survivors Insurance. The other was Old Age Assistance, which was a joint federal-state venture with the federal government matching state expenditures on a one-to-one basis up to a specified maximum per recipient. By 1940, all states had a program, and 22 percent of all individuals sixty-five and older were receiving benefits. Old Age Assistance remained the major income program supporting the elderly until 1950.[4]

The Social Security Old Age and Survivors Insurance program was initially small and inconsequential.[5] One-time lump-sum benefits were paid in 1937, but it was not until 1940 that monthly benefits first became payable. The program remained small until 1950, when coverage was extended to an additional 10 million persons, eligibility conditions were liberalized, and benefits were increased by 77 percent. The liberalization continued throughout the 1950s with increases in benefits, the expansion of coverage to farmers, farm laborers, domestic workers, and the self-employed, and the provision of monthly benefits to disabled workers aged fifty to sixty-four. The liberalization of qualifying rules for disability benefits and the increasing generosity of these benefits may be partially responsible for declines in labor force participation rates among workers aged fifty to sixty-four. In 1961 men were permitted to retire at sixty-two with reduced benefits, and in 1965 hospital insurance was provided to men sixty-five and over. Between 1968 and 1973 benefits were increased in every single year. Retrenchment did not come until 1977, when the indexation formula for benefits that produced an overadjustment was corrected, and until the 1980s, in the form of delays in cost-of-living adjustments, taxing half the benefits of upper-income recipients, and changes in the age of retirement for twenty-first-century retirees.

Most individuals today finance their retirement primarily through the Social Security system. Poterba, Venti, and Wise (1994) find that, for those aged sixty-five to sixty-nine in 1991, median Social Security wealth was three times as large as financial assets and employer-provided pensions combined. Hurd (1994) finds that, in 1986, 81 percent of elderly households received over half their income from Social Security, with 40 percent having no income from assets and 74 percent no income from private pensions or annuities. In 1987 Social Security was the only source of income for 14 percent of beneficiaries (Sherman 1989, 6). This need not be so. The elderly could finance their retirement through employer-provided pensions or private savings. Ultimately, what determines the amount of money available for retirement is income. The rise of private and government pensions, Social Security, and private savings reflects the growth of incomes. Those with higher incomes are better able to save and still maintain a high consumption standard while working. Pension and, to a lesser extent, Social Security benefits are determined by past wages. Individuals may simply have substituted away from other forms of savings (see, e.g., Ippolito 1986). After all, why keep money in a savings vehicle whose earnings are subject to taxation? But the form that workers' savings take does matter for retirement decisions. The growth of private and government pensions undoubtedly made savings more convenient and efficient and provided tax incentives for saving for old age. The first cohorts to collect Social Security benefits received unexpected retirement windfalls. In addition, both Social Security and most private pension plans incorporate substantial financial incentives to retire early. The incentives provided by firm pension plans are far greater than those provided by Social Security benefits. Workers who retire later do so under less advantageous conditions. In fact, the empirical estimates discussed below suggest that the magnitude of the effect of a dollar in private pension wealth is very different from that of a dollar in Social Security wealth, which in turn is very different from that of a dollar in asset holdings.

The financial incentives toward retirement incorporated in Social Security and private pension plans come in two forms. The wealth provided by Social Security and private pension plans encourages more retirement. But how benefits accumulate matters. Under Social Security, workers who retire after sixty-five do not receive an actuarially fair increase in benefits to account for the reduction in the number of years that they will be collecting benefits. Because Social Security accrual is a small proportion of wage earnings for high-wage workers but a significant proportion for low-wage workers, the inducement to leave the labor force at age sixty-five is inversely related to wage earnings. Because higher-paid workers are more likely to be covered by private pension programs, they are more likely to be affected by the work disincentives of private pension programs. The typical formulas used in determining firm pension benefits encourage continued employment until a given age, generally between fifty-five and sixty, and then provide incentives to leave the firm because the annual additions to retirement wealth are reduced or even negative. In most firms the addition to retirement wealth after age sixty-five is negative.

Estimates of the effect of private pensions on labor supply are typically large. For example, Stock and Wise (1990) estimate that raising the early retirement age from fifty-five to sixty would reduce the number of employees who are retired by age sixty by 35 percent.[6] Nonetheless, there is considerable disagreement about the overall effect of pensions on retirement trends. Anderson, Gustman, and Steinmeier (1997) attribute about a quarter of the trend toward earlier retirement by men in their early sixties from 1970 to the mid-1980s to the combined effects of private pensions and Social Security. One problem in trying to identify the effect of pensions is that nationally representative data cannot be used to draw inferences about labor supply behavior because they lack detailed pension plan information. But firm data tell us only whether a worker leaves the firm, not whether he withdraws from the labor force. An additional difficulty is that, if firms shape pensions to suit the tastes of workers, researchers may overestimate the effect of pension incentives on retirement. Finally, models that incorporate pension accrual patterns into the retirement decision may incorrectly assume that the exact details of pension plans and the complex calculation of accrual are fully understood by both workers and managers.

The accrual patterns of private pensions that provide incentives to retire at specific ages cannot explain why so many men retire at ages sixty-two and sixty-five. The economic inducements to retire at sixty-five, instead of sixty-four or sixty-six, are relatively small (Lumsdaine, Stock, and Wise 1996). Pension accrual patterns are an even less likely explanation for the increase in retirements at age sixty-two. Kotlikoff and Wise (1987) found that only 2 percent of the 988 pension plans that they surveyed exhibited any large change in pension accrual that would induce extra retirement at sixty-two. The availability of Social Security benefits may explain why so many men retire at sixty-two. If workers are liquidity constrained, they will retire only on becoming eligible to receive Social Security benefits.

Estimates of the effect of Social Security on labor supply tend to be smaller than those of private pensions and suggest that the existence of Social Security is an inadequate explanation of recent retirement trends. Hausman and Wise (1985) estimate that an extra $10,000 in Social Security wealth at ages sixty-two to sixty-four leads to only a 1.7 percent increase in the probability of retirement and at ages sixty-five or older to about a 4.0 percent increase. They estimate that increases in Social Security benefits from 1969 to 1973 could account for at most one-third of the decrease in labor force participation rates among men aged sixty to sixty-four and less for men sixty-five years of age or older. Burtless (1986) finds that these increases played an even smaller role.[7] Moffitt (1987) estimates that the growth of Social Security accounted for only 15 percent of labor force participation reductions in the 1970s. Krueger and Pischke (1992) use time-series data to examine cohorts whose Social Security wealth was reduced because of the 1977 amendments to the Social Security Act. They find that Social Security wealth had only a small and statistically insignificant effect on the retirement rate.

The labor force participation rates of men age sixty-five and over, as plotted in figure 2.2 above, provide no evidence that the institution of Social Security affected the trend in retirement. By the time Social Security began to pay monthly benefits in 1940, 58 percent of the total decline in male labor force participation rates from 1880 to 1990 had already occurred. No discernible effect of old-age insurance programs is seen in the participation rates of other countries either. In Britain the first means-tested old-age pensions were paid to people age seventy and over in 1909, but the British labor force participation rates plotted in figure 2.2 show no acceleration in trend. Beginning in 1928, contributory pensions were paid to workers over age sixty-five who had made the requisite number of contributions, but there was no retirement condition. It was not until the National Insurance Act of 1946 that workers were required to withdraw from full-time employment in order to qualify for benefits. But this date does not mark a deviation from the aggregate trend either. The deviation in trend in the German series coincides with the financial crisis of the Weimar Republic, not with changes in invalidity and old-age insurance. Although invalidity and old-age pensions were established in 1883 and 1889, respectively, participation rates barely declined between 1882 and 1895. In France voluntary old-age insurance was instituted in 1895 and made compulsory in 1910, but participation rates increased somewhat after 1910.

Researchers have found that increased assets also have a small effect on retirement rates and, for an equal discounted present value of wealth, a smaller effect than Social Security. Hurd and Boskin (1984) find that, although workers in the highest asset quartile retire more frequently, variation in retirement probability with assets is small. Hausman and Wise (1985) find that, on average, an extra $10,000 in liquid assets leads to only a 0.16 percent increase in the probability of retirement. Diamond and Hausman (1984) find that, on average, an extra $1,000 in wealth reduces time until retirement by 6 percent, whereas an extra $1,000 in Social Security wealth reduces time until retirement by about 15 percent. The observed effect of assets on retirement may be relatively small because, in contrast to Social Security wealth, assets holdings are more likely to be accurately predicted by individuals. That many Social Security increases were unexpected may have induced more retirements. Alternatively, assets may have little effect on the labor force participation decision because asset holdings are relatively small. A survey by Merrill Lynch ("Employees Need to Save More Money for Retirement" 1994) reported that only 61 percent of preretirees had savings and investments apart from an employer-sponsored pension plan.

The empirical evidence on the role of rising retirement income has been mixed. One problem has been that most research on the subject has used cross-sectional data for the period after the 1960s even though the labor force participation rates of older men have been declining since 1880. For men age sixty-five and over, 70 percent of the decline in participation rates occurred before 1960. If we are to understand the long-term trend, we cannot apply cross-sectional estimates from the period after the 1960s, when retirement rates were already high, to the past. In chapter 3 I therefore use data from 1900 and 1910 on Union army veterans receiving Union army pensions, data that allow me to examine the effect of the first major pension program in the United States.

In chapter 3 I argue that, at the beginning of the century, increased wealth had a substantial effect on retirement. This implies that rising incomes could account for much of the rise in retirement since 1880. But increasing incomes cannot be the only explanation. In chapter 3 I also show that the responsiveness of retirement to income has decreased, suggesting that the role of other factors—such as declining health, sectoral shifts in the economy, technological change, or an increased demand for retirement because it has become relatively more attractive and inexpensive—must be investigated.

2.3.2   Pushing Out the Old

The notion that older men were pushed out of the labor force by such factors as declining health, increased unemployment, sectoral shifts in the economy, and technological change has a long history. Early twentieth-century writers on the old argued that technological change in manufacturing was forcing older men out of the labor force. Machinery was increasingly operated at such fast speeds that older workers could not keep pace and were relegated to the "industrial scrap heap." They were condemned to be casual laborers or county charges because no firm would hire them. A manager interviewed by the Lynds in their study of Middletown in 1924 claimed that "in production work 40 to 45 is the age limit because of the speed needed in work" (Lynd and Lynd 1929, 33). The U.S. Committee on Economic Security (1935) justified the Social Security Act on the grounds that a worker's "advanced age or invalidity renders him incapable of an effective part in productive enterprise" (p. 137). The technological explanation persisted into later decades, becoming prominent in the writing of gerontologists in the 1960s.

But behind the indictment of technology lies the myth of a rural American past in which workers could labor into old age because there were always jobs for old men on farms or in leisurely self-employment. The Lynds described the older, rural world as one "where the physical decline is gradual and even the very old are useful," contrasting it with the rapid and abrupt superannuation faced by industrial workers (Lynd and Lynd 1929, 35). This appeal to a pastoral, rural past was echoed by Supreme Court Justice Cardozo when he upheld the constitutionality of Social Security in 1937, arguing that the number of the aged "unable to take care of themselves is growing at a threatening pace. More and more of our population is becoming urban and industrial instead of rural and agricultural." [8]

Trends in labor force participation rates arrayed by extent of urbanization belie the view that the experience of the elderly in urban areas represented a dramatic departure from that of the elderly in rural areas. Figure 2.9 plots labor force participation rates for men age sixty-five or older by farm residence, residence in a rural area but not on a farm (an unincorporated area or an incorporated area of fewer than twenty-five hundred people), residence in an urban area (an incorporated area of twenty-five hundred or more), and residence in a metropolitan area (either an area with a large agricultural population or an area integrated with a central city). These areas would differ not just in the extent of agricultural employment but also in the degree of self-employment. In 1910, 24 percent of older workers not living on a farm but living in a rural area were self-employed, as opposed to 19 percent in urban areas and 17 percent in metropolitan areas.

Labor force participation rates were falling for all men after 1880 regardless of residence, as figure 2.9 shows. Although the 1880–1940 decline was especially pronounced in metropolitan areas, there were declines in rural areas and among farm residents as well. When an aggregate participation rate is calculated for both farm residents and rural, nonfarm residents, this overall participation rate is higher than that observed in urban areas. The early social reformers' idealized view of rural employment might explain the difference in levels, but it cannot explain the trend common to both rural and urban areas.

One further aspect of the data presented in figure 2.9 must be mentioned. It

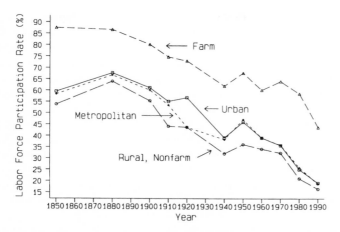

Fig. 2.9   Labor force participation rates for men aged sixty-five and over, by extent of urbanization, 1850–1990

Note: A rural area is defined as an unincorporated area or an incorporated area of fewer than 2,500 people, whereas an urban area is defined as an incorporated area of 2,500 or more people. After 1940 the definition of metropolitan areas varies slightly from year to year but basically covers areas with either large nonagricultural populations or areas integrated with a central city. Estimates of participation rates in rural, nonfarm, and urban areas are based on the current definition of the labor force from published census volumes and have been adjusted to account for differences in participation rates under the current definition and under the concept of gainful employment. All other labor force participation rates were estimated from the integrated public-use census samples (Ruggles and Sobek 1995) using the concept of gainful employment.

appears that men living on farms had remarkably high labor force participation rates—87 percent in 1880 and 62 percent in 1940, compared to those of non-farm men of 66 and 37 percent, respectively. Fifty percent of men age sixty-five and over were living on a farm in 1880, but by 1940 the proportion had fallen to 22 percent. Had the percentage of older men remained 50 percent in 1940, overall participation rates would have fallen by only 24 percent instead of 43 percent. This type of calculation has led researchers to argue that the fall in the participation rates of the elderly prior to 1940 was largely driven by the decline of farming. Farmers, however, were actually no less likely to retire than nonfarmers. Because they often retired by leaving their farms, the data cannot be used in this manner. This point will be taken up again in chapter 5.

Older men may have been pushed out of the labor force because, once they became unemployed, firms may have been unlikely to hire them. Wentworth (1945) reported that over half the individuals surveyed between 1941 and 1942 cited being laid off as their reason for retirement. The U.S. Committee on Economic Security (1935, 146) noted: "Once unemployed, older workers tend to have great difficulty in finding reemployment and their chances of reabsorption become less and less with advancing age." Slichter (1919, 155) wrote that "the loss of his job by a semi-skilled worker over 40 or 50 is likely to mean a permanent reduction in his earnings capacity, for he will have great difficulty in obtaining a job as good as his previous one." In the 1920s many firms began to prohibit or restrict the hire of new workers older than forty-five or fifty. In his ruling on Social Security Supreme Court Justice Cardozo cited a study reporting that, in 1930, "out of 224 American factories investigated, 71, or almost one third, had fixed maximum hiring age limits; in four plants the limit was under 40; in 41 it was under 46. In the other 153 plants there were no fixed limits, but in practice few were hired if they were over 50 years of age." A firm that needs to train its workers would much rather train a younger worker than an older worker because it can recoup its investment costs over many years. Younger workers had the advantage of physical strength at a time when many jobs were dangerous and physically exhausting. They also had an additional advantage. The rapid advances in high school education in the 1920s meant that younger workers had a much better general training.

The difficulties faced by older workers can be seen in the 1900 and 1910 census data. Margo (1993), for example, finds that the probability of long-term unemployment rose with age and that, the older a worker was when he became unemployed, the more likely he was to retire subsequently. A worker's probability of entering unemployment did not increase with age, but his probability of leaving unemployment declined with age. Lee (1996) finds that long-term unemployment in 1900 or 1910 greatly increased the odds of retirement within the next ten years. The difficulties faced by older workers may be even greater today because the probability that an unemployed worker will leave unemployment has decreased since 1910. In chapter 5 I examine the effect of increases in unemployment spells on retirement rates and investigate why unemployment spells have increased, concluding that the probability of leaving unemployment may have fallen because better income prospects now enable workers to reject the first job that becomes available, not because finding a new job has become increasingly difficult. Long-term unemployment could be a causal factor behind increasing retirement rates, but only if workers can afford to reject the first job that becomes available. Once unemployed, older workers will retire on not being able to find a satisfactory job, if they can afford to.

When firms adopted pension plans, many also adopted mandatory retirement provisions. One reason employers might want to impose mandatory retirement on their workers is if they offered wages tied to seniority rather than marginal product (Lazear 1979). Although such a wage structure would reduce turnover, it would lead younger workers to be paid less and older workers more than their marginal product. Compulsory retirement would allow firms to remove more expensive older workers and to offer younger workers incentives, in the form of promotions, to remain with the firm. The outlawing of mandatory retirement before age seventy by the 1978 Age Discrimination Act has allowed researchers to assess the effect of mandatory retirement (e.g., Burkhauser and Quinn 1983). On the whole, the effects of mandatory retirement appear to have been small, perhaps because it has been intertwined with financial incentives to retire and these have remained in place.

Another factor that pushes older men out of the labor force is poor health. One-third of the retirees studied by Wentworth (1945) between 1941 and 1942 stated that they had retired because of illness or failing health. Older men today still commonly cite poor health as one of their main reasons for withdrawing from the labor force. Recent data indicate that health plays an important role in retirement decisions.[9] Some researchers have pointed to increasing morbidity and disability rates as evidence that average health has worsened (e.g., Riley 1989; Verbrugge 1984) and therefore has led to rising retirement rates. According to this view, improvements in medical efficacy have led to an increased burden of chronic conditions by permitting the survival past age sixty-five of impaired individuals who in higher-mortality regimes would have died from acute diseases at earlier ages. I address the issue in chapter 4, in which I show that, not only has average health improved, but health has also become less, not more, important to the labor force participation decision.

2.4   Development of a Retirement Lifestyle

A man who retired in 1880 could expect a very different life from that of a man retiring today. In the past retirees were much more dependent on their families and friends for assistance. The 1919 Ohio Commission on Health Insurance and Old Age Pensions estimated that, in the cities of Hamilton and Cincinnati, 15–25 percent of people over age fifty were dependent on relatives or friends (cited in Epstein 1928, 50), a dependence necessitated by the fact that, at the turn of the century, a time when incomes were low, a large segment of the population had little in the form of savings, the only other source of retirement income. For example, around 1900, roughly one-fifth of working-class households had accumulated almost no financial savings (James, Palumbo, and Thomas 1997). Surveys of the nondependent aged in the Northeast in the mid-1920s suggest that 20 percent had assets and property worth less than $850 in 1917 dollars (Gratton and Rotondo 1991), a sum that could cover about one year's worth of a retired couple's expenditures.[10] Those who had accumulated more assets could not be assured that these were enough because either spouse might live longer than expected.

Dependence on the family is evident in elderly living arrangements. One useful indicator of household authority and of dependence is whether elderly males were household heads. Although there was little change from 1880 to 1940 in the probability that any man sixty-five years of age was the head of his household, there has been a steady increase since 1880 in the probability that a *retired* man was the head of his own household (see fig. 2.10). In fact, 48 percent of the increase in retired men heading their own households occurred between 1880 and 1940. The sharp differences in living arrangements by re-

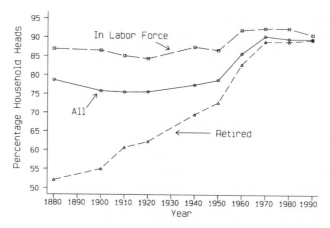

Fig. 2.10   Percentage of noninstitutionalized men aged sixty-five or older who were household heads, by retirement status

Note: Estimated from the integrated public-use census sample (Ruggles and Sobek 1995). The basic pattern remains unchanged if the institutionalized are included.

tirement status observed at the beginning of the century suggest that, in the past, only men who worked retained their independence. Those who did not either remained in the same household, relinquishing their position of authority to their children, or moved into the households of their children. I discuss these patterns in more detail in chapter 6, showing that, while the elderly of the past would have preferred to maintain their own households, the majority simply did not have the necessary income.

The elderly who retired were faced with a circumscribed choice, not just of living arrangements, but of activities as well. Old age, according to nineteenth-century essayists, was to be a time of rest and disengagement, serenity and peace (Fischer 1977, 122). Yeats imagined an elderly Maude Gonne as being "old and grey and full of sleep, And nodding by the fire." Advice given to the elderly in a 1904 article published in the medical journal *Practitioner* was to "lead an absolutely quiet and uneventful life." The old were to withdraw from all work, abandon all vigorous exercise, and prepare for the afterlife (Haber and Gratton 1994, 160–61). When Eleanor Roosevelt emphasized that the major benefit of Social Security would be to enable the elderly to remain in their own homes, she envisioned the old as resting in their chairs, content in familiar surroundings (see Graebner 1980, 200). She did not envision the large-scale development of retirement communities with residents putting to make par on a golf course.

Sleepy inactivity could not have been the lot of all the elderly. Local clubs founded by and for older people sprang up in the 1930s (Achenbaum 1978, 118). Retirement communities were already mushrooming in the 1920s and 1930s. Florida, where initially only wealthy New York families had winter homes, had become accessible to the middle class by the 1910s, when a railroad system was completed. It became accessible to an even larger segment of the population after highways were built in the 1930s and ownership of automobiles became more widespread. Once highways were built, California also received a major infusion of elderly migrants. The first census that provided information on migration in the past five years, that of 1940, showed that, between 1935 and 1940, the elderly were moving to the Pacific Coast and South Atlantic regions. This migration pattern has persisted to this day (Longino 1990). Some of the elderly clearly were enjoying recreational activities during their retirement, but, compared with the period after World War II, this was a relatively small group of well-to-do individuals. Isaac Rubinow could ask rhetorically in 1934, "Where will you and I be at 65? Behind an imposing desk of an executive office, shaping destinies of other people, or in an institution for mental disease? Clipping coupons while enjoying Florida in the winter and the Michigan lake in the summer, or in a comfortable old folks' home, or less comfortable poorhouse?" (p. 243). A recreation-filled retirement was limited to the fortunate few.[11]

Since the 1950s, a much more positive view of retirement has emerged, far removed from early reformers' conception of retirement as protection against the insecurities of an industrialized economy. Retirement is now viewed as a period of enjoyment and creative experience and as a reward for a lifetime of labor, increasingly shorter. Mass tourism, low-impact sports such as golf, and mass entertainment such as films, television, and spectator sports provide activities for the elderly at a low price. Data from the mid-1980s show that, among men, the amount of time spent on recreational activities increases with age (see table 2.1). Work occupied 26 percent of the time of twenty-five- to fifty-four-year-olds, 15 percent of the time of fifty-five- to sixty-four-year-olds, and 7 percent of the time of those older than sixty-four. About half the decline in work time was absorbed by recreation, which accounted for only 19 percent of time use at ages twenty-five to fifty-four but 28 percent after age sixty-four.

Table 2.1   Time Use in a 24-Hour Day for Men in 1985 (%)

Activity	Age		
	25–54	55–64	65+
Sleeping, including naps	32.5	34.4	34.9
On job or commuting	25.6	15.0	7.4
Recreation (including travel time)	18.6	24.0	27.8
Eating, preparing food	6.7	8.6	9.1
House cleaning, repair, gardening	4.6	5.3	7.4
Personal care, care for others (travel time excluded)	3.4	3.8	3.9
Shopping for goods and services	2.9	3.2	3.6
Other	5.5	5.7	5.9

Source: Calculated from Robinson (1993).

The remaining half was spread over several activities, some of which, such as leisurely meals, gardening, or certain forms of shopping, contain a recreational component. Increases in recreational activities with age are observed in other surveys as well. A 1978 survey of 1,031 retirees found that the retired sharply increased time spent on their favorite hobbies or recreational activities. The biggest increases were in active sports, general household repairs, gardening, and travel. Whereas only 13 percent of the sample claimed to have traveled frequently before retirement, 37 percent did so afterward (Morse and Gray 1980, 58–60).

As I argue in chapter 7, this new conception of retirement could not have been possible had it not been for increases in income, changes in technology, and the public provision of recreational goods. Rising income and technological change that has lowered the price of recreation has made recreational goods more affordable and thus increased access to them. The lower price and increased variety of recreational goods have made retirement much more attractive than it was in the past. This, in turn, may have induced more retirement.

An issue facing current generations is whether this new conception of retirement can continue to be the norm. The elderly have in part been able to finance retirement consumption by taxing younger generations. But, by 2029, if not sooner, the Social Security trust fund will be exhausted, and only payroll tax increases would maintain current benefit levels. Clearly, some reforms are needed. In chapter 8 I examine the history of old-age programs to determine what reforms are likely to produce a viable system, given that the political power of the elderly places demands for liberalization on old-age programs.

2.5 Summary

This chapter has shown that the decline in labor force participation rates among older men has proceeded at a steady pace since 1880. The downward trend was evident among many different subgroups of the population. Labor force participation rates fell among both white and black men, among both sixty-five- and seventy-five-year-olds, and among both rural and urban men. A review of explanations suggested that several factors could have contributed to the downward trend in labor force participation rates. After 1940 these factors included the provision of private pension plans and rising Social Security payments, both of which led to sharp increases in retirement probabilities at specific ages. Explanations for the decline prior to the establishment of Social Security have focused on the shift from agriculture to manufacturing. Finally, reasons for the decline in labor force participation observed from 1880 to the present included the worsening average health of the elderly population and an increased demand for leisure arising from higher incomes and from the growth of the entertainment and tourism industries. Although it was not possible to test competing explanations, the steady downward trend in labor force participation rates suggests that long-term factors may be at work.

Appendix 2A

Table 2A.1   **Labor Force Participation Rates of Men Aged 65 or over and of Men Aged 55–64**

Year	Age 65+ Gainful	Age 65+ Current	Age 55–64 Gainful	Age 55–64 Current
1850	76.6		92.2	
1860	76.0			
1880	78.0		95.2	
1890	73.8			
1900	65.4		91.0	
1910	58.1		91.1	
1920	60.1		89.1	
1930	58.0			
1940	43.5	41.8	82.2	86.1
1950	47.0	41.4	88.1	85.8
1960	40.8	30.5	83.8	84.6
1970	35.2	24.8	86.7	81.5
1980	24.7	19.9	77.4	71.9
1990	18.4	16.3	67.0	67.6

Sources: See fig. 2.1. The series for men aged 65 or over calculated under the concept of gainful employment is Moen's (1987) series extended backward to 1850 and forward to 1990 using the integrated public-use census samples (Ruggles and Sobek 1995). The series for men aged 65 or over based on the current definition of the labor force is from Series D 29-41 in U.S. Bureau of the Census (1975, 132) and from table 622 in U.S. Bureau of the Census (1993). The series for men aged 55–64 were estimated from the integrated public-use census samples (Ruggles and Sobek 1995).

Table 2A.2   **Labor Force Participation Rates of Men Aged 65 and over, 1850–1990, United States, Britain, France, and Germany**

Year	U.S.	Britain	France	Germany
1850	76.6			
1860	76.0			
1880	78.0			
1881		73.6		
1882				59
1890	73.8			
1891		65.6		
1895				58
1896			54.1	
1900	65.4			
1901		61.4		
1907				52
1910	58.1			
1911		56.9	51.1	
1920	60.1			
1921		58.9	53.5	
1925				47.4

(continued)

Table 2A.2   (continued)

Year	U.S.	Britain	France	Germany
1930	58.0			
1931		47.9	48.1	
1933				29.7
1936			42.7	
1939				29.5
1940	43.5			
1950	47.0			26.8
1951		31.1		
1954			36.2	
1960	40.8			
1961		24.4		22.9
1962			27.8	
1970	35.2			17.2
1973		18.6		
1975			10.6	
1980	24.7			
1982			5.0	
1985		8.2		5.1
1989			3.5	
1990	18.4			

Sources: See fig. 2.2. Participation rates for the United States are from Moen (1987) extended backward to 1850 and forward to 1990 using the integrated public-use census samples (Ruggles and Sobek 1995). Participation rates for Great Britain are from Matthews, Feinstein, and Odling-Smee (1982), and those for France are from Marchand (1991). Those for Germany for 1925 and later are from Jacobs, Kohli, and Rein (1991) and for 1882, 1895, and 1907 are Conrad's (1990) estimates based on participation rates for men aged 60–69 and 70 or older.

Table 2A.3   **Labor Force Participation Rates of Men Aged 65 and over, by Race and Nativity**

		White		
Year	All	Native Born	Foreign Born	Black
1880	76.7	76.6	70.5	87.3
1900	64.4	68.5	60.7	84.1
1910	58.5	58.6	52.9	86.0
1920	57.0	60.1	49.9	76.8
1940	44.1	45.4	36.1	54.6
1950	48.7	49.6	46.7	51.3
1960	40.3	41.6	36.2	37.3
1970	36.6	37.7	31.8	33.8
1980	27.1	27.9	22.1	23.7
1990	18.6	18.7	17.4	15.7

Sources: See figs. 2.3 and 2.4. Participation rates were calculated using the concept of gainful employment.

Notes

1. Median pension, Social Security, and liquid asset wealth was $123,400 in 1984 (Lumsdaine and Wise 1994).

2. The plans introduced by the railroads were typical. A worker received a pension equal to 1 percent of his wage multiplied by his years of service.

3. For a review of state old-age pension programs, see Weaver (1982, 54–75).

4. For studies of the effect of Old Age Assistance on the labor force participation rates of the elderly, see Friedberg (1996) and Parsons (1991).

5. For a history of Social Security, see Berkowitz (1991).

6. They examined only one firm.

7. Most other studies also find that the effect of Social Security is small. An exception is Hurd and Boskin (1984), whose estimates lead them to attribute all the change in retirement rates between 1968 and 1973 to increases in Social Security.

8. *Helvering v. Davis,* 1937, reprinted in National Conference on Social Welfare (1985, 129).

9. For a review, see Quinn and Burkhauser (1990).

10. Lee (1996) estimates that the needs of an elderly couple in 1917–19 were about $789 per year.

11. A retirement spent in an institution was limited to the unfortunate few. Less than 6 percent of the U.S. population age sixty-five or older has ever been institutionalized.

3   Income and Retirement

> But it is pretty to see what money will do.
>
> Samuel Pepys (1667)

Retirement requires income, whether in the form of state-provided retirement or disability benefits, private pensions, income from other family members, or assets. Researchers have investigated the role that each of these income sources plays in the retirement decision, largely using cross-sectional data for the years after the 1960s. But the applicability of cross-sectional estimates to periods outside the sample range is questionable. Seventy percent of the decline in the labor force participation rates of men age sixty-five or older occurred before 1960. Retirement rates were already high by 1960, and thus only large benefit increases could have enticed those remaining in the labor force to have withdrawn. To understand why retirement rates increased prior to 1960, we must examine earlier data.

An analysis of retirement requires information on retirement status, demographic characteristics (e.g., age), health, a proxy for the opportunity cost of not working (e.g., forgone income or occupation), and retirement income (e.g., pension amount). These are very strict data requirements. One of the few sources of information on the elderly of the past, the census, allows us to relate retirement status only to demographic characteristics, not to wealth. Fortunately, a data set that meets our requirements can be created from records generated by the Union army pension program.

This chapter will focus on the determinants of work levels in both 1900 and 1910 among white Union army veterans receiving Union army pensions. These men were the first cohort to reach age sixty-five in the twentieth century. They also represent a very broad cross section of the population. Eighty-one percent of all white, northern men born in 1843 served in the Union army during the Civil War. These men became eligible for an extremely generous pension, and the copious records generated by the Pension Bureau bureaucracy allow us to reconstruct their life histories. Additional information can be gathered by linking pension records to other sources, such as census manuscripts. The resulting data set provides a unique picture of the life of the elderly at the turn of the century.

The data set created from Union army records provides information on retirement income in the form of Union army pensions. The receipt or level of Union army pensions, which replaced about 30 percent of the income of an unskilled laborer, did not depend on current income or past wages. Rather, their generosity was determined by the pensioner's health. Because the amount received also depended on whether the veteran could trace his disability to the war and not just on the seriousness of his infirmity, the effect of pensions on labor supply can be disentangled from that of health. Therefore, Union army pensions can be used to estimate a pure income effect on labor supply, thus revealing the effect of income growth on retirement and bearing on income effects arising from the Social Security program.

3.1   The Economics of Retirement

Many factors are likely to affect the retirement decision. As health deteriorates with age, work may become more arduous, and therefore men's desire to leave paid labor may increase. After initially rising with age, earnings generally decline with age, thus increasing the incentive to retire. Earnings today peak at age fifty to fifty-nine, whereas in the past earnings peaked at ages thirty to thirty-nine and declined by almost 30 percent by age sixty (Haber and Gratton 1994, 76). In addition, retirement income tends to be lower than income while working. By continuing to work, not only do men enjoy a higher income than they would if they retired, but they are also able to accumulate more savings or increase their entitlements to Social Security and private pension benefits. They can thus support higher retirement consumption at a later date—a date when there will be fewer remaining years of life over which support would have to be provided. A richer society is able to support more years of retirement because, when wages are low, men find it hard to accumulate enough savings to finance their retirement.

Not all retirement income is earned during the working years. Some men inherit wealth from their parents, and today most receive retirement benefits from the state. Until recently, retiring cohorts have received aggregate Social Security benefits that far exceed the present value of the contributions made by them and their employers (Boskin and Shoven 1987). The Civil War cohort was even more fortunate. Union army pensions were given regardless of labor force participation status and therefore both directly increased the income of retired veterans and allowed them to accumulate more wealth during their working years, thus enabling them to retire earlier.

Union army pensions represent a pure income effect on labor supply and therefore should have induced more men to retire at any given age. The question I pose is by how much Union army pensions reduced labor supply for veterans in their later years. This question can be answered with the help of a simple model of the retirement decision. Although the model is so oversimplified that it cannot literally be true, when interpreted with care, it enables us to judge the effect of pensions on retirement rates.

At any date, a veteran can be thought of as making a choice between retirement and labor force participation. The well-being in each option will be determined by the income flows associated with each option, how enjoyable the veteran finds leisure and how unpleasant work, and the stigma costs of not working, among other factors. Well-being or utility when not working can be written as

$$U_w(Y + B + N, \overline{H}; \mathbf{Z})$$

and utility when not working as

$$U_l(B + N, 0; \mathbf{Z}),$$

where Y is labor market income, B is pension income, N is other non–labor market income, $\mathbf{Z}$ is a vector of demographic and socioeconomic variables likely to affect utility (such as age and number of children), and $\overline{H}$ is hours of market work. Then, assuming that the utility functions are linear in their arguments and that differences in tastes across individuals produce utility functions containing normally distributed random taste shifters, the individual can be thought of as evaluating the decision function

$$I^* = U_l(B + N, 0; \mathbf{Z}) - U_w(Y + B + N, \overline{H}; \mathbf{Z}).$$

Although the value of I^* is not observed, a discrete retirement indicator is observed, given by

$$I = \begin{cases} 0 & \text{if } I^* < 0, \\ 1 & \text{otherwise,} \end{cases}$$

where 1 represents retirement and 0 labor force participation. We do not know whether well-being when retired greatly or only narrowly outweighs well-being when not retired, nor are we even assuming that an individual can look forward to a comfortable retirement. However, if an individual is retired, then utility when retired must be greater than utility when not.

The decision function that the veteran evaluates can be rewritten as

$$I^* = U_l(B + N, 0; \mathbf{Z}) - U_w(Y + B + N, \overline{H}; \mathbf{Z})$$
$$= -X'\boldsymbol{\beta} + \varepsilon,$$

where X is a vector containing Y, B, N, $\overline{H}$, and $\mathbf{Z}$, $\boldsymbol{\beta}$ is a parameter vector, and ε is a standard normal error term. Recall that pensions might have two different effects on the retirement decision. Pensions will directly affect income flows, as captured by the incorporation of the term B in the utility functions, and the receipt of pensions in the past may affect the value of N, allowing veterans to retire earlier. Only the direct effect of pensions will be estimated. The estimated effect of pensions will therefore be a lower-bound estimate. Using the indicator function, I, the effect of characteristics such as pension amount included in X on the probability of retirement will be estimated by means of a probit,

$$\text{prob}(I = 1) = \text{prob}(\varepsilon < X'\beta) = \Phi(X'\beta),$$

where $\Phi(\ )$ is a standard normal cumulative distribution function. Knowing how the receipt and level of Union army pensions were determined, we can use this model to identify the effect of Union army pensions on retirement rates. The next section therefore provides a brief description of the Union army pension program and records. A more detailed description is given in appendix A at the end of the book.

3.2 Civil War Pensions and Union Army Records

By 1900 the scope of the pension program, run for the benefit of Union veterans and their dependent children and widows, was enormous. Benefits consumed almost 30 percent of the federal budget (Vinovskis 1990), and veterans lobbied vociferously for high tariffs to continue feeding the federal surplus (Glasson 1918a, 218–19). Even though Confederates were ineligible and immigration increased the population, a large percentage of the population was collecting benefits. Among all white males, 35 percent of those aged fifty-five to fifty-nine were on the pension rolls, 21 percent of those aged sixty-five to sixty-nine, 14 percent of those aged sixty-five to sixty-nine, and 9 percent of those aged seventy or older. The annual value of the average veteran pension was $135, or 53 percent of the annual income of farm laborers, 36 percent of that of nonfarm laborers, 20 percent of that of carpenters, blacksmiths, or salesmen, and 12 percent of that of landlords or merchants.[1]

The generosity of the Union army pension program arose from a number of causes. Like the elderly today, elderly Union veterans wielded considerable political might. Union pensions were a prominent election issue throughout the latter half of the nineteenth century and the beginning of the twentieth. While Union veterans constituted a relatively small group, they were, however, extremely well organized, again like the elderly today. The veterans' organization sent lobbyists to Congress and communicated with its members through local chapters and through newspapers. This organization was able to form an effective political alliance with manufacturing interests to maintain high tariffs and to redistribute the resulting revenue to its members. Because veterans had defended the Union, and because the federal treasury was relatively flush, veterans' pensions had the backing of many Americans.

Congress established the basic system of pension laws, known as the General Law pension system, in 1862 to provide pensions to both regular recruits and volunteers who were disabled as a direct result of military service. The dollar amount received depended on the degree of disability, where disability was determined by the applicant's capacity to perform manual labor. Under later reinterpretations the total disability standard soon meant incapacity to perform even lighter types of manual labor. In fact, men judged disabled continued to labor in physically demanding, manual occupations. Inability to perform manual labor remained the standard in this and all subsequent laws, regardless of the wealth of the individual or his ability to earn a living by other than manual means. Withdrawal from the labor force was not a necessary prerequisite for the receipt of a pension. If the claimant had lesser disabilities, then he received an amount proportionate to his disabilities. Application was made through a pension attorney, and the degree of disability was determined by a board of three local doctors employed by the Pension Bureau and following guidelines established by the bureau.

An act of 27 June 1890 instituted a universal disability and old-age pension program for Union veterans. According to the veterans' lobby, the new law would "place upon the rolls all survivors of the war whose conditions of health are not practically perfect" (quoted in Glasson 1918a, 233). In fact, within a year of the act's passage, the number of pensioners on the rolls more than doubled. Any disability now entitled a veteran to a pension. However, an applicant who could trace his disability to wartime service received substantially more for the same disability than his counterpart who could not. By 1900 men who could not claim a disability of service origin received from $6.00 to $12.00 per month or from 19 to 38 percent of the monthly income of a laborer, while men who could claim a war-related disability generally received a pension ranging from $6.00 to $35.00 per month or up to 109 percent of the monthly income of a laborer. Although few men were eligible, pensions for war-related disabilities could be as much as $100 per month, close to one-third the yearly income of a laborer. By 1900, 58 percent of veterans who were Union army pensioners were collecting a pension for disabilities unrelated to wartime service (U.S. Bureau of Pensions 1900).

Table 3.1 illustrates differences in pension amounts according to whether a veteran could trace his disability to the war and thus fell under the 1862 law rather than the 1890 law. Controlling for health, men who fell under the 1862 rather than the 1892 law received much larger pensions. Fifty-six percent of the very disabled were receiving pensions of over $12.00 and 44 percent pensions of $12.00 or less. That individuals of the same health status received different pension amounts will prove to be very important to my subsequent estimation strategy. The difference in pension amount will allow me to identify the effect of pensions and of health on the retirement decision.

The Pension Bureau instructed the examining surgeons in 1890 to grant a minimum pension to all men at least sixty-five years of age, unless they were unusually vigorous. At age seventy-five men became eligible for an even larger pension. In 1904, Executive Order 78 officially authorized the Pension Bureau

Table 3.1   **Monthly Pension Means and Pension Rates by Percentile, by Health Status and Law, 1900 ($)**

	Mean	\multicolumn{5}{c}{Percentile}				
		10	25	50	75	90
All veterans	12.9	6	8	12	14	24
General Law	17.6	8	12	14.5	24	30
1890 law	9.4	6	8	10	12	12
Health:						
Good	9.8	6	8	8	12	12
Fair	11.4	8	8	12	12	16
Poor	17.5	10	12	15	24	30
General Law and:						
Health good	14.3	8	8	12	15	18
Health fair	14.1	10	12	12	16	17
Health poor	20.1	12	15	17	24	30
1890 law and:						
Health good	8.6	6	6	8	12	12
Health fair	9.6	6	8	10	12	12
Health poor	10.9	8	10	12	12	12

Source: Calculated from the data used in the estimation. The health variable used is based on the ratings of the examining surgeons.

to grant pensions on the basis of age. The Service and Age Pension Act of 6 February 1907 marks official congressional recognition of age as sufficient cause to qualify for a pension. Veterans aged sixty-two to sixty-nine now received $12.00 per month, those aged seventy to seventy-four $15.00 per month, and those older than seventy-four $20.00 per month. Because most eligible veterans were already on the rolls, this act mainly induced pensioners to switch from the 1890 law to the 1907 law; it did not increase the total number of pensioners. Whereas in 1900 slightly more than half of all veterans were collecting a pension under the 1890 law, by 1910 64 percent of all veterans were collecting under the 1907 law, 22 percent under the General Law, and only 14 percent under the 1890 law (U.S. Bureau of Pensions 1910). Pension amount now depended primarily on age and whether a veteran could trace his disabilities to the war (see table 3.2).

The samples of veterans that I use are random samples of the veteran population and contain disproportionate numbers of rural, native-born men.[2] Nonetheless, as discussed in greater detail in appendix A, we can draw inferences from these samples for the entire population. The men in these samples do not differ in observable characteristics (e.g., home ownership, marital status, literacy, and age) from the male population in northern states. Controlling for rural residence, they resemble the northern population of men in occupation and foreign birth. The samples are also representative of the northern population in terms of mortality and wealth.

Table 3.2   **Monthly Pension Means and Pension Rates by Percentile, by Age, Health Status, and Law, 1910 ($)**

		Percentile				
	Mean	10	25	50	75	90
All veterans	16.5	12	12	15	20	24
General Law	22.3	17	17	24	24	30
1890 law	11.7	12	12	12	12	12
1907 law	14.5	12	12	12	15	20
Good health	16.6	12	12	15	20	24
Poor health	18.0	12	12	15	20	30
Age < 70	15.0	12	12	12	17	24
Age ≥ 70	18.8	15	15	17	20	30
Age < 70 and:						
General Law	21.3	14	17	17	24	30
1890 law	11.7	12	12	12	12	12
1907 law	12.2	12	12	12	12	12
Age ≥ 70 and:						
General Law	23.9	17	17	24	30	30
1890 law	11.5	10	12	12	12	12
1907 law	16.9	15	15	15	20	20

Source: Calculated from the data later used in estimation. The health variable used was based on the ratings of the examining surgeons.

The reconstruction of the life histories of men who fought for the Union army in the American Civil War represents a unique data source on a past population. Because such a large percentage of the male population fought in the Civil War, we can generalize from this sample to the population as a whole. Because the peculiar rules of the Union army pension program led to men who were equally disabled receiving very different pension amounts, we can identify the effect of pensions on the retirement behavior of veterans. Because neither demographic nor occupational characteristics nor the lawyer through whom the pensioner applied predicts either the ratings of the examining surgeons or pension amount, we can be sure that our results are not tainted by past fraud. Furthermore, whether a man could trace his disability to the war can be used to identify the relation between retirement and pension amount free from the confounding effects of potential endogeneity between pension amount and retirement status. This is because the ability to claim war-related disabilities or receive a pension under the General Law, and therefore to receive a larger pension, is arguably unrelated to unobservable determinants of retirements. Whether a veteran received a pension under the General Law depended on the often incorrect medical theories of the time.

3.3   Pensions and Retirement

Compared with the general population, Union army veterans retired at a greater rate at all ages. This is evident in figure 3.1, which compares retirement

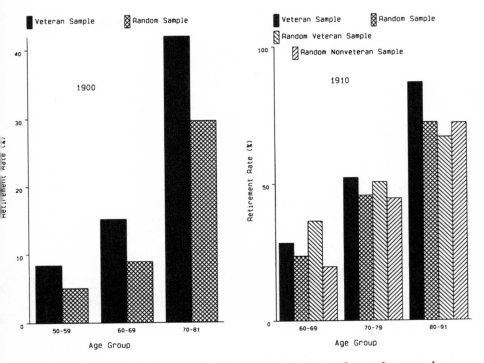

Fig. 3.1   Comparison of retirement rates among veterans and a random sample of white men, 1900 and 1910

Note: To ensure comparability with the veteran sample, the random samples were reweighted to have the same age distribution as the veteran sample and were restricted to men who were either born in a Union state or who, if foreign-born, immigrated prior to the Civil War. The random samples contain both veterans and nonveterans. Because one of the questions asked in the 1910 census was veteran status, by type of veteran, retirement rates for both veterans and nonveterans in the random sample are given in 1900. The random samples were drawn from Ruggles and Sobek (1995). All samples were limited to the noninstitutionalized.

rates by age group among men in the Union army sample with the general population in both 1900 and 1910. Thus, among men aged sixty to sixty-nine in 1900, retirement rates among veterans were 15 percent, whereas they were only 9 percent in the general population. Among men of the same age in 1910, they were 28 percent among veterans but only 22 percent in the general population. In 1910, when veteran status of the general population is known, retirement rates of veterans in the general population can be compared to those of nonveterans. With the exception of ages eighty to ninety-one, an age group of which veterans composed a relatively small fraction in 1910, the retirement rates of veterans are sharply higher than those of nonveterans. This difference between veteran and nonveteran retirement rates is underestimated because undernumeration of veterans in the 1910 census implies that the retirement rates of nonveterans are overestimated.

Figure 3.1 suggests that retirement rates were higher for veterans because of Union army pensions, but other reasons could explain this finding. Morbidity rates may have been higher for veterans, and poor health, not the pension, may have been the driving factor. After all, 31 percent of veterans claimed to have had an injury or gunshot wound while in service. Even those who had not been injured may still have suffered long-term effects from the infectious diseases endemic in the army. Over three-quarters of men paid a visit to the camp hospital or saw a camp surgeon during their service. The effect of pensions therefore needs to be distinguished from that of health by comparing retirement rates of veterans with similar health status but different pension levels within the Union army sample.

I use the ratings of the examining surgeons to construct health variables. The surgeons rated each specific disability, and I use the surgeons' ratings to classify each veteran as being in good, fair, or poor health. Other health proxies could have been used, but the results remain unchanged regardless of whether the surgeons' ratings, the Body Mass Index (see sec. 4.1.1), or the presence of a chronic disease is used.

Figure 3.2 shows that men younger than seventy were more likely to be retired either if they were receiving higher pensions or if they were in poorer

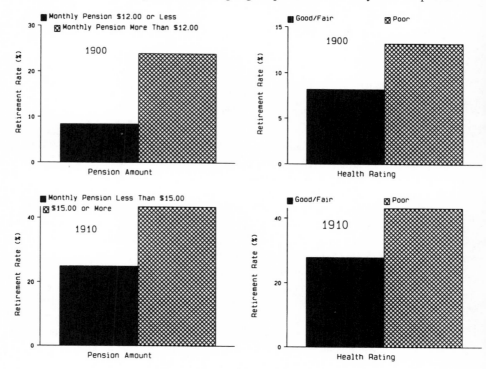

Fig. 3.2   Retirement rates among veterans under seventy years of age by pension amount, 1900 and 1910

health. In 1900, 8 percent of veterans receiving a monthly pension of $12.00 or less were retired, as opposed to 24 percent of those receiving a pension of more than $12.00. In 1910, 43 percent of veterans receiving a monthly pension of $15.00 or more were retired, as opposed to only 25 percent of those receiving a pension of less than $15.00. Retirement rates were about 40 percent higher among those in poor health than among those in good or fair health.

Figure 3.2 does not provide conclusive proof that veterans were responding to increased income. The receipt of a large pension and disability were correlated because of the rules of the pension program. Therefore, figures 3.3 and 3.4 show retirement rates by health category and by pension amount among

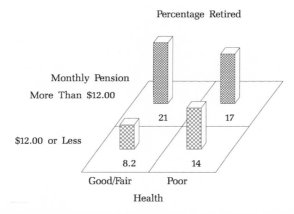

Fig. 3.3   Retirement rates by disability status among veterans under seventy years of age, 1900

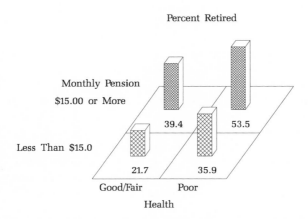

Fig. 3.4   Retirement rates by disability status among veterans under seventy years of age, 1910

men younger than seventy years of age. Retirement rates were higher at higher pension amounts among those in good or fair health and for those in poor health, and the difference in retirement rates by health status is statistically significant in 1910. But, because men with war-related disabilities, and thus those eligible for a large pension, were not a random sample, this evidence is still insufficient proof of a relation between income and retirement.

Men with war-related disabilities had different service, occupation, and health histories. Compared with men whose disabilities were not service re-lated, men who claimed a disability of service-related origin were more likely to have been discharged for a disability, to have been prisoners of war, and to have been volunteers. They were also more likely to have been farmers and less likely to have been professionals and proprietors. Interestingly, there is no significant difference in the percentage claiming injury or gunshot wounds, but men without service-related disabilities were more likely to claim rheumatism, gastrointestinal disorders other than diarrhea, respiratory disorders, hernias, and conditions that could not be classified. Men who could trace their disabili-ties to the war entered the rolls earlier, were judged by the surgeons to be in worse health, and were less likely to live out their expected life span. Even though men who could trace their disabilities to the war had different charac-teristics than those who could not, an income effect from pensions can still be identified provided that I can control for these characteristics.

Recall that the empirical specification that will be estimated is a probit,

$$\text{prob}(I = 1) = \text{prob}(\varepsilon < X'\beta) = \Phi(X'\beta),$$

where I is equal to one if the individual is retired and 0 otherwise; X is a vector containing both labor and nonlabor income, pension income, and demographic and socioeconomic variables; β is a parameter vector; and $\Phi(\ )$ is a standard normal cumulative distribution function. Although direct evidence on earnings and wealth is not available, several proxies are. I use past occupation as a proxy for the opportunity cost of not working, where occupation is classified as farmer, professional or proprietor, artisan, and semiskilled or unskilled laborer, including farm laborer. For men in 1910 this is either occupation in 1900 or, for those retired in 1900, occupation at an earlier date as given in the pension records. For men in 1900 this is either occupation in 1900, if working, or past occupation as given in the pension records. Men whose occupation could not be discerned from the pension records were assigned to an occupation class on the basis of their occupation at enlistment and their probability of switching occupation category given their individual characteristics. These men could just as well have been assigned to random occupations; the results on pension amount remain unchanged. Past occupation may be a poor proxy for opportu-nity cost if the ill are no longer able to work in their usual occupation, and for these men the opportunity cost of retirement is underestimated. Therefore, the effect of pensions may be overestimated.

Other indicators of lower earnings are illiteracy and foreign birth. Marital status may also be measuring earnings if employers favored married men or if married men were more skilled. In 1900, married males in manufacturing earned 17 percent more than unmarried males, controlling for the observable characteristics of workers and their jobs (Goldin 1990, 102). Among home owners in cities, letting rooms to boarders increased family income but may be symptomatic of economic difficulties (Modell and Hareven 1973). The hire of a servant is an indicator of affluence, but servants may have played an important role in family market enterprises, particularly among farmers or small business owners. Home ownership meant that the person had wealth because a substantial down payment, generally equal to half the value of the purchased property, was required (Haines and Goodman 1992).[3] Because long-term unemployment was often a prelude to retirement, higher unemployment in the veteran's current state, available in 1900 but not in 1910, may have induced more retirement.[4] Additional control variables are region of residence, extent of urbanization, and whether the veteran was discharged for disability from the army, a measure of early health status.

The probit results for 1900 are presented in table 3.3. It should not come as a surprise that the older were more likely to retire. Note that a single linear term in age is included because tests revealed that in 1900 the probability of retirement did not increase sharply at a specific age.[5] Those living in states with high unemployment rates and those in poor health were significantly more likely to retire. Those who owned no property were also significantly more likely to retire, but, because property ownership is known only for household heads, this variable is also an indicator of living arrangements. Having servants, boarders, and four or more dependents in the household reduced the probability of retirement, but not significantly so, as did being married, foreign born, or illiterate. Nonfarmers were less likely to retire than farmers, and, in the case of professionals and proprietors, the difference in retirement rates was statistically significant. I discuss the effect of occupation on retirement, particularly of farm occupation, in more detail in chapter 5. Interestingly, those who had been discharged from the service for disability were significantly less likely to be retired in 1900 even though they were in worse health than men who had not been discharged for disability. These men changed to a less physically demanding occupation after enlistment, which may have enabled them to remain in the labor force longer.

The effect on the probability of retirement of a unit change in one of the independent variables is given by the partial derivative of the probability function P with respect to that independent variable. Thus, a $10.00 increase in monthly pension income raises the retirement probability by 0.09.[6] Coefficients on interactions of pension amount with poor health and dummies for older ages and an above-average unemployment rate are small and insignificant.

As previously noted, those with higher pensions may have been less healthy,

Table 3.3   **Probit of Determinants of Probability of Retirement, with Retirement Status as the Dependent Variable, 1900 (526 observations, pseudo $R^2 = .22$**

Variable	Mean	Est.	S.E.	$\partial P/\partial x$
Dummy = 1 if retired	.17			
Intercept		−12.14‡	2.24	
Monthly pension	12.94	.05‡	.01	.0090
Age	61.28	.05‡	.01	.0106
Dummy = 1 if does not own home	.34	.35†	.17	.0695
Discharged disability	.25	−1.63‡	.19	−.1229
Health good	.22			
Health fair	.35	.39*	.23	.0765
Health poor	.25	.37*	.25	.0717
Health status unknown	.18	.46*	.26	.0905
Farmer	.46			
Professional or proprietor	.18	−.48†	.24	−.0935
Artisan	.14	−.09	.23	−.0168
Laborer	.22	−.02	.21	−.0046
Servant in house	.02	−.96	.67	−.1891
Boarder in house	.05	−.26	.41	−.0515
4 or more dependents	.14	−.46	.29	−.0895
Married	.85	−.25	.20	−.0486
Foreign-born	.10	−.13	.25	−.0249
Illiterate	.06	−.02	.31	−.0031
Lives in East	.21			
Lives in Midwest	.73	.42*	.24	.0828
Lives in other region	.06	−.28	.47	−.0540
Urban county	.37	.41†	.17	.0799
Mean duration of unemployment for manufacturing workers by state	3.62	1.86‡	.63	.3644

Note: The omitted dummies are good health, farmer, and eastern residence. The symbols *, †, and ‡ indicate that the coefficient is significantly different from zero at at least the 10 percent, 5 percent, and 1 percent levels, respectively. $\partial P/\partial x = \beta(1/n) \sum \phi (x'\beta)$, where ϕ is the standard normal density, and $\partial P/\partial x$ is in probability units.

but their poorer health may be unobservable. Furthermore, although pensions were awarded regardless of participation status, nonparticipation may have been viewed by employees of the Pension Bureau as evidence of an inability to perform manual labor. It is therefore unclear whether we are measuring the effect of pensions on retirement rates or the effect of retirement on pensions. Pension status is potentially endogenous, and all coefficients may be biased. Fortunately, unbiased estimates of the coefficients can be obtained through the use of a proxy that is highly correlated with pension amount but uncorrelated with the error term appearing in the regression equation. Such a proxy is known as an *instrumental variable.*

The instrumental variable that I use is whether the veteran received a pension under the General Law, that is, whether he could trace his disability to his wartime service. Recall that the ability to establish that a disability was related to wartime service depended on the recruit's record of military service and prevailing medical theory. The ability to establish whether a disability could be traced to wartime service predicts pension amount and is arguably not related to unobserved retirement determinants conditional on measured health status. Although the war disabled entered the pension rolls eight years earlier than those not war disabled, the war disabled were not necessarily disabled earlier in life and therefore did not necessarily receive less job training and therefore have lower opportunity costs of not working. Whether a recruit could trace his disability to the war does not predict whether his occupation in 1900 was of lower socioeconomic status than his occupation at enlistment. Furthermore, the fraction of men who were property owners does not vary by ability to establish whether a disability was war related. A dummy variable indicating whether a recruit could trace his disability to the war, that is, whether he fell under the General Law, is therefore used as an instrumental variable.

Assuming that whether a recruit could trace his disability to the war is a legitimate instrument, consistent estimates of pension amount on retirement can be obtained easily. In the first stage, pension amount is regressed on the exogenous variables, that is, all variables except for pension amount, and a dummy equal to one if the recruit could trace his disability to the war. In the second stage, a probit is estimated in which a retirement dummy is regressed on pension amount, the exogenous variables, and the residuals from the first stage. This method, known as two-stage conditional maximum likelihood, was developed by Rivers and Vuong (1988).[7] A convenient feature of this estimation procedure is that it becomes possible to test statistically whether pension amount is determined by retirement status.[8] If pension amount is not determined by retirement status, then the coefficient on the residuals will be equal to zero when uncorrected standard errors are used. In fact, the hypothesis that the coefficient on the residuals is not equal to zero can be rejected only at the 85 percent level of significance, suggesting that endogeneity is not a problem.

Table 3.4 compares probit estimates with those from a two-stage conditional maximum likelihood procedure among men for whom information on whether the disability can be traced to the war is available.[9] The first-stage estimates are also presented. The two columns that should be compared are those giving the derivatives and marked $\partial P/\partial x$. These columns show that the change in the coefficient on pension amount is small, with the estimated mean effect of a dollar increase in monthly pension amount on retirement probability rising from 0.0092 when a probit is estimated to 0.0101 when two-stage conditional maximum likelihood estimation is used. As in the simple probit, coefficients on interactions of pension amount with other variables are small and insignificant.

Endogeneity is not the only source of potential bias. Another possible source of bias is that from sample selection. If pensions affected survivorship, then the men surviving to 1900 will be a selected sample, and the coefficient on

Table 3.4   Comparison of Probit and Two-Stage Conditional Maximum Likelihood Estimates of Determinants of Probability of Retirement, 1900 (485 observations)

| | | Two-Stage Conditional Maximum Likelihood | | | | |
| | | First Stage:
Adj R^2 = .33 | | Second Stage:
Pseudo R^2 = .22 | | |
Variable	Probit: $\partial P/\partial x$	Est.	S.E.	Est.	S.E.	$\partial P/\partial x$
Intercept		22.36‡	8.49	−12.48‡	2.57	
Monthly pension	.0092			.05†	.03	.0101
Age	.0116	.06	.05	.06‡	.01	.0115
Dummy = 1 if does						
not own home	.0651	−1.00	−1.00	.34*	.18	.0664
Discharged						
disability	−.1342	.91	.72	−.69‡	.21	−.1358
Health good						
Health fair	.0651	.15	.84	.34	.24	.0658
Health poor	.0745	3.42‡	.94	.33	.29	.0692
Health status						
unknown	.0921	2.12‡	.96	.45*	.27	.0892
Farmer						
Professional or						
proprietor	−.0802	−1.06	.85	−.40	.25	−.0787
Artisan	−.0255	−.64	.95	−.12	.24	−.0246
Laborer	.0190	−1.27	.83	.11	.22	.0246
Servant in house	−.2207	9.23‡	2.22	−1.15	.70	−.2269
Boarder in house	−.0617	−.06	1.34	−.31	.41	−.0621
4 or more						
dependents	−.0892	−1.22	.88	−.45	.29	−.0890
Married	−.0185	−.84	.90	−.10	.22	−.0189
Foreign born	−.0381	.03	1.00	−.19	.26	−.0376
Illiterate	−.0301	−.08	1.33	−.15	.32	−.0296
Lives in East						
Lives in Midwest	.0921	1.43*	.85	.49*	.25	.0961
Lives in other region	−.0447	3.14†	1.48	−.24	.48	−.0467
Urban county	.0893	−.62	.67	.46‡	.18	.0905
If disability						
traceable to war		6.83‡	.66			
Mean duration of						
unemployment in						
manufacturing by						
state	.3563	−4.73†	2.26	1.83‡	.65	.3615
Residuals first stage				−.01	.03	−.0010

Source: Costa (1995b).

Note: The first stage is a regression of pension amount on the exogenous variables and whether the disability was traceable to the war, that is, whether the veteran fell under the General Law. The second stage is a probit with the exogenous variables, pension amount, and the first-stage residuals as explanatory variables. The standard errors have been corrected. The symbols *, †, and ‡ indicate that the coefficient is significantly different from zero at at least the 10 percent, 5 percent, and 1 percent levels, respectively. $\partial P/\partial x = \beta(1/n) \sum \phi(x'\beta)$, where ϕ is the standard normal density, and $\partial P/\partial x$ is in probability units.

pensions will be biased.[10] I tested whether pension amount affects life expectancy using a proportional hazards model where the dependent variable was the number of years lived after 1900. Controlling for health, pension amount did not affect the probability of mortality. Neither did date of entry, suggesting that duration of the receipt of a pension was not an important predictor of mortality.

Now that we can be confident that our results are not tainted by bias, we can estimate how responsive retirement rates are to changes in pension income. One way of measuring responsiveness is to calculate elasticities of labor force nonparticipation with respect to pension income from mean derivatives and retirement probabilities. In the probit specification in table 3.3 above, and at the pension mean of $12.90, the elasticity is 0.73 (= 0.0090 [12.9/0.1589]), indicating that a 1 percent increase in pension amount increases retirement by 0.73 percent. Evaluated half a standard deviation below and above the pension mean, the elasticities are 0.53 (= 0.0076 [9.0/0.1289]) and 0.88 (= 0.0104 [16.8/0.1990]), respectively. Hence, the larger the pension income, the larger the elasticity. Using the two-stage conditional maximum likelihood method used in table 3.4, and evaluating at the pension mean, the elasticity of labor force nonparticipation with respect to pension income rises slightly to 0.80 (= .0101 [12.9/0.1625]).

The results obtained for 1900 should be compared with those for 1910, when veterans were ten years older. Probit results for 1910 are given in table 3.5. As in 1900, the older, those in poor health, and those who owned no property are significantly more likely to be retired. Having either a servant or two or more dependents in the household becomes a significant predictor of retirement. In contrast to the 1900 results, being foreign born raised the probability of retirement in 1910, a finding consistent with the pattern seen in the general population. Although the coefficient on whether a veteran was discharged for disability was no longer significant, those so discharged were still less likely to be retired. Professionals, proprietors, and artisans were less likely to be retired than farmers, and the difference between farmer and artisan retirement rates was statistically significant. Compared with farmers, laborers were more likely to be retired, but the difference in retirement rates is not statistically significant.

A $10.00 increase in monthly pension income raises the retirement probability by 0.112. Once again, coefficients on interactions of pension amount with poor health and age dummies are small and insignificant, but the coefficients on the interactions of pension amount with the age dummies suggest that the effect of pensions is lower among older men. Two-stage conditional maximum likelihood estimation, using the 1862 law as an instrument, yielded coefficients almost identical to those obtained from the probit estimates. The estimated elasticity for 1910, evaluated at the pension mean of 16.94, is 0.47 (= 0.0112 [16.94/0.3989]), somewhat lower than the elasticity estimated for 1900.

Although an interaction between pension amount and age in the regression

Table 3.5   **Probit of Determinants of Probability of Retirement, with Retirement Status as the Dependent Variable, 1910 (923 observations, pseudo $R^2 = 0.16$)**

Variable	Mean	Est.	S.E.	$\partial P/\partial x$
Dummy = 1 if retired	.40			
Intercept		−6.42‡	.71	
Monthly pension	16.94	.03‡	.01	.0112
Age	69.19	.08‡	.01	.0246
Dummy = 1 if does not own home	.28	.34‡	.11	.1101
Discharged disability	.18	−.14	.12	−.0458
Health good or fair	.53			
Health poor	.34	.22†	.11	.0703
Health status unknown	.13	−.17	.16	−.0552
Farmer	.49			
Professional or proprietor	.19	−.11	.13	−.0360
Artisan	.14	−.39‡	.14	−.1249
Laborer	.17	.16	.13	.0527
Servant in house	.05	−.87‡	.25	−.2796
Boarder in house	.05	−.16	.21	−.0530
2 or more dependents	.21	−.30‡	.12	−.0976
Married	.78	.12	.12	.0385
Foreign born	.08	.34†	.17	.1114
Illiterate	.05	.14	.22	.0441
Lives in Midwest	.86	.21	.14	.0680
Urban county	.18	−.04	.13	−.0141

Note: The omitted dummies are good or fair health and farmer. The symbols *, †, and ‡ indicate that the coefficient is significantly different from zero at at least the 10 percent, 5 percent, and 1 percent levels, respectively. $\partial P/\partial x = \beta(1/n) \sum \phi\,(x'\beta)$, where ϕ is the standard normal density, and $\partial P/\partial x$ is in probability units.

equations was insignificant, there is some suggestion that the effect of pensions on retirement varied by age. When the 1910 sample is divided into those aged seventy or less and those older than seventy, the respective elasticities, evaluated at the pension means, are 0.62 (= 0.0123 [15.3/0.3033]) and 0.28 (= 0.0083 [20.2/0.5930]). The elasticity is lower in the older sample both because the increase in the probability of retirement for a dollar increase in monthly pension amount is smaller than in a younger sample and because the probability of retirement is much higher. At older ages, men's participation decision is less sensitive to changes in income.

Figure 3.5 simulates the effect on retirement rates of eliminating Union army pensions, showing that retirement rates in the Union sample and in the general population, which contains veterans collecting Union army pensions, would have fallen—which they did in fact do.[11] The resulting narrowing of differentials in retirement rates between the general population and the Union army sample suggests that much of the difference in retirement rates between veterans and the general population is due to pensions.

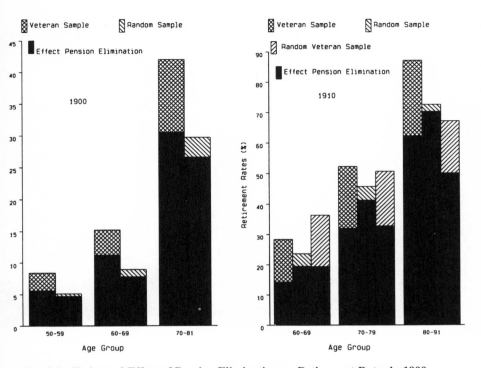

Fig. 3.5   Estimated Effect of Pension Elimination on Retirement Rates in 1900 and 1910

Note: Retirement rates assuming a pension elimination were calculated using the coefficients in tables 3.3 and 3.5. The random samples were drawn from Ruggles and Sobek (1995) and were limited to men who either were born in a Union state or, if foreign born, immigrated prior to the Civil War. The random samples contain both veterans and nonveterans and were reweighted to have the same age distribution as the veteran sample. Estimates of the fraction collecting Union army pensions were used to calculate retirement rates under a pension elimination. For details, see Costa (1995b).

3.4   Confederate and Union Veterans

Variation in pension amount by whether a recruit was able to trace his disability to the war has enabled me to separate the effect of pensions from that of health. Another source of variation in the Union army pension program was disparate treatment by type of veteran. Confederates were ineligible. In 1910 Union pensioners were collecting an average pension of $171.90 per year, and about 90 percent of all Union veterans were collecting a pension. Although some Confederate states provided pensions, the average pension amount was just $47.24 per year, and fewer than 30 percent of all Confederate veterans were collecting a pension.[12] Because the Union army pension was extremely generous while Confederate pensions were honorariums, then, if pensions matter, the difference in retirement rates between Union veterans and nonveter-

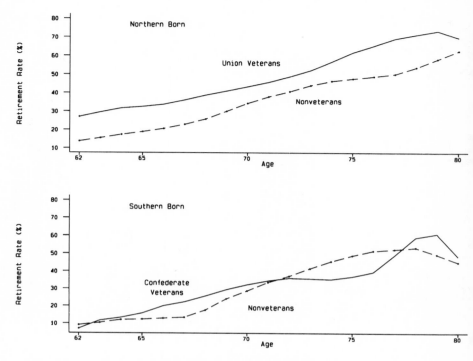

Fig. 3.6   Retirement rates by veteran status among northern-born and southern-born men aged sixty-two to seventy-nine in 1910

Note: Estimated from Ruggles and Sobek (1995). The trend in retirement rates was smoothed using Cleveland's lowess running line smoother with a band width of 0.4.

ans should be large and that between Confederate veterans and nonveterans small. This pattern is indeed observed in figure 3.6, where to control for differences in regional characteristics the sample was divided into those born in a Union state, that is, those at risk to serve in the Union army, and those born in a Confederate state, that is, those at risk to serve in the Confederate army. Because disability rates were probably higher among Confederate veterans than among Union veterans, relative differences in retirement rates between veterans and nonveterans in the two samples cannot be explained by health status.[13]

An alternative way to compare retirement rates among veterans and nonveterans within northern- and southern-born samples is to estimate two probits in which retirement status is the dependent variable. The advantage is that individual characteristics such as marital status, illiteracy, property ownership, region of residence, extent of urbanization, and whether servants or boarders are in the household can be controlled for. Table 3.6, which gives the probits, bears

Table 3.6 Probit Predicting Probability Retirement for Northern-Born and Southern-Born Aged 62–79 in 1910, with Retirement Status as the Dependent Variable (from Public-Use Census Sample)

Variable	Northern Born (4,517 Observations, Pseudo R^2 = .10)				Southern Born (1,224 Observations, Pseudo R^2 = .17)			
	Mean	Parameter Est.	S.E.	$\partial P/\partial x$	Mean	Parameter Est.	S.E.	$\partial P/\partial x$
Dummy = 1 if retired	.31				.24			
Intercept		−5.37‡	.30			−7.07		
Dummy = 1 if:								
Union veteran	.23	.36‡	.05	.1160				
Confederate veteran					.38	.03	.09	.0071
Married	.71	−.10*	.05	−.0305	.77	−.29‡	.11	−.0767
Illiterate	.04	−.11	.10	−.0345	.12	−.15	.13	−.0380
Has servant	.07	−.15*	.08	−.0484	.04	−.22	.22	−.0577
Takes in boarder	.13	−.11*	.06	−.0361	.11	−.22	.14	−.0568
Owns no property	.40	.14‡	.05	.0461	.39	.28‡	.10	.0723
Lives in South	.03	−.10	.12	−.0308	.78	−.03	.11	−.0085
Lives in urban county	.31	−.07	.05	−.0218	.07	−.05	.16	−.0127
Age	68.22	.07‡	.00	.0233	67.84	.09‡	.01	.0227
Number of dependents	1.24	−.14‡	.02	−.0454	1.63	−.20‡	.04	−.0527

Source: The sample consists of white, noninstitutionalized, native-born men aged 62–79 drawn from the integrated 1910 Census (Ruggles and Sobek 1995).

Note: The symbols *, †, and ‡ indicate that the coefficient is significantly different from zero at at least the 10 percent, 5 percent, and 1 percent levels, respectively. $\partial P/\partial x = \beta(1/n) \sum \phi (x'\beta)$, where ϕ is the standard normal density, and $\partial P/\partial x$ is in probability units.

out the results of figure 3.6. In the southern-born sample Confederate veteran status is not a significant predictor of retirement. In the northern-born sample, Union army veteran status is, suggesting that Union pensions led to higher retirement rates among veterans. There were a few Confederate veterans in the northern-born sample and a few Union veterans in the southern-born sample (classified as nonveterans in table 3.6).[14] Although no strong conclusions can be drawn from such a small fraction of men in either category, when dummies are included for these men, the coefficient on Confederate status in the northern-born sample is insignificant and that on Union veteran in the southern-born sample is significant, suggesting once again that the receipt of a pension was an important determinant of retirement status.

The results presented in table 3.6 can also be used to estimate whether the difference in participation rates between the northern- and the southern-born sample is largely due to differences in observable characteristics or in participation behavior. When retirement rates from the northern-born sample are compared with those from the southern-born sample, then the difference in retirement rates should consist of two components. The first will be the component due to observable differences, such as region of residence or fraction of veterans in the population. The second component should be due to differences in participation behavior. Union army pensions will lead to differences in the participation functions. So might other variables. For example, the northern born who lived in the South may have differed in unobservable retirement determinants. More formally, let R^n be the probability of retirement among the northern born, R^s the probability among the southern born, and X^n and X^s the vectors of northern- and southern-born characteristics, respectively. Then

$$R^n - R^s = [R^n(X^n) - R^n(X^s)] + [R^n(X^s) - R^s(X^s)],$$

where the first term is predicted using the northern-born participation equation for both samples, and the second term is the residual component due to differences in participation behavior between northern and southern born using the southern-born sample. The actual difference in retirement rates is 0.0722. Using the northern-born participation equation for both samples yields a value of 0.0445 for the second term, suggesting that differences in participation behavior and thus pensions account for about 62 percent of the difference in retirement rates between the southern and the northern born. When men aged eighty to ninety-one are included in the sample, regressions on the northern- and southern-born samples suggest that differences in participation behavior account for about 39 percent of the difference in retirement rates between the southern and the northern born. Although the coefficient on an interaction term between age and Union army veteran was statistically significant only at the 20 percent level, it was negative, suggesting that being a Union army veteran had a smaller effect on the participation decision of older relative to younger veterans.

3.5   Implications

I have demonstrated that Union army pensions exerted a large effect on male labor force participation rates. The elasticity of labor force nonparticipation with respect to pension income was 0.73 in 1900 and 0.47 in 1910. I argued that these estimates were unbiased. They can therefore be used to calculate the effect of a secular increase in income on the secular decline in male labor force participation rates, under the assumption that the elasticity of labor force nonparticipation with respect to pension income remained constant after 1900. The retirement rate for men sixty-five years of age or older rose from 35 percent in 1900 to 83 percent in 1990, and per capita fixed reproducible tangible wealth rose by 415 percent.[15] Therefore, using the 1910 pension elasticity of nonparticipation, an increase in income, holding wages constant, could explain 60 percent of the decline in labor force participation rates.

Mounting evidence, however, suggests that the elasticity of labor force nonparticipation with respect to income was lower in the period after 1940 than in my estimates. According to my results, the elasticity of labor force nonparticipation was 0.73 in 1900, when the median age of veterans was fifty-six, and 0.47 in 1910, when the median age was sixty-six. But others find far lower estimates for the period after 1940.

Friedberg's (1996) estimates of the effect of Social Security Old Age and Assistance in 1940 and in 1950, given to those age sixty-five and older, imply an elasticity of labor force nonparticipation with respect to benefits of around 0.25–0.42. The majority of studies using data from the late 1960s on find a similar or smaller effect on labor force participation rates of either assets or Social Security retirement and disability payments (Bound 1989; Bound and Waidmann 1992; Hausman and Wise 1985; Haveman and Wolfe 1984a, 1984b; Krueger and Pischke 1992). Among men in their early sixties Hausman and Wise (1985) estimate an elasticity of 0.23 and Krueger and Pischke (1992) one of 0. Elasticities of labor force nonparticipation with respect to assets in these studies are close to 0. Bound (1989) finds an elasticity of labor force nonparticipation with respect to Social Security disability of 0.16 among men aged forty-five to sixty-four. Studies finding a more sizable effect of Social Security payments on labor force nonparticipation are those of Hurd and Boskin (1984), Leonard (1979), and Parsons (1980). For example, Parsons (1980) calculates an elasticity with respect to Social Security disability of 0.63. The results of selected studies are summarized in table 3.7.

Statistical problems may bias some of the estimates presented in table 3.7 upward. Leonard (1979) and Parsons (1980) compare the labor force participation rates of those whose potential disability benefits would replace a relatively large fraction of their predisability earnings to those whose potential benefits would not. Since replacement rates for disability benefits are decreasing functions of past earnings, it is difficult to determine whether generous replacement

Table 3.7   Elasticities of Labor Force Nonparticipation in Selected Studies

Study	Age of Sample	Year Studied	With Respect to	Elasticity
Costa (this chapter)	Median age is 56	1900	Union army pensions	.73
Parsons (1980)	48–62	1969	Social Security Disability (SSDI)	.63
Leonard (1979)	45–54	1972	SSDI beneficiary status	.35
Haveman and Wolfe (1984a, 1984b)	45–62	1978	SSDI	.21–0.06
Bound (1989)	45–64	1972 and 1978	SSDI	.16
Costa (this chapter)	Median age is 66	1910	Union army pensions	.47
Friedberg (1996)	66–80	1940 and 1950	Old Age Assistance	.25–0.42
Hurd and Boskin (1984)	60–64		Old Age and Survivors Insurance (OASI)	.71
Hausman and Wise (1985)	58–63 in 1969	1969–79	OASI	.23
			Assets	≈0
Krueger and Pischke (1992)	60–68	1976–88	OASI	≈0

Source: The elasticities given for Friedberg (1996), Hurd and Boskin (1984), and Hausman and Wise (1985) were estimated using the information provided by the authors.

rates or low earnings induce the individual to leave the labor force. Haveman and Wolfe (1984a, 1984b) try to avoid the problem of the endogeneity of the replacement rate through the use of an instrumental variables procedure in which they first predict disability benefits as a function of exogenous information and then incorporate these predicted values into the final estimation equation. They estimate an elasticity of 0.06–0.21. Bound (1989) avoids the endogeneity problem by using those who applied for disability benefits but were rejected as a control group for beneficiaries. He also estimates a low elasticity (0.16).

Some of the estimates of the effect of Social Security retirement benefits on retirement may also be biased upward. A potential problem with most studies is that the source of variation across individuals, differing levels of Social Security benefits, arises because of past earnings history. Past earnings are likely to be correlated with present labor supply and thus bias upward estimates of the effect of Social Security.[16] A few studies use other sources of variation. Friedberg (1996) uses state variation in benefits to identify the influence of Old Age Assistance on labor supply. Krueger and Pischke (1992) examine an unexpected legislative change that substantially reduced benefits to individuals born after 1916, leading to a worker who retired at age sixty-five after a career of earning the average wage to receive Social Security benefits that were 13 percent lower than he would have received had he been born in 1916. They concluded that Social Security wealth had a negative, but insignificant, effect on the probability of retirement. The income elasticity of retirement therefore appears to have fallen from 0.47 in 1910, to 0.25–0.42 in 1940 and 1950, to 0 in recent years.

What therefore needs to be explained is why elasticities estimated from the Union army sample are so much higher than elasticities with respect to transfer income estimated from recent data. One possibility is that there has been a change in the income elasticity of retirement. Another is that elasticities of nonparticipation with respect to assets or Social Security benefits may not be comparable to those calculated with respect to Union army pensions. Assets are not necessarily exogenous, and Social Security payments will have both an income and a substitution effect. With the exception of the unique circumstances examined by Krueger and Pischke (1992), it is plausible to assume that the future stream of Social Security payments was predicted with greater accuracy by men in their working years than was the future stream of Union army payments. Another difference exists because Union army pensions represented a larger fraction of earnings than do Social Security disability payments today, the former constituting 36 percent of the annual earnings of nonfarm laborers in 1900, the latter 36 percent. Furthermore, Union army pensions were the only available retirement program, whereas Social Security disability payments represent 75 percent of all transfer payments (estimated from Center for Human Resource Research 1985).

If noncomparability of elasticities calculated with respect to Union army pension income and those calculated with respect to Social Security payments arises from Union army pensions being at the time the only available transfer program, then the retirement elasticity with respect to Union army pensions can be adjusted to account for this. Thus, if total transfer income were $12.90 per month in 1900, which is what the average Union army pension paid, a program equivalent in scale and scope to Social Security Disability would have paid $9.70 per month in 1900 (or 0.75 [$12.90]). Retirement income includes not only transfer income but also private pensions. Disability payments represent 67 percent of the sum of transfer income and private pensions today, translating into $8.60 of $12.90 per month in 1900. Using the 1900 regression produces an elasticity of 0.56 (= 0.0078 [9.7/0.1343]) for the equivalent of Social Security disability and one of 0.51 (= 0.0075 [8.6/0.1259]) for that of transfer income plus private pensions.[17] Similar calculations using the 1910 regression estimates yield an elasticity of 0.40 (= 0.0112 [12.4/0.3473]), also substantial.[18] Furthermore, the average Union army pension in 1900 and 1910 was about as generous as the average Social Security retirement benefit.

The elasticities given in table 3.7 therefore suggest that the responsiveness of retirement to income has fallen since 1900. Workers may now be less responsive to changes in transfer income because they are no longer close to subsistence levels; instead, they reach retirement age with enough to satisfy their consumption needs. Each additional dollar of income will therefore have less of an effect on their decision. Alternatively, workers' choices may now be constrained by a retirement ethos. Once a sizable fraction of older men are retired, unresponsiveness to pension payments may be the outcome of a "bandwagon" effect or of a desire to conform to societal expectations. By establishing age sixty-five and later age sixty-two as an "official" retirement age, Social Security may have led individuals to want to retire at that age and therefore reduced the effect of income on the work decision. The men remaining in the labor force may be those who are greatly attached to work and who can be induced to leave the labor force only by a very large sum of money.

Workers may also be less responsive to changes in transfer income because leisure has become relatively more attractive and less expensive. In chapter 7 I discuss how in the 1920s and 1930s new technologies such as the car, the phonograph, the radio, and movies increased the variety of recreational activities and lowered their price. These new goods diffused rapidly throughout the population. At the same time public recreational facilities, such as parks, golf courses, and swimming pools, put recreational sports within the reach of more and more individuals. In 1934 the pension advocate Isaac Rubinow noted that wintering in Florida and summering on Michigan lakes was how many of the well-to-do spent their lives after age sixty-five (Rubinow 1934, 243). Even during the 1930s large numbers of the elderly migrated to the Pacific Coast and South Atlantic regions. Their numbers increased after the Second World War. By 1940 private insurance companies offering retirement income plans advertised those plans as offering "freedom from money worries. You can have all the joys of recreation or travel when the time comes at which every man wants them most."[19] Graebner (1980, 215–41) argues that there was a national effort to glorify retirement in the 1950s and describes how retirement was aggressively marketed as a consumable commodity by corporations, labor unions, and insurance companies that were pension plan trustees. Companies established retirement preparation programs, and journals aimed at retired employees were increasingly filled with idyllic depictions of the retired life. What is not known is the extent to which increased retirement induced the marketing and the extent to which the marketing induced retirement.

The marketing of retirement in the 1950s, however, was accompanied by the continued growth of leisure industries. Now mass tourism and mass entertainment, such as films, television, golf, and spectator sports, provide activities for the elderly at a low price. As the desirability of leisure increased, the elasticity of labor force nonparticipation with respect to pension income may have decreased. I take this point up again in chapter 7. Once retirement was seen as a period of personal fulfillment rather than a period before death when men were too ill to work, more men may have found retirement desirable, even if their retirement activities were limited.

A fall in the income elasticity of retirement implies that, while secular increases in income explain a larger share of the rise in retirement rates at the beginning of the century, they explain much less at the century's end. The 1910 estimate of the elasticity of nonparticipation implies that 90 percent of the decline in labor force participation rates between 1900 and 1930 could be attributed to secularly rising incomes. Friedberg's (1996) estimates suggest that at least half the decline between 1930 and 1950 can be accounted for by secularly rising incomes. In contrast, rising incomes may explain none of the 1950–80 decline.[20] The findings also suggest that, as leisure continues to grow more attractive, changes in transfer policies alone may not be enough to induce large increases in labor force participation rates among the elderly.

3.6 Summary

This chapter investigated the effect of Union army pensions on veterans' retirement rates, finding that the elasticity of nonparticipation with respect to Union army pension income was 0.73 in 1900 and 0.47 in 1910, when veterans were older and their participation decision was less sensitive to changes in income. The findings suggest that secularly rising income explains a substantial part of increased retirement rates, particularly before 1940. Rising incomes cannot, however, account for most of the recent increase in retirement rates. Comparisons with elasticities of nonparticipation with respect to Social Security income imply that the income elasticity of retirement has decreased with time, either because of changing societal expectations or because of increasingly attractive leisure-time opportunities. Not only can most men now afford to retire, but, when they do retire, they can look forward to a variety of low-cost leisure activities.

Notes

1. Imputations for annual incomes are given in Preston and Haines (1991, 212–20, table A.1). The pension represented an even greater proportion of the earnings of older men because of the sharp decline in the age-earnings profile.
2. The pension records, which include the successive reports of the examining surgeons of the Pension Bureau, are currently being linked to the 1850, 1860, 1900, and 1920 censuses and to army service records to reconstruct the life histories of a random sample of men who served in the Union army. The collection of these data is still ongoing; therefore, nonrandom subsamples of the data are used in the statistical analysis.
3. However, because property was one of the primary modes of savings, men who had retired might already have liquidated their property.
4. The statewide unemployment numbers are from Keyssar (1986, 340–41, table A.13).
5. The coefficients on a spline in age are insignificant, and the use of a spline leaves the regression results unchanged. Similarly, the use of a quadratic term in age does not affect the results.
6. The values of $\partial P/\partial x$ were calculated as $\beta(1/n) \sum \phi(x'\beta)$, where $\phi(\ )$ is a standard normal density function, β is the probit coefficient, and n is the number of observations.

7. Using symbols,

$$I_i^* = \alpha P_i + \mathbf{Z}_{1i}'\beta + u_i,$$

$$P_i = \Pi'\mathbf{Z}_i + V_i,$$

where I_i^* is not observed, only the dummy variable, $I_i = 1$ if retired and 0 otherwise, is. P_i is pension amount; $\mathbf{Z}_{1i}$ is the vector of exogenous variables (all variables except for pension amount) and is a subset of $\mathbf{Z}_i$, which also contains the instrumental variable indicating whether a recruit fell under the General Law. The instrumental variable is not included in the retirement equation. The normally distributed error terms are represented by u_i and V_i. Rivers and Vuong (1988) present formulas for the standard errors. When the coefficient on the residuals in the second stage is equal to zero, the standard errors are the usual probit standard errors. There was little difference between the corrected and the uncorrected second-stage standard errors.

8. A Hausman test for exogeneity of pension amount is used.

9. Men for whom such information is unavailable do not differ in observable characteristics from men for whom this information is available.

10. The bias could go either way.

11. Among the white male population in 1900, 15 percent of those aged fifty to fifty-nine, 18 percent of those sixty to sixty-nine, and 9 percent of those seventy to eighty-one were collecting a Union army pension. Among the white male population either born in a Union state or, if foreign born, who immigrated prior to the Civil War, 28 percent of those aged fifty to fifty-nine, 33 percent of those sixty to sixty-nine, and 22 percent of those seventy to eighty-one were collecting a Union Army pension (for sources, see Costa 1995b). Retirement rates among nonveterans in 1900 are calculated from

$$R_g = R_v(\text{fraction veterans}) + R_{nv}(\text{fraction nonveterans}),$$

where R_g is the retirement rate of the general population, R_v that of veterans, and R_{nv} that of nonveterans. Assuming that a pension elimination affects only veteran retirement rates, new retirement rates for the veteran general population can be estimated.

12. Glasson (1918a, 1918b) gives the number of Civil War veterans on the pension rolls in 1910. Because of undernumeration of veterans in the 1910 census, the total number of Union army veterans is estimated from a life table and is from Series Y 957–970 in U.S. Bureau of the Census (1975, 1145). Assuming that undernumeration of veterans did not vary among Union and Confederate veterans, the number of Confederate veterans can be calculated from the 1910 public-use sample.

13. Although disability levels for Confederate veterans are unavailable, young men in the South were almost three times as likely to die during the Civil War as were young northern men (Vinovskis 1990).

14. If these men are classified as either Confederate veterans in the northern-born sample or as Union army veterans in the southern-born sample, then the coefficients in table 3.6 do not change.

15. The increase in per capita fixed reproducible tangible wealth was calculated from U.S. Bureau of Economic Analysis (1986, 322–70). Retirement incomes have kept pace with per capita wealth between 1950 and 1990, increasing by 90 percent, but between 1900 and 1990 rose by more than per capita wealth.

16. An additional problem arises with Hurd and Boskin's (1984) study. Their high elasticity may be an artifact of the way they selected the population at risk to retire (see Diamond and Hausman 1984).

17. Of course, savings, wages of family members, and income from part-time work are now greater than in 1900. Therefore, a monthly transfer is likely to have a smaller effect at high than at low levels of retirement.

18. Hurd and Shoven (1982) estimated that Social Security retirement benefits account for 73 percent of nonwage income, excluding Medicare and Medicaid payments. Including Medicare and Medicaid payments, Social Security payments account for 37 percent of nonwage income, and the elasticity becomes 0.24 (= 0.0103 [6.7/0.286]).

19. Insurance company advertisement from a 1940 issue of *Newsweek,* reproduced in Haber and Gratton (1994, 64).

20. Secular increases in income were proxied by increases in per capita fixed reproducible wealth.

4   Work and Disease

Illnesses were more important than any other cause in bringing
about premature superannuation.

Ohio Health and Old Age Insurance Commission (1919)

Health is a critical component of labor supply. Among middle-aged men today
chronic conditions such as heart disease, arthritis and other musculoskeletal
conditions, and respiratory disorders substantially reduce hours worked and
the probability of participation, and this reduction in labor supply accounts for
up to 45 percent of the decline in earnings observed among middle-aged men
(Bartel and Taubman 1979; Burkhauser et al. 1986; Pincus, Mitchell, and
Burkhauser 1989). Because the prevalence of chronic disabilities rises with
age, the effects of health at older ages are especially pronounced. In virtually
all studies, poor health leads to retirement.[1]

I begin this chapter by reviewing long-term trends in health. Some researchers have argued that average health has worsened both over the last twenty
years and over the last hundred years because improvements in medical efficacy have permitted the survival of those afflicted with chronic conditions
(Riley 1989; Verbrugge 1984). Their arguments imply that worsening average
health may explain rising retirement rates and underscore the importance of
establishing health trends. I then proceed to investigate whether health has become more or less important to the retirement decision since the nineteenth
century. Participation rates were higher in the past, but were they uniformly
higher, or were the disabled more or less likely to work relative to the healthy?
The shift from the manufacturing and agricultural to the service sectors, increasing mechanization, and the shortening of the workday have lessened the
expenditure of physical energy required for jobs, thus easing the incorporation
of the disabled into the labor force. Improved control or alleviation of chronic
conditions provided by innovations such as hypertensive drugs used in the care
of arthritis has also eased the incorporation of the disabled into the labor force.
But the low retirement incomes that prevailed at the beginning of the century
meant that men may not have been able to afford to consider themselves
disabled. As a result, men who by today's standards would be clearly disabled

60

may have been participating in the labor force even if they were working with pain.

4.1   Trends in Health

Scholars have compared the health of modern and past populations using data on life expectancy, time lost from work, prevalence of chronic conditions, and anthropometric measures such as height and weight adjusted for height. The difficulty in using life expectancy as a measure of health is that life expectancies can be high and health poor if advances in medical technology lead to the increased survival of people suffering from chronic conditions. Using time lost from work avoids these problems, but this measure may be affected by cultural factors, economic incentives, or the distribution of income or wealth. For example, an individual from a poor household may be more likely to work when ill or disabled than an individual from a rich household. This section therefore examines trends in prevalence rates of chronic conditions, in heights, and in weight adjusted for height.

4.1.1   Chronic Conditions

Few surveys of past populations provide detailed information on chronic conditions that is comparable to recent data. Although early health surveys are available, they often confounded acute and chronic conditions and recorded only chronic conditions that caused an illness. Thus, an individual with arthritis might be listed as having arthritis only if the condition temporarily flared up and disabled him for a few days. These surveys were based on self-reported data, and health awareness may have been much lower in the past. One early data source that does not share these problems is the Union army records. Only chronic conditions, neither acute conditions nor bouts of illness brought on by chronic conditions, qualified a man for a pension. Physicians, not veterans, judged the presence of a chronic condition.

Table 4.1 contrasts disease rates among Union army veterans sixty-five years of age or older in 1910 with disease rates, adjusted to account for differences in the age distribution, among World War II veterans in the 1980s. Disease rates for World War II veterans are estimated from a 1983 survey that reports whether a veteran ever had a disease and from successive years of the National Health Interview Survey (NHIS), 1985–88, which reports whether an individual had a condition in the twelve months prior to the interview. Because nineteenth-century medical technology could not cure chronic conditions, disease rates for Union army veterans are estimated under the assumption that, if an examining surgeon ever judged a veteran to have a specified chronic condition, that condition was permanent. The Union army data are therefore most comparable to the 1983 survey. Although prevalence rates of chronic diseases that occurred during the twelve months preceding the National Health Interview are not directly comparable to the Union army data, a comparison with

Table 4.1   Comparison of the Prevalence of Chronic Conditions among Union
Army Veterans in 1910, Veterans in 1983 (reporting whether they
ever had specific chronic conditions), and Veterans in NHIS 1985–88
(reporting whether they had specific chronic conditions during the
preceding 12 months), Aged 65 and above (%)

Disorder	Union Army Veterans	1983 Veterans	Age-Adjusted 1983 Veterans	NHIS 1985–88 Veterans
Skin or musculoskeletal	68.4	48.1	47.5	45.8
Musculoskeletal	67.7	47.9	47.2	42.5
Digestive	84.0	49.0	48.9	18.0
Hernia	34.5	27.3	26.7	6.6
Diarrhea	31.9	3.7	4.2	1.4
Genitourinary	27.3	36.3	32.3	8.9
Central nervous, endocrine, metabolic, or blood	24.2	29.9	29.1	12.6
Circulatory	90.1	42.9	39.9	40.0
Heart	76.0	38.5	39.9	26.6
Varicose veins	38.5	8.7	8.3	5.3
Hemorrhoids	44.4			7.2
Respiratory	42.2	29.8	28.1	26.5
Neoplasms	2.2	13.1	11.5	9.2

Note: Among veterans in 1983, the prevalence of all types of circulatory diseases will be underestimated because of underreporting of hemorrhoids. The variable indicating whether the 1983 veteran ever had hemorrhoids is unreliable. Neoplasms in the NHIS are estimated as the sum of
prevalence rates of neoplasms of the skin, digestive systems, prostate, and respiratory systems. No
allowance is made for the fact that an individual may have multiple kinds of neoplasms, so this
number should be interpreted as an upper bound. However, people with multiple neoplasms are
more likely to be institutionalized and hence not included in the NHIS.

the 1983 data that report whether a veteran ever had a chronic condition might
explain why chronic conditions among the elderly have declined since 1910.

Musculoskeletal, heart, and digestive disorders were the major chronic conditions among the elderly in 1910 and still remain so to this day. Table 4.1
shows that the prevalence rates of musculoskeletal, digestive, heart, and respiratory disorders and of varicose veins were considerably higher among Union
army veterans than among the veterans surveyed in 1983 or in the NHIS survey.
Although neoplasms and genitourinary conditions were much more common
among veterans surveyed in 1983 than among Union army veterans, physicians
in 1910 were unable to diagnose these disorders at early stages. The large difference in prevalence rates for conditions of the digestive, genitourinary, central nervous, endocrine, metabolic, and blood and blood-forming systems, according to whether those conditions are reported as being ever experienced or
as existing during the previous twelve months, indicates that many conditions
in these categories that could not be cured in 1910 can now be treated effectively.

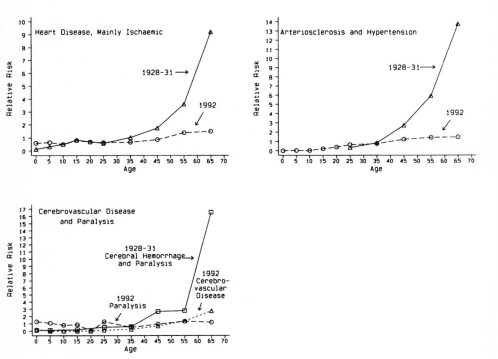

Fig. 4.1   Relative risk of ischaemic heart disease, arteriosclerosis and hypertension, and cerebrovascular disease and paralysis among whites, both sexes, 1928–31 and 1992

Note: Calculated from Collins (1935) and the 1992 National Health Interview Survey. Relative risk of a specific form of heart disease, R_i, at age i is calculated as $R_i = H_i/(\sum N_i H_i/N) = H_i/\bar{H}$, where H_i is the prevalence rate of heart disease at age i, N_i is the number of individuals of age i, $N = \sum N_i$, and $\bar{H}$ is the prevalence rate over all ages.

The health of the elderly relative to their counterparts today remained poor for several decades after 1910. The National Health Survey of 1935–38 and the Committee on the Costs of Medical Care's 1928–31 survey, both random surveys of households within selected cities, provide suggestive evidence. Although prevalence rates for most chronic conditions listed in the two surveys are not comparable to recent data because of different definitions that produce undercounting in the older data, prevalence rates for specific conditions such as blindness are unlikely to be undercounted.[2] Furthermore, it is possible to compare the prevalence rates of the elderly with those of the general population. If the relative risk of a specific condition rose much more sharply with age in the past than today, then, relative to the general population, the elderly of the past fared worse than the elderly today.

Figure 4.1 performs this comparison, plotting the relative risk of ischaemic heart disease, arteriosclerosis and hypertension, and cerebrovascular disease and paralysis by age group for white men and women in 1928–31 and in 1992.

Table 4.2   Rates of Blindness in Both Eyes per 100,000 Persons, 1935–38
                   and 1992

Age	1935–38		1992	
	Men	Women	Men	Women
55–64	213	163	38	162
65–74	522	405	158	61
75–84	942	1,213	385	159
85–89	2,010	3,536	1,683	1,437

Note: The 1935–38 rates are from Britten (1941). Although prevalence rates are given for earlier ages as well, those prevalence rates are an underestimate because many children born blind were previously institutionalized. The 1992 prevalence rates are calculated from the 1992 National Health Interview Survey. Because the percentage of the population that is blind in both eyes is relatively small, the rate of blindness does not increase continuously in 1992. For comparison with the 1935–38 survey, the 1992 NHIS was restricted to men below 90 years of age. Note that, when no age restriction is imposed, the rate of blindness rises to 2,049 for men and 1,389 for women.

Provided that undercounting in the 1928–31 survey does not depend on age, figure 4.1 accurately represents increases in relative risk with age and tells us that the increase in cardiovascular disease with age was much sharper in the past than it is today.

The elderly of the 1930s were much more likely to be blind. Table 4.2 compares rates of blindness in both eyes per 100,000 persons by age as estimated from the 1935–38 National Health Survey (Britten 1941) and from the 1992 National Health Interview Survey. Especially striking is the sharp increase in blindness at older ages in 1935–38 relative to 1992. Britten (1941) calculated that, in 1935–38, the annual incidence of new cases of blindness among men rose from 11 per 100,000 at ages fifty to fifty-nine to 31 at ages sixty to sixty-nine, 42 at ages seventy to seventy-nine, and 107 at ages eighty to eighty-nine. Among women the annual incidence of new cases of blindness rose from 9 per 100,000 at ages fifty to fifty-nine to 24 at ages sixty to sixty-nine, 81 at ages seventy to seventy-nine, and 232 at ages eighty to eighty-nine. The most common causes of blindness in 1935–38 were cataracts (34 percent), degenerative diseases (23 percent), glaucoma (18 percent), and general infectious diseases (11 percent). Today cataracts can be treated easily, and causes of glaucoma, such as diabetes, are now more readily controlled.

Reductions in occupational hazards have also contributed to the improving health of the elderly. In 1935–38, when 70 percent of losses of fingers arose from occupational injuries, 25 percent of men and 3 percent of women age sixty-five or older had lost one or more fingers (U.S. Public Health Service 1938). In contrast, the respective figures were only 7 and 1 percent in 1992 (estimated from the National Health Interview Survey).

Not only did earlier cohorts suffer high rates of chronic disease in old age, but they also suffered high rates of chronic disease at young adult ages. Among the Union army cohort the prevalence of tuberculosis, hernias, varicose veins, deafness, epilepsy, clubfoot, and deformities of the hand was higher in

1861–65 than in 1985–88. At ages thirty-five to thirty-nine hernia rates, for example, were more than three times as prevalent in the 1860s as in the 1980s. Of special note is the much higher prevalence of clubfoot in the 1860s, a birth anomaly that suggests that damage during the fetal stage and during birth was more likely in the past than it is today (Fogel 1994).

My comparison of chronic disease rates among Union army veterans and recent veterans, of blindness rates in the 1930s and today, and of the relative risk of heart disease in the 1930s and today suggests that average health has improved considerably, but many chronic conditions cannot be compared over such a long time span. Different disease definitions used in the past sometimes confounded acute and chronic conditions. Chronic conditions were enumerated only if they resulted in illness. Changes in prevalence rates within disease categories that, for example, have led to arteriosclerosis displacing valvular heart disease as the most common form of heart disease may invalidate comparisons of prevalence rates over three-quarters of a century. In addition, the comparison of prevalence rates by itself does not give much insight into how the large decline in chronic conditions occurred. Fortunately, anthropometric measures provide insight. Height and weight adjusted for height permit me to relate disease prevalence to cumulative nutritional status during developmental ages as measured by height and to current nutritional status as measured by the Body Mass Index (BMI), or the Quetelet Index, which is defined as body weight in kilograms divided by the square of body height measured in meters. These anthropometric health proxies have the additional advantage of being measured consistently across time.

4.1.2 Height

Adult height is a measure of cumulative nutritional status over all the growing years, including the fetal stage and early infancy. Mean heights are consistently lower in deprived populations. This does not necessarily imply that the level of nutrient intake is lower in a deprived population, but it may mirror a worse disease environment, overcrowding, a harsher climate, greater physical exertion, or the mother's poor health. Large height differentials are present between high- and low-income groups in developing countries, were present in the Western world in the past century, and still persist in the West, albeit in much diminished magnitude.[3]

Height and mortality are related. Mortality first declines with height, to reach a minimum at heights close to 185 centimeters, and then starts to rise (see fig. 4.2). This is true not only among modern Norwegians, the largest population for which both height and subsequent mortality are known, but also among Union army veterans. In the case of Union army veterans, the relation between height and mortality remains unchanged when controlling for such socioeconomic covariates as occupation, nativity, and urbanization. A similar relation is found between height and self-reported health status among modern American males and between height and the probability of rejection for military service among Union army soldiers (Fogel 1994). Height appears to be

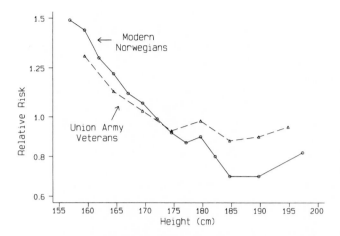

Fig. 4.2   Comparison of relative mortality risk by height among modern Norwegian males and Union army veterans circa 1900

Source: Costa and Steckel (1997).

Note: Height for 309,554 modern Norwegians was measured at ages forty to fifty-nine, and the period of risk was seven years. Height of 322 Union army veterans aged twenty-three to forty-nine was measured at enlistment, and the period of risk was from age fifty-five to age seventy-five. Calculated from the data in Waaler (1984) and from the Union army sample.

inversely related to heart and respiratory diseases and positively related to the hormonal cancers (Barker 1992), suggesting that the high relative risk of heart disease at older ages observed in 1928–31 may be partially related to poor conditions early in life.

Data from developing countries imply that the effect of height on productivity is substantial. Using data for rural south India, Deolaliker (1988) finds that the elasticity of wage rates with respect to heights is in the range of 0.28–0.66. Haddad and Bouis (1991) report that wages in the rural Philippines are strongly influenced by height. In an extension, Foster and Rosenzweig (1992) find that height and calories have particularly large effects on piece-rate wages. Data from the antebellum American South show that height and weight were positively associated with slave market value, suggesting that better-fed, healthier slaves were more productive (Margo and Steckel 1982).

Americans born in the past century and at the beginning of this century were stunted by today's standards. Men who served in the Union army were almost four centimeters shorter than men born in 1970. The Norwegian height curve suggests that, had the distribution of heights in the Union army sample been the same as among American males in 1991, older-age mortality rates would have fallen by 9 percent. Some subsequent cohorts fared even worse. Average heights for the native born reached a nadir in the 1880s, and those born in that decade were almost nine centimeters shorter than cohorts born in 1970. Thereafter, average height improved rapidly (see fig. 4.3).

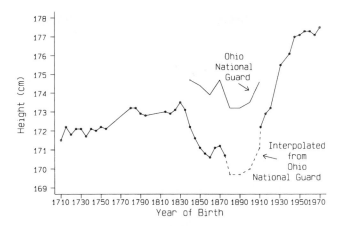

Fig. 4.3   Mean heights of white, native-born males by birth cohort, 1710–1970
Source: Costa and Steckel (1997).

4.1.3   Body Mass Index

Body Mass Index (BMI), a measure of current nutritional status, may be an even stronger predictor of productivity, morbidity, and mortality than height. It measures not only nutritional intake but also the effect of illness, climate, and physical exertion. The relation between weight and mortality among Union army veterans measured at ages fifty to sixty-four and observed from age fifty until age seventy-five resembles that seen among modern Norwegian males (Costa and Steckel 1997). Mortality risk first declines rapidly at low weights as BMI increases, stays relatively flat over BMI levels from the low to the high twenties, and then starts to rise again, but less steeply than at very low BMIs (see fig. 4.4). The similar mortality pattern across these two very different populations suggests that standards derived from recent populations can be applied to past populations. Therefore, had it been possible to shift the BMI distribution of Union army veterans one standard deviation to the right so that the mean would be equivalent to that prevailing in modern Norway, the 14 percent reduction in the mortality rate implied by the Norwegian curve would explain roughly 20 percent of the total decline in mortality above age fifty from 1900 to 1986, a percentage greater than that explained by changes in height.

When height and weight are simultaneously related to mortality through a mortality surface, it becomes obvious that optimal weight varies with height. To minimize their mortality risk, the shorter should be heavier and the taller leaner (Fogel 1994). When BMI curves are plotted by cause of death, there is a strong U shape for obstructive lung disease, stomach cancer, and cerebrovascular disease, a very slight U shape for cardiovascular disease and diabetes, and none at all for colon cancer, tuberculosis, and lung cancer (Waaler 1984). When Waaler (1984) deleted from his sample men who died within five years

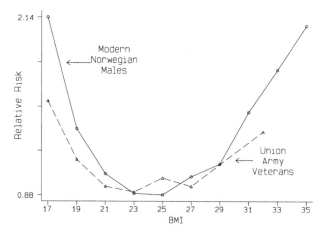

Fig. 4.4   Comparison of relative mortality risk by BMI level among men fifty years of age, Union army veterans circa 1900 and modern Norwegians
Source: Costa and Steckel (1997).
Note: In the Norwegian data BMI for 79,084 men was measured at ages forty-five to forty-nine, and the period of risk was seven years. BMI of 550 Union army veterans was measured at ages forty-five to sixty-four, and the observation period was twenty-five years. Calculated from the data in Waaler (1984) and from the Union army sample.

after measurement, the U shape was even more pronounced. A thirty-two-year follow-up study of a cohort measured at age eighteen found that the most obese men had higher mortality rates from coronary heart disease, whereas the leanest men had higher mortality rates from cancer (Hoffmans, Kromhout, and de Lezenne Coulander 1989).

BMI is also correlated with ill health. A plot of BMI against self-reported health status shows the same U-shaped pattern for males aged fifty to sixty-four as seen for mortality risk (see fig. 4.5). When height and weight are simultaneously related to ill health through a surface, the resulting surface is similar to that for mortality and predicts a decline of 6 percent per decade in ill health among the elderly from 1910 to the 1980s (Fogel 1994). This predicted decline is consistent with Manton, Corder, and Stallard's (1993) findings on the decline in disability rates among the elderly between 1982 and 1989 and is consistent with the decline in chronic conditions observed among veterans age sixty-five or older between 1910 and the present. BMI is also related to more objective measures of ill health. The prevalence of hypertension, heart disease, and other circulatory disorders and of diabetes and chronic neck pain rises with obesity. Chronic respiratory disorders show a U-shaped relation to BMI (Makela et al. 1991; Negri et al. 1988; Roman Diaz 1992). The incidence of pulmonary tuberculosis is greater at lower BMI levels (Tverdal 1988). BMI is also related to the number of chronic conditions, bed days, hospitalizations, and doctors' visits (see fig. 4.6).[4]

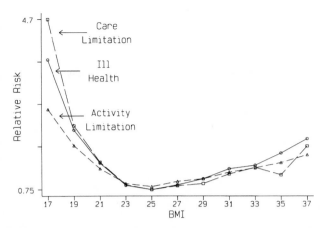

Fig. 4.5 BMI and relative risk of ill health, as measured by presence of self-reported activity or care limitation or of self-reported ill health among white men aged fifty to sixty-four

Source: Costa (1996).

Note: An individual with an activity or care limitation indicated that he could not perform certain basic activities of daily living or needed help with personal care, respectively. Individuals were also asked whether they were in poor, fair, good, or excellent health. An individual who answered poor or fair is considered to be in ill health. All observations are centered at the marks.

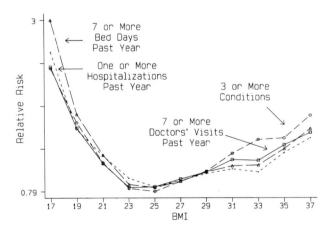

Fig. 4.6 BMI and relative risk of chronic conditions, bed days, hospitalizations, and doctors' visits among white males aged fifty to sixty-four

Source: Costa (1996).

Note: All observations are centered at the marks.

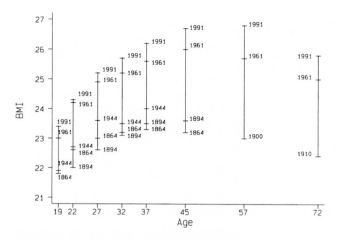

Fig. 4.7   Mean BMI by age group and year, 1863–1991

Source: Costa and Steckel (1997).

Note: The age groups are centered at the marks and are ages eighteen to nineteen, twenty to twenty-four, twenty-five to twenty-nine, thirty to thirty-four, thirty-five to thirty-nine, forty to forty-nine, fifty to sixty-four, and sixty-five to seventy-nine. For some years BMI is not available for a specific age group.

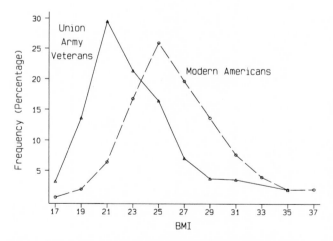

Fig. 4.8   BMI distribution among Union army veterans and modern, white American males, aged fifty to sixty-four

Source: Costa (1996).

Note: All observations are centered at the marks.

Not only were men born in the nineteenth century stunted by today's standards, but their BMIs at adult ages were also about 13 percent lower than current U.S. levels (see figs. 4.7 and 4.8). Mean BMI for modern Americans aged fifty to sixty-four is 26.4, while that for Union army veterans was 23.0. This was not necessarily because Americans today are more obese; they also have greater muscle and bone mass (Costa and Steckel 1997). Men in the past were thin by today's standards, perhaps because chronic disease rates were so high, nutritional intakes lower, physical activity greater, and exposure to occupational hazards higher. The corrosive effects of occupation were well recognized by contemporaries: "Castin'? No I never did that. It's a hell of a job. The fires burn a man out. Lots of them get burnt out. That heat is no good for a man. You know Charley Buckland? He's burnt out. That man used to be as fleshy as I am, but look at him now. Skinny as a rail" (WPA Life Histories Collection, interview with Robert White). Differences in BMI between men today and men in the past widened with age, perhaps because chronic disease rates increased more rapidly with age in the past or because differences in nutritional intakes, physical activity, and exposure to occupational hazards have cumulative effects. Insufficiency of contemporaneous income was probably not the major determinant of BMI. Mean BMI at older ages did not differ among farmers, artisans, and laborers. At younger ages, it did not differ among professionals and proprietors, artisans, and laborers.

The next section uses BMI as a health proxy to examine the relation between health and labor force participation. BMI is used as a proxy, rather than height or specific chronic conditions, because the relation between labor force participation and either height or specific chronic conditions among Union army veterans is relatively weak.

4.2 Health and Labor Force Participation

Despite the large health differential between Union army veterans and recent populations, the relation between BMI and labor force participation is similar among Union army veterans and modern American men found in successive years of the 1985–91 National Health Interview Survey (NHIS).[5] Figure 4.9 shows that the relative risk that a man aged fifty to sixty-four would be out of the labor force in 1985–91 falls precipitously from a BMI level of 17, levels off at 22–28, and then rises gradually. Among Union army veterans in 1900 for whom BMI was measured at ages fifty to sixty-four, the probability of participating was also at its peak at a BMI of 22–28 (see fig. 4.10). Although sampling error warrants some caution, among Union army veterans the probability of nonparticipation increased sharply, not just at low BMIs, but also at high BMIs.

The relation between BMI and labor force participation is weaker at older ages among both modern Americans and Union army veterans in 1910, even though there is still a strong relation between BMI and other health proxies,

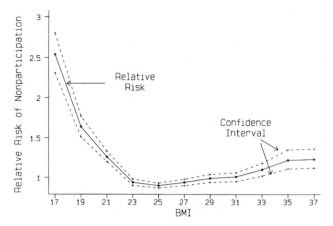

Fig. 4.9   Relation BMI and relative risk of nonparticipation, white, modern, American men, aged fifty to sixty-four, 1985–91
Source: Costa (1996).
Note: All observations are centered at the marks.

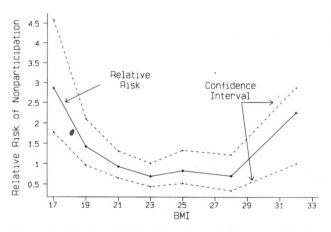

Fig. 4.10   Relation BMI and relative risk of nonparticipation, Union army veterans, 1900
Source: Costa (1996).
Note: All observations are centered at the marks.

such as the relative risk of self-reported ill health or of seven or more bed days within a year (see fig. 4.11). Among modern Americans, the relation between BMI and labor force participation is flatter at ages sixty-five to seventy-nine than at ages fifty to sixty-four, and the relative risk that the lean are not in the labor force is lower. Among Union army veterans, the distinctive U-shaped

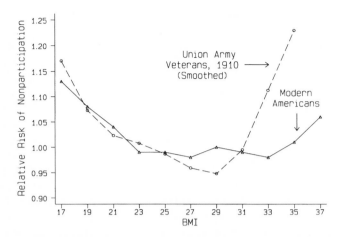

Fig. 4.11   Relation BMI at ages sixty-five to seventy-nine and relative risk of nonparticipation, modern American males, 1987–92, and Union army veterans, 1910
Note: Calculated from the 1987–92 NHIS and the Union army sample.

relation between BMI and labor force participation persists, but the U shape is less deep and the relative risk of being out of the labor force lower both for the lean and for the obese. Health appears to have less of an effect on the labor supply decision at older ages. This conclusion is tentative because sampling error problems are even more acute among older Union army veterans. To avoid working with excessively small samples, I will focus on men aged fifty to sixty-four.

In investigating the relation between BMI and labor force participation, it is necessary to control for socioeconomic and demographic characteristics because these variables are correlated with BMI. Among Union army veterans, wage income, as proxied by occupation, and BMI were positively correlated, while pensions and BMI were negatively related. Among modern Americans, the correlation between wage income and BMI is slightly negative, while that between disability benefits and BMI is likely to be strongly negative. Provided that I control for socioeconomic and demographic conditions, I can derive estimates of the BMI levels that maximize the probability of participation among both modern Americans and Union army veterans. Once I derive these BMI levels, I can then determine whether the BMI level that maximizes the probability of labor force participation has changed over the last ninety years. I can also derive estimates of the elasticity of labor force nonparticipation with respect to BMI for the two groups of men. Changes in this elasticity provide some indication of whether health, as proxied by BMI, is now more or less important to the retirement decision than in the past.

The BMI level that maximizes the probability of participation can be derived using a regression framework similar to that employed in the previous chapter. There is an additional complication in the estimation of the participation-maximizing BMI level among modern Americans. Recall that an individual's decision to retire depends on both the income he expects to receive when working and the income he expects to receive when not working. In the case of Union army veterans, pensions did not depend on labor force status, and unobserved income flows were proxied by occupation. For modern Americans, income flows are observed, but the income flows under either the retirement or the participation option are observed only if the respective choice was made. If an individual is in the labor force, then we do not know how much in Social Security disability payments he would receive were he to withdraw from the labor force. Alternatively, if an individual is out of the labor force, then we do not know how much in income he would receive were he to enter the labor force. These income flows can be estimated, provided that a correction is made that accounts for differences in characteristics between those who choose work and those who choose nonparticipation. First, a participation probit is estimated where the explanatory variables are BMI, age, education, veteran and marital status, year of survey, extent of urbanization, geographic region, foreign birth, and the presence of a care limitation (i.e., whether the individual reported needing help with personal care). Then income is estimated for both participants and nonparticipants using the same explanatory variables, with the exception of the presence of a care limitation, and the inverse Mill's ratio to account for selection (see table 4.3).[6] Estimated nonparticipation income will therefore include income from disability programs as well as from family members. In the final step, the probability of labor force nonparticipation is then estimated by means of a probit in which the dependent variable is a dummy equal to one if the individual is not participating, and the independent variables are estimated family income when working, estimated family income when not working, BMI, marital status, age, and survey year (see table 4.4).[7]

The effect of BMI on the probability of participation is fairly large and significant.[8] The elasticity of nonparticipation with respect to BMI is 0.28. The BMI level that maximizes the probability of participation is 25.4—statistically indistinguishable from the BMI level that at the sample mean height of 1.78 meters minimizes mortality risk. When dummies are used for BMI levels, the risk of nonparticipation is minimized at BMI levels of 23–26, and the risk of nonparticipation is much greater at lower BMI levels, as in figure 4.9 above.

The regression specification includes no interactions between BMI and income. But it is certainly plausible to assume that the effect of health on the probability of participation varies by income. The poor cannot always afford to withdraw from the labor force even when they are ill. When BMI is interacted with a dummy for household income of less than $20,000 per year when not participating in the labor force, the BMI level that maximizes the probability of participation of men in households where this income is less than $20,000 per year is 25.9, compared to 24.7 among men in households where

Table 4.3   **Participation Probit and Earnings Equations Used to Estimate Income in and out of the Labor Force, NHIS, Men Aged 50–64**

Variable	Mean	Participation Probit Parameter	S.E.	Participant Income Parameter	S.E.	Nonparticipant Income Parameter	S.E.
Probability of participation	.23						
Log of participant income	10.41						
Log of nonparticipant income	9.83						
Intercept		22.713‡	1.856	8.792‡	.949	3.804*	1.936
BMI	26.4	−.894‡	.112	.189†	.055	.119	.088
BMI^2	712.24	.029‡	.004	−.006‡	.002	−.003	.003
BMI^4/10	1,959.45	.003‡	.000	.001†	.000	.000	.000
Age	56.86	−.628‡	.054	−.036	.027	.107*	.060
Age squared	3,233.06	.007‡	.000	.000	.000	−.001	.001
Dummy = 1 if:							
Care limitation	.03	1.780‡	.044				
Less than high school	.39						
High school graduate	.36	−.121‡	.018	.047‡	.008	.177‡	.018
Some college	.14	−.200‡	.024	.143‡	.010	.366‡	.026
Graduate school	.11	−.468‡	.029	.328‡	.011	.651‡	.034
Married	.86	−.397‡	.021	.372‡	.011	.587‡	.020
Veteran	.65	.020	.017	.098‡	.007	.135‡	.019
Foreign born	.03	−.045	.047	−.104‡	.019	−.306‡	.049
Non-MSA	.27						
MSA 1 million or more	.38	−.097‡	.020	.276‡	.008	.242‡	.021
MSA ≤ 1 million	.35	−.033*	.020	.182‡	.008	.151‡	.020
Northeast	.22						
Midwest	.27	−.045†	.023	−.060‡	.009	−.009	.024
South	.31	.119‡	.022	−.078‡	.009	−.083‡	.023
West	.20	.100‡	.100	−.028†	.010	−.020	.025
1985	.14						
1986	.09	.009	.034	.009	.014	.080†	.034
1987	.16	.031	.029	.070‡	.012	.088‡	.029
1988	.16	.022	.029	.111‡	.012	.112‡	.029
1989	.15	.047	.029	.156‡	.012	.219‡	.030
1990	.15	.040	.030	.196‡	.012	.249‡	.030
1991	.15	.065†	.029	.214‡	.012	.286‡	.030
Inverse Mills ratio				−.221‡	.032	−.121‡	.020

Source: Costa (1996).

Note: The symbols *, †, and ‡ indicate significance at the 10 percent, 5 percent, and 1 percent levels, respectively. The participation probit was run on 39,923 observations. The likelihood ratio test for all coefficients except the intercept being different from zero is 9,062. The participant income regression was run on 25,665 observations, adjusted R^2 = .19. The nonparticipant income regression was run on 7,517 observations, adjusted R^2 = .25. The standard errors in the income regressions are unadjusted, but, since the equations are used only for prediction, this is unimportant to interpretation.

Table 4.4   **Probit of Determinants of Probability Nonparticipation with Nonparticipation as the Dependent Variable, NHIS 1985–91**

Variable	Mean	Parameter	S.E.	Mean Derivative
Nonparticipating	.23			
Intercept		20.230‡	1.811	
Family income/10,000:				
If nonparticipant	2.15	.292‡	.031	.033
If participant	3.33	−.595‡	.031	−.111
Age	56.86	−.537‡	.522	−.133
Age squared	3,251.86	.005‡	.000	.001
Dummy = 1 if married	.86	−.052†	−.024	−.015
Dummy = 1 if year is:				
1985	.12			
1986	.09	−.019	.033	.000
1987	.17	.082‡	.028	.020
1988	.16	.133‡	.029	.030
1989	.15	.161‡	.029	.041
1990	.15	.209‡	.030	.050
1991	.16	.233‡	.030	.057
BMI	26.43	−.733‡	.108	−.208
BMI^2	712.36	.024‡	.004	.007
$BMI^4/10$	1,959.90	−.003‡	.000	−.001
39,923 observations				

Source: Costa (1996).

Note: The symbols *, †, and ‡ indicate significance at the 10 percent, 5 percent, and 1 percent levels, respectively. The likelihood ratio for the test that the coefficients on all variables except for the intercept are equal to zero is 6,773. Family income was estimated by means of the Heckman two-step selection correction. Additional variables that were included in the income and participation regressions were the extent of urbanization, education, geographic region, foreign birth, and the presence of a care limitation.

this income is more than $20,000. But recall that, to minimize their mortality risk, the shorter should be heavier and the taller leaner (Fogel 1994). Those in high-income households are taller, and the difference in BMI levels that maximize the probability of participation is accounted for by differences in height. When dummies for a low BMI (under 22) and a high BMI (over 30) are included in the regression and interacted with income both in and out of the labor force, the resulting coefficients are small and insignificant. The evidence thus suggests that the effect of health on the probability of participation does not vary by income.

The retirement problem of Union army veterans in 1900 is investigated using the same econometric specification as in the previous chapter, with the exception that BMI replaces the health dummies on the basis of the ratings of the examining surgeons. Because figure 4.10 above indicated that the risk of labor force nonparticipation was strongly U shaped in BMI levels, a quadratic rather than a cubic specification was employed.[9]

Table 4.5　　　　**Probit of Determinants of Probability of Nonparticipation with Nonparticipation as the Dependent Variable, Union Army Sample**

Variable	Mean	Parameter	S.E.	Mean Derivative
Nonparticipating	.16			
Intercept		−6.257*	3.337	
BMI	22.97	−.551‡	.160	−.107
BMI²	540.56	.011‡	.003	.002
Age	61.32	.054‡	.012	.011
Monthly pension	12.73	.030‡	.010	.006
State unemployment	3.62	2.168‡	.708	.419
Dummy = 1 if farmer	.46			
Professional or proprietor	.17	−.552†	−.107	−.119
Laborer	.22	−.083	.227	−.016
Artisan	.15	.135	.234	.026
Does not own residence	.31	.319*	.178	.062
Atlantic seaboard	.20			
Midwest	.74	.583†	.279	.113
Other region	.06	−.146	.547	−.028
Urban county	.36	.363*	.177	.070
4 or more dependents	.14	−.538	.314	−.104
Servant present	.02	−.747	.663	−.144
Boarder present	.04	−.034	.421	−.007
Illiterate	.06	.079	.330	.015
Foreign born	.10	−.065	.272	−.012
471 observations				

Source: Costa (1996).

Note: The symbols *, †, and ‡ indicate significance at the 10 percent, 5 percent, and 1 percent levels, respectively. The likelihood ratio for the test that all coefficients except for the intercept are equal to zero is 96.11. Mean duration of unemployment in months for manufacturing workers is from table A.13 in Keyssar (1986, 340–41).

Once again the effect of BMI on retirement is substantial and significant (see table 4.5). The elasticity of nonparticipation with respect to BMI was 1.07. The BMI level that maximizes labor force participation is 25.2—well within the range that maximizes labor force participation in figure 4.10. This BMI level is statistically indistinguishable from that which for the sample mean height of 1.73 meters minimizes mortality risk. Coefficients on the interactions of BMI dummies with pension amount were small and insignificant. The BMI level that maximizes the probability of participation remains unchanged when an instrumented probit is estimated using whether a disability could be traced to the war as an instrumental variable.

In contrast to modern American males the body build of Union army veterans placed them at relatively high risk of nonparticipation. The mean BMI of modern Americans is 26.4, within half a standard deviation of the level that maximizes the probability of participation within the sample of modern Americans. However, the mean BMI in the Union army sample is 23.0, not within

half a standard deviation of the level that maximizes the probability of participation within the Union army sample.[10]

Figures 4.9 and 4.10 above showed that low BMI levels have a large effect
on the nonparticipation probability of both Union army veterans and modern
American men. It is therefore not surprising that, among Union army veterans,
for whom mean BMI is low, the elasticity of nonparticipation with respect to
BMI is larger than it is for modern Americans. Some adjustment to the elasticities can be made by evaluating the Union army elasticity at the mean BMI of
modern Americans. This calculation yields an elasticity of 0.88, still much
larger than the elasticity of 0.28 found among modern Americans. The regressions produce results similar to those of figures 4.9 and 4.10, which show that,
in 1900, the excessively lean and the excessively obese were at relatively
greater risk of being out of the labor force compared to their present-day counterparts.

The regressions have shown that, in both 1900 and 1985–91, the BMI that
maximizes the probability of participation was about 25 and that the relative
risk of nonparticipation first fell with increasing BMI and then rose. But the
elasticity of nonparticipation with respect to BMI has fallen since 1900, implying that the retirement decision is now less dependent on health.

4.3   Interpreting BMI

BMI depends on individual characteristics such as smoking status, exercise
habits, and illness. If we do not control for these characteristics in estimating
the effect of BMI on retirement, then we may confound the effect of BMI with
that of other factors. The problem may be particularly acute when we try to
estimate whether the BMI level that maximizes the probability of being in the
labor force has remained constant throughout the shifts in the work and disease
environment and in health habits that occurred over the century. The occupational structure has shifted from one in which physically strenuous occupations
are common to one in which sedentary occupations are. The percentage of
muscle mass may therefore differ across the two samples. Cigarette smoking
became a widespread practice after World War II. The higher risk of nonparticipation among thin, modern Americans could arise from the thinner being
smokers and therefore in worse health.[11] As smoking rates fall, the BMI level
that maximizes participation rates could change. Among Union army veterans,
a group of men suffering from much higher rates of respiratory disorders and
diarrhea than men today, the BMI levels that maximize participation rates may
have been high because infectious diseases were so prevalent.

Although information on muscle mass is unavailable, the 1985, 1990, and
1991 National Health Interview Surveys provide information on exercise habits. Figure 4.12 shows the relation between labor force participation and BMI
in the entire sample when the sample is divided into those who exercise regularly and those who do not. Note that the relation between labor force partici-

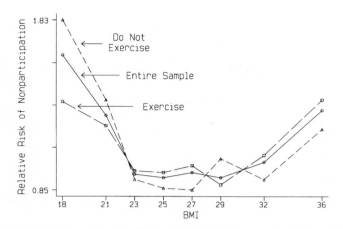

Fig. 4.12   BMI and relative risk labor force nonparticipation by exercise habits among modern white Americans, 1985, 1990, and 1991
Source: Costa (1996).
Note: All observations are centered at the marks.

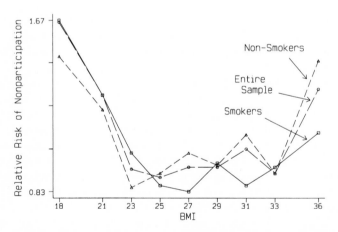

Fig. 4.13   BMI and relative risk labor force nonparticipation by smoking status among modern white Americans, 1985, 1987, 1990, and 1991
Source: Costa (1996).
Note: All observations are centered at the marks.

pation and BMI does not change by that much, suggesting that the estimated relation is not confounded by differences in muscle mass.[12]

Nor does the relation between labor force participation and BMI change when a sample consisting of the NHIS in the years 1985, 1987, 1990, and 1991 is divided into smokers and nonsmokers (see fig. 4.13). Furthermore,

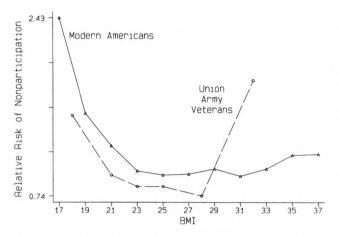

Fig. 4.14   BMI and relative risk labor force nonparticipation, Union army veterans and modern white American males, deleting the very ill
Source: Costa (1996).
Note: All observations are centered at the marks.

controlling for other characteristics, the addition of smoking status as an explanatory variable in predictions of labor force participation does not change the coefficients on dummies for BMI levels or the coefficients on the cubic specification for BMI.[13]

The relation between BMI and labor force participation among modern American men and Union army veterans is unchanged when the very sick are deleted from the sample, suggesting that the relation between BMI and labor force participation does not arise from current illness alone (see fig. 4.14).[14] Rather, BMI measures the stock of health. When men who reported at least one condition are deleted from the sample of modern Americans, the obese are no longer at greater risk of nonparticipation than those of average weight for height, suggesting that BMI partially reflects chronic conditions.[15]

Changes in relative chronic disease rates may have changed the relation between BMI and retirement. The effect of chronic conditions on labor force participation differs greatly by chronic condition (Bartel and Taubman 1979). If chronic conditions that are now correlated with a high BMI do not have as large an effect on labor force participation as conditions that in the past were correlated with high BMI, then high BMI levels will no longer have as large an effect on participation rates. Most of the heart disease observed among Union army veterans was valvular rather than arteriosclerotic, and among these men prevalence of heart disease decreased with increasing BMI. Today prevalence increases with BMI.

The constancy of the BMI level that maximizes the probability of being in the labor force, even when personal characteristics such as smoking, exercise habits, and the extent of chronic conditions are controlled for, suggests that the lessened effect of BMI on retirement rates cannot be accounted for by changes in personal characteristics. Although we cannot say with certainty, perhaps the changing nature of chronic conditions, technological advances in the control of chronic conditions, and improvements in the workplace that now enable those in poor health to participate in the labor force more actively may explain the reduced role of health in the retirement decision.

4.4 Implications

One of the most significant findings of this chapter has been that rates of chronic disease among the elderly in the first half of this century were extremely high. Heart disease was almost three times as prevalent, musculoskeletal and respiratory diseases were one and a half times as prevalent, and digestive diseases were more than four times as prevalent among veterans aged sixty-five or over in 1910 as in 1985–88. The elderly also suffered from high rates of blindness and from occupational injuries. Their risk of specific forms of heart disease relative to the general population was much greater than that of the elderly today.

The findings suggest that chronic conditions were far more prevalent throughout the life cycle for those born in the nineteenth century than is suggested by the theory of the epidemiological transition. This theory has characterized the past as a period when chronic conditions were relatively rare because the predominance of acute conditions ensured that those individuals susceptible to them would not survive. Support for this characterization of the past has come from cause-of-death data, which indicate that in the past few individuals died of chronic disease, whereas today chronic diseases are the most common causes of death. But reliance on cause-of-death information to characterize the epidemiology of the past may have led to a significant misrepresentation of the distribution of health conditions among the living. Only 61 percent of Union army veterans observed at age sixty-five died of one of the causes listed in a surgeons' exam. The chronic disease rates of Union army veterans suggest that any genetic advantage to having survived the deadly infectious diseases of childhood and adolescence was offset by a lifetime of socioeconomic and biomedical stress that left health in old age badly impaired and that sharply curtailed the life expectations of the elderly.

The trend in prevalence rates of chronic conditions, in the relative risk of chronic conditions at older ages, and in anthropometric measures suggests that the secular rise in retirement cannot be attributed to an increase in chronic disorders, as implied by the work of Riley (1989) and Verbrugge (1984). Retirement rates increased despite, not because of, improving health. Furthermore, because the average sixty-five-year-old today is much healthier than a sixty-five-year-old at the beginning of the century or even at the middle of the century, a retirement age first established by Bismarck and later enshrined in the Social Security Act may no longer be an appropriate demarcation of old age. What is more, health now appears to be less important to the labor force decision. Although the relation between BMI and the risk of labor force nonparticipation in 1900 was remarkably similar to that in 1985–91, men in 1900 were much more responsive to changes in health than they are now, perhaps because of changes in the relation between chronic conditions and BMI, improved control of chronic conditions, and reduced job requirements brought about by the rise of the clerical sector, the increased mechanization of manufacturing, greater safety in the workplace, and the shortening of the workday.

Had the distribution of BMI in the Union army sample been the same as that in the NHIS, the probability of nonparticipation among men age forty-five to sixty-four would have fallen by 6 percent, thereby increasing the total output of all male workers by 1 percent.[16] But how could such a shift in BMI have been achieved? Advances in medical care, public health investments in sanitation, improved working conditions, and rising incomes have ameliorated both early childhood and adult environmental conditions. The mounting body of evidence of a relation between chronic conditions at late adult ages and early childhood environmental factors suggests that better early life conditions have improved adult health (Barker 1992, 1994). However, these improvements may have changed the relation between BMI and the relative risk of nonparticipation. If the increase in BMI was accompanied by a shift in the relation between BMI and the relative risk of labor force nonparticipation, then, because the effect of high BMI on retirement is relatively small in recent data, if the distribution of BMI in the Union army sample had been the same as that in the NHIS, the probability of nonparticipation would have fallen by 10 percent (rather than 6 percent), and the total output of male workers would have increased by 1.7 percent.[17]

The findings do not necessarily imply that, as the population grows increasingly healthier, jobs become less physically demanding, control over chronic conditions improves, and greater efforts are made to increase the incorporation of the old and disabled into the labor force, labor force participation rates among older men will rise. Secularly rising incomes lower participation rates and, according to chapter 3, explain up to 60 percent of the fall in labor force participation rates among men sixty-five years of age or older. Moreover, because it affects wage levels, improved health may lower labor force participation rates. Recent cross-sectional evidence indicates that the male labor supply curve is gently backward sloping (Killingsworth 1983, 12–13). In the nineteenth century, the labor supply curve for working men was strongly backward bending (Whaples 1990). If BMI were a strong predictor of wages in the nineteenth century, the strongly backward-bending labor supply curve implies that early improvements in health may have produced a substantial rise in retirement.[18] The findings thus suggest that, although health is now less important to the retirement decision than in the past, and although there have been improvements in the health of the elderly population, these factors might not induce greater labor force participation.

4.5 Summary

At the beginning of the century the health of men older than sixty-four was very poor compared with that of men today, who have benefited from advances in medical technology, lessened occupational hazards, and better early life conditions. Despite improvements in average health, and despite the decreasing importance of health to the retirement decision, retirement rates rose. An individual today looks forward to a long retirement, much of which is spent in good health. Age sixty-five may therefore no longer be as appropriate a demarcation of old age as it was in the first half of the century, when the health of a typical sixty-five-year-old was very poor.

Notes

1. For a review, see Quinn and Burkhauser (1990).
2. For example, in the 1928–31 survey no attempt was made in the published results to distinguish between acute and chronic conditions, thus limiting the set of conditions that could be examined. Not only were conditions in that survey self-reported and therefore dependent on health awareness (probably much higher in 1992); a condition is enumerated in the survey only if it resulted in illness during the survey year. More than one illness from the same cause within the year was rare, suggesting the undernumeration rather than overnumeration is the more likely problem.
3. Height differentials at adult ages have disappeared in Scandinavia and the Netherlands (Eveleth and Tanner 1990, 199).
4. When height and weight are jointly related to the presence of an activity, work, or care limitation or to the number of chronic conditions, bed days, hospitalizations, and doctors' visits, once again the resulting surface is similar to the mortality surface. However, in the case of the chronic conditions, bed days, hospitalizations, and doctors' visits, the relation with height is greatly diminished.
5. I examine the relative risk of nonparticipation, R_i, which at BMI level i is defined as

$$R_i = L_i / \left(\sum N_i L_i / N \right) = L_i / \bar{L} ,$$

where L_i is the probability of nonparticipation at BMI level i, N_i is the number of individuals of age i, $N = \sum N_i$, and $\bar{L}$ is the probability of nonparticipation over all BMI levels.
6. The inverse Mill's ratio is $\phi(\gamma w)/\Phi(\gamma w)$, where $\Phi(\ )$ is a standard normal cumulative distribution function, $\phi(\ )$ is a standard normal density function, γ is the vector of coefficients from the participation probit, and w is the vector of variables used in the participation probit. When the presence of a care limitation and BMI are included in the income equations, the coefficient on the presence of a care limitation is insignificant. The presence of a care limitation is therefore used to ensure statistical identifiability.

7. Provided that not all the variables used in the two-step selection correction are included in the final probit, the model will be identified. The covariance matrix is approximated as if estimated family income were the exact exogenous variable.

8. Tests revealed that a quadratic specification for age and a cubic specification for BMI fit the data. The use of dummy variables for age and BMI indicated that interactions between age and BMI were small and insignificant. The use of a spline indicated that retirement did not rise abruptly at age sixty-two, perhaps because the effect of Social Security benefits is captured by income when out of the labor force. I also tested whether height had any effect on retirement by including the log of height as an explanatory variable. The coefficient on height was insignificant, perhaps because height is correlated with income.

9. When either a cubic or a dummy variable specification is used, the coefficients on BMI are no longer significant. Work with the NHIS indicates that the significance of coefficients on BMI is more sensitive to sample size when a dummy variable rather than a continuous specification is used.

10. The standard deviation of BMI in the Union army sample is 3.6, whereas that in the sample of modern Americans is 3.7. The observed relation between BMI and labor force participation is not an artifact of distance of the mean from the level that maximizes the probability of participation. When the sample of modern Americans is randomly restricted to have the same fraction of men in BMI categories as the Union army sample, the relation between health and participation remains unchanged.

11. Lee et al. (1993) argue that the influence of cigarette smoking can skew weight recommendations that are optimal in terms of subsequent mortality.

12. In both fig. 4.12 and fig. 4.13 below, the relative risk of nonparticipation is lower than in fig. 4.9 above. Because of missing information, few men in the sample had a BMI of less than 18.

13. When smoking is interacted with BMI, the coefficient on the resulting variable is insignificant. Once again, the coefficients on BMI remain unchanged.

14. Among men who are in the labor force, the relation between BMI and sick days is U shaped and similar to that between BMI and labor force participation.

15. However, the thin still face a greater risk of nonparticipation, perhaps because the strong focus in the medical literature on the problems of obesity means that the obese are more likely to be diagnosed as having a chronic condition.

16. The increase in labor force participation rates would have added 31,806 male workers in the labor force in 1900. Assuming that each of these workers would produce the average annual output per employee in 1900, the increase in the total output of male workers forty-five to sixty-four would have been 0.6 percent. Assuming that the probability of nonparticipation among all men in 1900 would have fallen by 6 percent had they had modern BMIs, 226,674 more workers would have been added to the labor force, increasing the total output of male workers by 1 percent (estimated from the nonparticipation graph and Series D 29-41 in U.S. Bureau of the Census 1975, 131–32). This calculation absts from any complications caused by the substitutability of healthy and unhealthy workers and the impact of increases in labor force participation among older men on the employment prospects of the young.

17. Repeating the previous calculation, the total output of male workers age forty-five to sixty-four would have increased by 0.8 percent. Again assuming that the probability of nonparticipation among all men would have fallen by 10 percent, the total output of male workers would have increased by 1.7 percent.

18. In the NHIS the effect of BMI on income was substantial among low-income families and declined as family income rose. Estimates from quantile regressions indicate that the elasticity of family income with respect to BMI ranges from 0.50 for the tenth income decile, to 0.11 for the fiftieth, and to 0 for the eightieth.

5   The Older Worker

> If he got no reward whatever, the artist would go on working just
> the same; his actual reward, in fact, is often so little that he almost
> starves. But suppose a garment-worker got nothing for his labor:
> would he go on working just the same? Can one imagine his sub-
> mitting voluntarily to hardship and sore want that he might ex-
> press his soul in 200 more pairs of ladies' pants?
>
> H. L. Mencken (1922)

Occupation plays a crucial role in the retirement decision. Older men employed
in physically demanding, unpleasant jobs might prefer to retire rather than take
easier but lower-paying and less prestigious jobs. The less physically demanding the job, and the more hours flexibility it provides, the lower the likelihood of retirement. The self-employment occupations, particularly farming,
are widely perceived not only as providing greater hours flexibility than wage
work but also as having the additional advantage of permitting assistance by
family members or hired help. Yet both the farm and the nonfarm self-
employment sectors have declined in size since the beginning of the century.

Changes in the structure of industry may also have worsened the employment prospects of older workers. The skill and education mix demanded by
employers depends on the production technology within an industry. Older
workers who started their careers in growing industries might find themselves
in declining industries at the end of their careers. Once these older men are
laid off, they face great difficulties finding a new job. Firms might prefer to
hire younger workers because they can recoup their training costs over a much
longer period, because younger workers are better educated and trained, or
simply because they prefer younger workers. Because the average length of an
unemployment spell has risen for all workers, older workers, discouraged by
their labor market prospects, might retire rather than continue to search for a
new job.

In this chapter I investigate whether changing labor markets have worsened
the employment prospects of older workers. Do certain occupations, particularly farming, permit workers to remain in the labor force longer? Has a decline in these occupations increased retirement rates? Can rising retirement
rates be explained by the increased difficulties faced by unemployed older
workers in finding a new job?

5.1   Who Retires?

At the end of the last century the typical workingman older than sixty-four was a farmer. The typical workingman today is a white-collar worker and a very different type of white-collar worker from his counterpart one hundred or even fifty years ago, when most white-collar workers were proprietors or managers of businesses rather than professional or technical workers. Table 5.1 illustrates. Over half of older men were farmers in 1880, but by 1990 only 7 percent were. The elderly labor force employed in a white-collar job grew from one-tenth in 1880 to over half in 1990. The elderly labor force employed in the service sector increased sixfold, from less than 2 percent in 1880 to 13 percent by 1990. The one seemingly constant figure is that for manual occupations, consistently the second most common occupational category. But, even within this occupational grouping, skill and education levels have increased, as evinced by the decline in the percentage of common laborers.

All workers, not just the old, experienced the trends described in table 5.1. However, older workers always have been disproportionately concentrated in farm or manual occupations, while the young have dominated white-collar and service jobs. Within the broad occupational categories used in Table 5.1, older workers have been disproportionately concentrated in certain jobs within the broad occupational categories as well. In 1880, both younger and older crafts workers were shoemakers, but by 1910, when shoemaking had largely become a factory trade, older workers predominated in the older, artisanal tradition. Some jobs, such as those of janitor, guard, or watchman, always have been and still remain old men's jobs, constituting half of all nonhousehold service jobs in 1880, 60 percent in 1940, and 41 percent in 1990. The professional occupa-

Table 5.1   Occupational Distribution of Men Older than 64, 1880–1990

	1880	1910	1940	1970	1990
White collar	9.7	18.3	26.0	41.2	52.4
Professional, technical	3.2	3.8	5.5	11.5	18.9
Managers, officials, proprietors	4.8	9.4	12.2	12.4	14.8
Clerical	.6	2.3	3.5	7.4	7.5
Sales	1.1	2.9	4.7	9.8	11.2
Service	1.5	3.8	8.0	14.7	12.8
Private household	.6	.7	.6	.3	.1
Other service	.9	3.1	7.4	14.4	12.7
Manual (except service)	28.4	29.2	28.7	32.3	26.0
Crafts, supervisors	11.2	12.2	13.4	15.0	10.9
Operatives	4.9	6.7	7.2	11.4	10.1
Laborers (except farm, mine)	12.3	10.3	8.0	5.9	5.0
Farm	60.4	48.7	37.3	11.8	8.8
Farmers, farm managers	54.1	39.0	32.5	8.9	6.8
Farm laborers, supervisors	6.3	9.7	4.8	2.9	2.0

Note: Calculated from the integrated public-use census samples (Ruggles and Sobek 1995).

tions also have always contained older men's jobs: clergyman, physician, or surgeon and, since 1940, lawyer or judge.

Older workers might predominate in certain jobs either because there is little new entry, because workers move into these jobs as they age, or because older workers are less likely to retire from these jobs. The first cause, little new entry, can be disentangled from the last two by arraying census data by cohort. If workers are less likely to retire from certain occupations or move into certain occupations as they age, then, as a cohort ages, the proportion of the cohort employed in those occupations should increase. Tables 5.2, 5.3, 5.4, and 5.5 therefore illustrate the experiences of several cohorts with the four broad occu-

Table 5.2   **Percentage of Native-Born Men in Labor Force Who Are Farmers, by Age Group and Cohort**

Cohort Aged 25–34 in:	% Farmers at Ages:					Cohort Aged 65–74 in:
	25–34	35–44	45–54	55–64	65–74	
1870		41.3		45.3	42.4	1910
1880	34.9		41.7	39.4	40.9	1920
1900	25.0	27.8	31.1		34.9	1940
1910	21.3	26.8		24.4	25.0	1950
1920	21.1		18.7	16.4	17.4	1960
1930		13.6	12.7	9.4	9.4	1970
1940	9.9	10.0	7.0	5.1	7.7	1980
1950	7.5	5.1	3.4	3.7	5.8	1990

Source: Calculated from the integrated public-use census samples (Ruggles and Sobek 1995).

Note: Missing values indicate unavailability of a public-use census sample. Prior to 1940 the labor force was defined under the gainful definition of the labor force and in 1940 and later under the current definition.

Table 5.3   **Percentage of Native-Born Men in Labor Force Who Are Professionals or Proprietors, by Age Group and Cohort**

Cohort Aged 25–34 in:	% Professionals/Proprietors at Ages:					Cohort Aged 65–74 in:
	25–34	35–44	45–54	55–64	65–74	
1870		16.6		18.6	19.7	1910
1880	13.8		18.5	20.6	15.8	1920
1900	18.8	24.7	21.1		26.4	1940
1910	22.2	22.2		27.4	28.8	1950
1920	20.4		30.1	31.4	37.1	1960
1930		30.1	32.9	34.5	40.0	1970
1940	27.5	31.8	34.4	36.4	46.4	1980
1950	29.7	36.7	40.1	44.9	53.3	1990

Source: Calculated from the integrated public-use census samples (Ruggles and Sobek 1995).

Note: Missing values indicate unavailability of a public-use census sample. Prior to 1940 the labor force was defined under the gainful definition of the labor force and in 1940 and later under the current definition.

Table 5.4   **Percentage of Native-Born Men in Labor Force Who Are Artisans, by Age Group and Cohort**

Cohort Aged 25–34 in:	% Artisans at Ages:					Cohort Aged 65–74 in:
	25–34	35–44	45–54	55–64	65–74	
1870		12.6		12.3	11.0	1910
1880	10.9		12.4	12.6	11.3	1920
1900	13.7	15.6	15.6		12.4	1940
1910	14.3	16.2		16.4	14.4	1950
1920	17.3		18.0	19.9	15.3	1960
1930		17.5	20.7	21.8	15.3	1970
1940	13.7	20.6	23.1	22.6	13.2	1980
1950	19.7	23.4	24.1	21.0	11.3	1990

Source: Calculated from the integrated public-use census samples (Ruggles and Sobek 1995).

Note: Missing values indicate unavailability of a public-use census sample. Prior to 1940 the labor force was defined under the gainful definition of the labor force and in 1940 and later under the current definition.

Table 5.5   **Percentage of Native-Born Men in Labor Force Who Are Laborers, by Age Group and Cohort**

Cohort Aged 25–34 in:	% Laborers at Ages:					Cohort Aged 65–74 in:
	25–34	35–44	45–54	55–64	65–74	
1870		29.6		23.8	27.0	1910
1880	40.4		27.4	27.5	32.0	1920
1900	42.5	31.9	32.1		26.3	1940
1910	42.2	34.8		31.8	31.8	1950
1920	41.2		33.2	32.3	30.2	1960
1930		38.9	33.7	34.4	35.4	1970
1940	49.0	37.7	35.6	35.8	32.6	1980
1950	43.3	34.8	32.5	30.4	29.6	1990

Source: Calculated from the integrated public-use census samples (Ruggles and Sobek 1995).

Note: Missing values indicate unavailability of a public-use census sample. Prior to 1940 the labor force was defined under the gainful definition of the labor force and in 1940 and later under the current definition.

pational categories *farmer, professional or proprietor, artisan,* and *laborer,* respectively. Consistent with my previous use of these occupational classifications, most white-collar workers are classified as professional or proprietor, and semiskilled, farm, and service-sector laborers are classified as laborers.

Table 5.2 shows that, although farming has always contained a disproportionate number of older men, for most of the twentieth century farmers did not have a high propensity to remain in the labor force. For cohorts aged sixty-five to seventy-four in 1910, 1920, and 1950, the percentage of men in the labor force who were farmers remained virtually unchanged from the preceeding ten years. For the cohort that reached age sixty-five to seventy-four in 1940, farmers were somewhat more likely to remain in the labor force, a phenomenon associated with the Great Depression (Schultz 1945, 191–93). Only beginning with the cohort that reached age sixty-five to seventy-four in 1970 do farmers retire later than men in other occupations.

Professionals' and proprietors' propensity to retire has fallen relative to that of artisans or laborers. Beginning with the cohort that reached age sixty-five to seventy-four in 1960, professionals and proprietors started to leave the labor force at later ages relative to men in other occupations. Artisans are the ones who now retire early. Laborers, who used to be disproportionately represented at older ages relative to their numbers at younger ages, no longer are. Perhaps artisans now retire earlier than professionals or proprietors because Social Security benefits replace a larger share of their income or because they now find their jobs less satisfying.

The disproportionate number of laborers observed at older ages in the past arises from nonlaborers becoming laborers at older ages. Tables 5.6 and 5.7,

Table 5.6   **Entry into 1910 Occupational Group, Union Army Veterans, 1900–1910 (restricted to men in the labor force in both 1900 and 1910)**

	Occupation in 1910			
Occupation in 1900	Farmer	Professional/ Proprietor	Artisan	Laborer
Farmer	84.1	**5.6**	**6.2**	**23.7**
Professional/proprietor	**6.3**	72.9	**12.3**	**21.7**
Artisan	**3.2**	**9.4**	66.7	**3.2**
Laborer	**6.3**	**12.2**	**14.8**	42.3

Note: The table indicates the percentage of men within an occupational class in 1910 entering from another occupation between 1900 and 1910. The percentage of new entrants is highlighted in bold.

Table 5.7   **Exit out of 1900 Occupational Group, Union Army Veterans, 1900–1910 (restricted to men in the labor force in both 1900 and 1910)**

	Occupation in 1910			
Occupation in 1900	Farmer	Professional/ Proprietor	Artisan	Laborer
Farmer	86.2	**2.4**	**2.0**	**9.3**
Professional/proprietor	**12.8**	62.4	**8.0**	**16.8**
Artisan	**9.5**	**11.9**	64.3	**14.3**
Laborer	**19.5**	**15.9**	**14.6**	50.0

Note: The table indicates the percentage of men within an occupational class in 1900 who changed occupatons by 1910. The percentage of exits is highlighted in bold.

which examine transitions across broad occupational categories between 1900 and 1910, illustrate. New entrants constituted 16, 27, 39, and 58 percent, respectively, of farmers, professionals or proprietors, artisans, and laborers in 1910 (see table 5.6). At a time when retirement incomes were low, men remained in the labor force even if they could do so only by switching to a less physically demanding but lower-paying occupation. This is less likely to happen today. Although a small amount of job switching either at the end of men's careers or after retirement has been observed in recent data (Fuchs 1982; Ruhm 1990), the most common employment pattern, particularly for white males, is lifetime employment. Today only one in six older men works fewer than ten years on any one job (Ruhm 1990), and three-quarters of men who retire from a job switch from full-time work to being out of the labor force (Rust 1990). Of course, even at the beginning of the century occupational change was not for the majority. The percentages of men who were farmers, professionals or proprietors, artisans, or laborers in 1900 and who were still in that occupational class in 1910 were 86, 62, 64, and 50 percent, respectively (see table 5.7).[1]

The inclusion of retirement as an occupational category clarifies retirement patterns by different occupational groups at the beginning of the century. Table 5.8 shows that retirement rates were highest among laborers (45 percent), followed by farmers (37 percent) and professionals or proprietors (31 percent), while artisans had the lowest retirement rates (28 percent). Interestingly, it was men within the most physically demanding occupational categories, those of laborer and farmer, who were most likely to retire. When specific jobs were classified by the likely degree of physical exertion that would be required for job performance, there was a tendency for men in poor health to switch to an easier job, but this effect was not statistically significant. Many men continued to labor in physically demanding occupations; only 22 percent of laborers and 27 percent of artisans switched to an easier job. Older men therefore did not commonly move into less physically demanding occupations as an alternative to retirement. Although certain occupations such as janitor and guard or watch-

| Table 5.8 | Exit out of 1900 Occupational Class, Union Army Veterans 1900–1910 (including retired as an occupational category) |

	Occupation in 1910				
Occupation in 1900	Farmer	Professional/ Proprietor	Artisan	Laborer	Retired
Farmer	54.5	**1.5**	**1.3**	**5.9**	**36.8**
Professional/proprietor	**8.8**	43.1	**5.5**	**11.6**	**30.9**
Artisan	**7.0**	**8.7**	46.1	**10.4**	**27.8**
Laborer	**10.8**	**8.1**	**8.1**	27.7	**45.3**
Retired	**12.1**	**10.5**	**4.0**	**8.1**	65.3

Note: The table indicates the percentage of men within a occupational class in 1900 who either changed occupations or retired by 1910. The percentage of exits is highlighted in bold.

man have had a disproportionate number of older men within them since 1880, such jobs were relatively few and in 1910 provided employment for at most 2 percent of the male labor force sixty-five years of age or older. These jobs have remained relatively unimportant, providing employment for only 4 percent of the male labor force older than sixty-four in 1990.

Table 5.8 illustrates that 35 percent of men who were retired in 1900 had reentered the labor force by 1910, a reentry rate only slightly higher than the rate of 28 percent observed in recent data among men younger than seventy years of age (Rust 1990). In the past men who reentered the labor force had lower pensions and were younger than those who did not. These men may have found that they could no longer afford to be retired. Wentworth (1945) reported that some Social Security beneficiaries in 1941–42 quit their employment and filed for benefits only to realize that their retirement incomes would be insufficient. Although she cited instances of reentry caused by boredom with retirement, such cases were few. Today, those who reenter the labor force tend to be the most highly educated (Sum and Fogg 1990), suggesting that workers are now motivated by either the high returns to education in today's labor market, job satisfaction, or both.

Ability to continue within an occupation depends not just on physical job requirements but also on hours flexibility and the ability to hire assistants. Hurd and McGarry (1993) found that, among workers today, physical job requirements had only a small influence on prospective retirement, whereas job flexibility had a large effect. Haber and Gratton (1994, 97) cite the recollections of James J. Davis, U.S. secretary of labor in the 1920s, who began his work life as a boy helper "when an aged puddler devised a scheme to enable himself to continue the physically arduous exertion of the trade." Self-employment may provide just such hours flexibility and just such an ability to continue working with the help of apprentices. In the early 1970s the self-employed were significantly more likely to work, partly by reducing their work week to under thirty-five hours (Fuchs 1982). Exactly why wage and salary workers find it harder than the self-employed to reduce their weekly hours is unclear, but the problem might arise from the demands of team production or from firms' needs to minimize payments on fixed costs per worker.

The decline in the self-employed nonfarm labor force from 15 percent in 1910 to 9 percent in 1990 suggests that opportunities for self-employment may now be lower. But, when the data are arrayed by cohort, it becomes evident that only beginning with the cohort that reached age sixty-five to seventy-four in 1960 were the self-employed more likely to remain in the labor force than wage and salary workers (see table 5.9). Carter and Sutch (1996) even argue that, between 1900 and 1910, the nonfarm self-employed had a slightly higher retirement propensity than wage and salary workers. If the hours flexibility provided by self-employment enabled workers to remain in the labor force longer, then this hours flexibility has been a factor only in recent decades. Private pension plans may have changed the retirement patterns of the self-

Table 5.9   Percentage of Native-Born Men in Labor Force Who Are Self-Employed, but Not Farmers, by Age Group and Cohort

Cohort Aged 55–64 in:	% Self-Employed at Ages:		Cohort Aged 65–74 in:
	55–64	65–74	
1910	26.0	26.6	1920
1940	19.5	20.6	1950
1950	16.1	21.5	1960
1960	14.8	21.0	1970
1970	14.1	23.9	1980
1980	14.9	26.1	1990

Source: Calculated from the integrated public-use census samples (Ruggles and Sobek 1995).
Note: Prior to 1940 the labor force was defined under the gainful definition of the labor force and in 1940 and later under the current definition.

employed relative to wage and salary workers because the self-employed today are less likely to be covered by private pension plans. The similar retirement propensities of wage and salary workers and the self-employed suggest that a decline in self-employment opportunities cannot explain the rise of retirement before 1950. That there was no change in self-employment at ages fifty-five to sixty-four after 1950 implies that a decline in self-employment opportunities cannot explain the rise after 1950.

Another way for the elderly to continue working, but to work fewer hours, is to work in part-time or part-year jobs. Modern survey data suggest that older workers would prefer part-time work to early retirement (Kennedy 1980), but, if fixed costs per employer have been increasing, then fewer employers may now be willing to offer part-time or part-year work. Fewer part-year jobs are now available—the percentage of the labor force older than seventeen in part-year work has fallen from 38 percent in 1940 to 30 percent in 1990. But the percentage of the labor force in part-time work has increased from 13 percent in 1940 to 20 percent in 1990, suggesting that more, not fewer, part-time jobs are now available.

Table 5.10 shows that, among the elderly still in the labor force, both part-time employment and part-year employment have been rising. Among employed men age sixty-five to seventy-four in 1940, only 15 percent worked fewer than thirty-five hours per week and only 30 percent fewer than fifty weeks per year, whereas, in 1990, 47 percent worked fewer than thirty-five hours per week and 37 percent fewer than fifty weeks per year. In contrast, among employed men age fifty-five to sixty-four, the proportion employed in a full-year job increased between 1940 and 1990, while the fraction working part-time remained relatively constant. Not only have older men increasingly been leaving the labor force, but, when they remain in the labor force, they have been reducing hours of work as well.

Table 5.10   **Percentage of Native-Born Men in the Labor Force Who Are Employed Part-Time and Percentage Who Are Employed for Part of the Year, by Age Group and Cohort**

| Cohort Aged 55–64 in: | % Employed, by Age: | | | | Cohort Aged 65–74 in: |
| | Part-Time: | | Part Year: | | |
	55–64	65–74	55–64	65–74	
1930		14.5		29.6	1940
1940	10.9	20.8	32.5	33.0	1950
1950	10.8	30.6	31.4	37.7	1960
1960	10.7	38.0	28.6	40.1	1970
1970	11.3	46.4	22.3	37.2	1980
1980	9.6	48.1	19.5	37.0	1990

Source: Calculated from the integrated public-use census samples (Ruggles and Sobek 1995).
Note: The current definition of the labor force was used. Part-time workers are defined as those working fewer than 35 hours per week. Part-year workers are defined as those working fewer than 50 weeks a year.

Why more older men do not move into part-time employment rather than retire completely, despite their expressed preference for part-time work, is not because these jobs are unavailable; perhaps the reason is that they want part-time work at their old wage and can find jobs only at lower pay. Companies that hire part-time employees report great difficulty recruiting older workers (Belous 1990), perhaps because older workers remaining with the same employer experience an hourly wage loss of 10 percent on becoming part-time workers and those switching employers an hourly wage loss of 30 percent (Jondrow, Brechling, and Marcus 1987).

Although no data are available on part-time work for earlier periods, the opportunities for part-time work among wage and salary workers were probably no better in the first half of the nineteenth century than in the second. The policy of most nineteenth-century firms was to have workers begin and end their day at the same time. Entry and exit were controlled, and penalties were imposed for tardiness (Atack and Bateman 1990).

Tables 5.9 and 5.10 implied that the rise of retirement cannot be attributed to declines in opportunities for self-employment or part-time work, jobs that might enable the elderly to continue in the labor force by reducing hours of work. The fraction of prime-aged males employed in part-time work has been relatively stable since 1940. Prior to 1960 the nonfarm self-employed retired at the same rate as wage and salary workers. But what of self-employment as a farmer? Table 5.2 above, showing that, until 1970, farmers retired at the same rate as nonfarmers, implies that the decline in the size of the agricultural sector does not explain the rise in retirement. Because this finding is contrary to most researchers' perceptions, and because the decline in the size of the agricultural sector has been such a common explanation for the rise in retirement, the next section discusses farmer retirement in greater detail.

5.2   Farmers and Retirement

Farming is frequently cited as an occupation that provides older workers with great flexibility. It has been thought that farmers remain in the labor force longer because they can continue to operate their farms with the help of family members and hired labor (e.g. Durand 1948; Ransom and Sutch 1986; Taietz, Streib, and Barron 1956; cf. Carter and Sutch 1996). Epstein (1922, 2) wrote that "in an agricultural society men and women are still useful in their old age, and their activities rarely cease before actual senility has set in." In fact, labor force participation rates of men living on a farm have been consistently higher than those of men not living on a farm. As pointed out in chapter 2, participation rates for men living on a farm were 87 percent in 1880 and 62 percent in 1940, whereas those for nonfarm men were 65 and 37 percent, respectively. High labor force participation rates among farm men are one reason why retirement has traditionally been regarded as an urban phenomenon and why researchers have concluded that the sectoral shift away from agriculture is the most important explanation of the secular decline in labor force participation rates of men prior to World War II (Dorfman 1954; Durand 1948; Mushkin and Berman 1947). Using estimates of participation rates among farm men, Moen (1987, 56) argues that the move away from agriculture accounts for 71 percent of the decline in labor force participation rates of males at least sixty-five years of age between 1900 and 1950.

Comparing the labor force participation rate of men who lived on a farm with that of men who did not can be misleading. Durand (1948, 68–69) first noted that the higher rates of labor force attachment among farm men may be an artifact of the way in which the rural farm population is defined. Because farmers who withdrew from the labor force often moved into a nonfarm residence or ceased to cultivate their land, they were eliminated from the rural farm population. Thus, the only older men who remained in the rural farm population were employed as farmers. However, Durand did not believe that the withdrawal of farmers from a farm and to a nonfarm residence could lead to retirement rates among farmers as high as those among nonfarmers. Dorfman (1954) also noted that there was a substantial tendency for older people to migrate away from the farm on leaving the labor force but added that migration was unlikely to be the entire explanation for the high rate of labor force participation in rural farm communities.

Just how misleading a calculation based on residence rather than past occupation can be is shown in figure 5.1, which compares retirement rates by farm residence and by farm occupation among Union army veterans. When the retirement rates of Union army veterans in 1900 and 1910 are compared by residence, farmers' retirement rates are at least half those of nonfarmers. However,

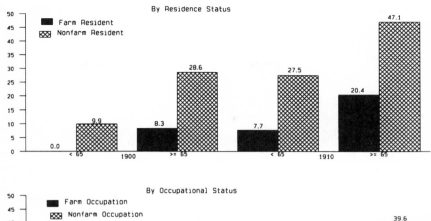

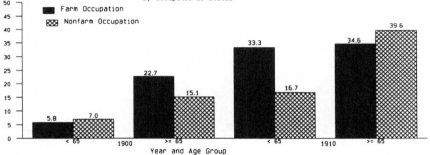

Fig. 5.1   Percentage retired, Union army veterans, by farm residence and farm occupation

Note: Residence is residence during the current census year. Occupation is based on past occupation as given in either pension or census records.

when retirement rates are compared by past occupation, as given in either the pension or the census records, farmer and nonfarmer retirement rates cannot be distinguished statistically. The same phenomenon is observed among non-veterans as well (Costa 1995a). Carter and Sutch's (1996) estimates of new flows into occupations between 1900 and 1910 suggest that the retirement rates of farmers and of others were similar.

Differences in retirement rates need to be examined controlling for socio-economic and demographic characteristics not only because farmers were slightly older but also because, among Union army veterans, they were in slightly worse health and were collecting larger pensions. This was done in chapter 3, and the results for 1900 and 1910 are reproduced in tables 5.11 and 5.12. In 1900 farmers were less likely to be retired than nonfarmers and significantly more likely than professionals and proprietors. In 1910 farmers were more likely to be retired than professionals or proprietors or artisans but were less likely to be retired than laborers.

The immediate explanation for the high retirement rate of farmers is that

Table 5.11   **Probit of Determinants of Probability of Retirement, with Retirement Status as the Dependent Variable, 1900 (526 observations, pseudo $R^2 = .22$)**

Variable	Mean	Est.	S.E.	$\partial P/\partial x$
Dummy = 1 if retired	.17			
Intercept		−12.14‡	2.24	
Monthly pension	12.94	.05‡	.01	.0090
Age	61.28	.05‡	.01	.0106
Dummy = 1 if does not own home	.34	.35†	.17	.0695
Discharged disability	.25	−1.63‡	.19	−.1229
Health good	.22			
Health fair	.35	.39*	.23	.0765
Health poor	.25	.37*	.25	.0717
Health status unknown	.18	.46*	.26	.0905
Farmer	.46			
Professional or proprietor	.18	−.48†	.24	−.0935
Artisan	.14	−.09	.23	−.0168
Laborer	.22	−.02	.21	−.0046
Servant in house	.02	−.96	.67	−.1891
Boarder in house	.05	−.26	.41	−.0515
4 or more dependents	.14	−.46	.29	−.0895
Married	.85	−.25	.20	−.0486
Foreign born	.10	−.13	.25	−.0249
Illiterate	.06	−.02	.31	−.0031
Lives in East	.21			
Lives in Midwest	.73	.42*	.24	.0828
Lives in other region	.06	−.28	.47	−.0540
Urban county	.37	.41†	.17	.0799
Mean duration of unemployment for manufacturing workers by state	3.62	1.86‡	.63	.3644

Note: The omitted dummies are good health, farmer, and eastern residence. The symbols *, †, and ‡ indicate that the coefficient is significantly different from zero at at least the 10 percent, 5 percent, and 1 percent levels, respectively. $\partial P/\partial x = \beta(1/n) \sum \phi(x'\beta)$, where ϕ is the standard normal density, and $\partial P/\partial x$ is in probability units.

they moved away from the farm on retirement. Eighty-four percent of the retired farmers in the 1900 census would not have been classified as part of the farm sector since they were no longer living on a farm. Among men who were farmers in 1900, 69 percent were living in a house in 1910, 59 percent had moved to a different town, 21 percent to a different county, and 14 percent to a different state. Moves across state lines averaged 1,128 miles and those across county lines, but within a state, fifty-six miles. This pattern of retirement on the part of farmers accompanied by moves, frequently to a nearby town, has been noted before (Bauder and Doerflinger 1967; Bogue 1971; Haber and Gratton 1994; Salamon 1992; Sauer, Bauder, and Biggar 1964). Figure 2.9 above, which plotted estimates of labor force participation rates among men sixty-five years of age by residence, showed that labor force participation rates

Table 5.12   **Probit of Determinants of Probability of Retirement, with Retirement Status as the Dependent Variable, 1910 (923 observations, pseudo $R^2 = .16$)**

Variable	Mean	Est.	S.E.	$\partial P/\partial x$
Dummy = 1 if retired	.40			
Intercept		−6.42‡	.71	
Monthly pension	16.94	.03‡	.01	.0112
Age	69.19	.08‡	.01	.0246
Dummy = 1 if does not own home	.28	.34‡	.11	.1101
Discharged disability	.18	−.14	.12	−.0458
Health good or fair	.53			
Health poor	.34	.22†	.11	.0703
Health status unknown	.13	−.17	.16	−.0552
Farmer	.49			
Professional or proprietor	.19	−.11	.13	−.0360
Artisan	.14	−.39‡	.14	−.1249
Laborer	.17	.16	.13	.0527
Servant in house	.05	−.87‡	.25	−.2796
Boarder in house	.05	−.16	.21	−.0530
2 or more dependents	.21	−.30‡	.12	−.0976
Married	.78	.12	.12	.0385
Foreign born	.08	.34†	.17	.1114
Illiterate	.05	.14	.22	.0441
Lives in Midwest	.86	.21	.14	.0680
Urban county	.18	−.04	.13	−.0141

Note: The omitted dummies are good or fair health and farmer. The symbols *, †, and ‡ indicate that the coefficient is significantly different from zero at at least the 10 percent, 5 percent, and 1 percent levels, respectively. $\partial P/\partial x = \beta(1/n) \sum \phi(x'\beta)$, where ϕ is the standard normal density, and $\partial P/\partial x$ is in probability units.

were highest among men living on a farm and lowest among rural nonfarm men, suggesting that the rural nonfarm population contained many retired farmers.[2] Movement off the farm is also evident in the 1900–20 censuses. Among rural men aged fifty-five to sixty- four in 1900 and 1910, 64 and 63 percent, respectively, were living on a farm, but ten years later only 56 and 57 percent of the men in these two cohorts were.

Movement off the farm on retirement explains why past researchers were misled into thinking that the retirement rates of farmers were low, but it does not explain why farmers did not continue to operate the farm with the help of family members and hired labor. Farmers' high retirement rates were not the result of the great physical exertion required by farming. When health was interacted with farm occupation in the regression presented in table 5.11, the coefficient on the resulting variable was insignificant. Coefficients on the interactions of farm occupation with age and pension amount were small and insignificant. One possibility is that, if farmers were wealthier than nonfarmers, then they may have had less need to remain in the labor force. Eighty-nine percent of active farmers owned their own farms in 1900, 93 percent in 1910.[3]

But, when farmers who left their farms are compared with nonfarmers in either 1900 or 1910, home-ownership rates between retired farmers and retired non-farmers were not significantly different.[4] Of course, because farms represented a sizable asset, farmers may still have been wealthier than nonfarmers, holding their wealth in a form other than home ownership on retirement.

Deed and probate records provide direct evidence of farmers' wealth. But success in linking the farmers who retired between 1900 and 1910 to their probate records and their deed records between 1900 and 1910 has been mixed. Only the deed records for twenty men of fifty-five searched have been found. The deeds that were found recorded both sales and purchases. Ten men frequently bought land from and sold it to nonrelatives, and three of these only purchased and never sold land. Seven men transferred land to their children for a nominal sum, one for a discounted price, and one as an outright gift. The remaining man purchased land from his wife for a nominal sum. None of the sales were of the entire farm property, suggesting that outright sales were rare. Only nine of the men have been linked to probate records, and these men held substantial amounts of wealth until their death.

Other researchers have also argued that farmers who retired still possessed farmland. Bogue (1971) finds that, when farmers left the land to retire to county towns, they accepted mortgages for a portion of the sale price of their land. Moen (1994) finds that, in 1860, older men who lived in rural nonfarm households held considerable amounts of real estate wealth and suggests that that is because retired farmers still possessed farmland. What farmers did with their land on retirement depended on their ethnicity.

Native-born or Yankee farmers were the most likely to retire and liquidate the farm, either renting it for a while or selling it to a non–family member (Conzen 1985, 269, 283). In these cases retirement seldom occurred before age sixty-five (Salamon 1992). The number of farmers who sold their property probably increased during the nineteenth century. In Bucks County, Pennsylvania, the proportion of all testators who passed their farm or other business to their heirs was 70 percent in the 1790s but only 30 percent in the 1890s (Haber and Gratton 1994, 32). Like Yankees, Danish farmers in Wisconsin also sold the farm, moving to a nearby town (Pedersen 1950, 59).

In contrast, German families commonly transferred land to their children through inter vivos transfers when the household head was around age fifty-five, with the aging parents establishing new households (Conzen 1985, 272–79; Friedberger 1983; Salamon 1992). This pattern appears to have persisted at least until the 1940s. Parsons and Waples (1945) examined a low-tenancy area of Wisconsin around 1940 and found that a frequently employed method for retaining the farm in the family was for parents aged fifty-five to sixty-five to transfer the farm to a son about twenty-seven years of age. The transfer might be accompanied by a mortgage, which gave the parents an income and was automatically canceled on their deaths. The parents might live in town on the interest from the mortgage, or the children might care for the parents on the farm, without any kind of formal agreement. Although Parsons and Waples did not examine the living arrangements of the retired farmer by ethnicity, Pederson's (1950) work on Wisconsin suggests that farmers who remained in the farm household were more likely to be Poles rather than Germans.

Union army veterans who retired from farming and transferred land to their children rarely moved in with their children. Only one of the seven men who transferred land to children lived with his daughter and her family, and he moved out on remarrying. The average distance of within-county moves suggests that contact between children who received land and parents was limited. Land does not appear to have been exchanged for children's care within the same household. In fact, for the country as a whole, when retired farmers moved to nearby towns, they set up households independent of those of their children. In 1910, 79 percent of retired men sixty-five years of age or older headed their own nonfarm households in rural areas, compared to 26 percent of men living on a farm and 64 percent of men living in an urban area. Among those who were household heads only 40 percent of men in rural, nonfarm households had a child living with them, compared to 60 percent of men living on a farm and 56 percent of men in urban areas.[5]

In 1900 and 1910 farmers' retirement may have been enhanced by the unusually high appreciation of real estate, livestock, and other farm property that occurred during the years 1895–15.[6] Farmers' retirement was sensitive to wealth. Parsons (1986) finds that, from 1930 to 1950, the labor force participation of the aged within the agricultural sector was significantly lower in wealthy than in poorer farm states. In 1910, labor force participation rates of older men were significantly lower in wealthy farm counties.[7] A $10,000 increase in the average value of a farm in 1910 increased the average county retirement rate of 0.60 by 0.07. Farmers retiring after 1915 may have begun to change their retirement behavior. The Danish farmers in Wisconsin studied by Pederson (1950) adopted a system of gradual retirement in response to the agricultural depression of the 1920s, renting or selling land in parcels until they were left with only a few acres for subsistence farming. In response to the Great Depression almost 110,000 more farm operators over fifty-five years of age had delayed retirement as of 1940 than did farm operators in the 1920s (Schultz 1945, 191–93). Nonetheless, as table 5.2 above showed, even when agriculture was not in its golden years high retirement rates among farmers were common.

Although farmers had the means to retire, they may not have retired had it not been for the declining importance of agriculture. The proportion of the labor force employed in agriculture was falling throughout the twentieth century. From 1900 to 1910, the fraction of men in the labor force who were farmers fell across all age groups by 12–15 percent. In Union states, the proportion declined by 15–17 percent. For older farmers, with few skills outside the farm sector, retirement may have been a better option than reemployment in the manufacturing sector. Table 5.6 above showed that, although farmers rarely changed occupations, when they did, they experienced downward occupational mobility, becoming laborers. Retirement may have been preferred to downward mobility. But, because table 5.2 showed that the retirement rates of farmers were not rising relative to those of nonfarmers prior to 1960, a declining agricultural sector cannot explain the increase in retirement rates before 1960.

5.3   Displaced Workers

The previous sections demonstrated that, by replacing farming and self-employment artisanal occupations with factory production and office work, technological change did not destroy the only types of jobs the elderly could perform and thereby condemn them to a miserable retirement. Technological change did, however, increase the probability of retirement by displacing workers from their current jobs. For example, the Linotype machine turned the printing industry from a classic craft in which type was set by hand in thousands of small shops into an industry that required relatively less skill but greater speed. Among machinists, the increased division of labor made broadly based training unnecessary, leaving displaced workers with skills that could not easily be transferred across industries (Graebner 1980, 21–24). Older workers were placed at an additional disadvantage as employers turned to high schools as a source for job training. Epstein (1922, 4–5) wrote,

> The problem facing the aged today is largely the creation of the modern machine industry with its components of specialization, speed, and strain. It is a result of the elimination of large numbers of workers as soon as they are unable to keep up fully with the demands of modern methods of production. The introduction of new inventions and more specialized machinery, inevitable in the evolutionary process, while resulting in an ultimate good always involves the replacing of men, which in the case of the aged, has an absolutely harmful effect, as it leaves them destitute. For, in addition to preventing their continuity in regular work, it precludes also their adaptability to newer processes of work.

The older a worker was when he became unemployed, the lower his probability of leaving unemployment, and the higher his probability of retiring (Lee 1996; Margo 1993). Firms might be reluctant to hire older workers. Older workers are more likely to be concentrated in declining industries, and their skills may not be readily transferred to new industries. Older workers might therefore prefer to retire rather than take a new job at reduced pay or migrate to a new region with better job opportunities. Thus, an older worker's probability of retiring is especially likely to be sensitive to local labor market conditions. Among Union army veterans, the higher the mean months of unemployment for manufacturing workers within the state, the more likely a veteran was to retire (see table 5.11 above). An increase of a week in the mean months of unemployment within a state (less than a standard deviation increase) would have raised his probability of retirement by 0.09, an amount equivalent to the effect of a $10.00 increase in pension amount.

Survey evidence suggests that job loss should be a less important determinant of retirement now than it was in the past. Over half of retired men aged sixty-five or older in 1941 and 1942 cited being laid off—whether because of mandatory retirement, job discrimination, or other company reasons—as their reason for retirement (Wentworth 1945), whereas in 1951 only 46 percent did so. By 1963 the figure was down to 39 percent and by 1982 to 20 percent (Palmore 1964; Reno and Grad 1985). That unemployment now has a lessened effect on retirement can be seen in table 5.13, which reports the effect of mean months of unemployment within a state on men's probability of being retired in both 1900 and in 1980, controlling for age, race, marital status, foreign birth, and region.[8] Mean months of unemployment within state of residence had a substantial effect on the retirement probability of men older than sixty-four in 1900 but a much smaller one in 1980. In terms of elasticities, the elasticity of retirement with respect to months of unemployment was 1.18 in 1900 but only 0.32 in 1980. Because so few men older than sixty-four are now still in the labor market, those who are left are likely to be the highly motivated. They are also more likely to be white-collar workers and therefore less affected by cyclic downturns in the economy.

It is not just those older than sixty-four who retire when faced with job loss. Both at the beginning of the century and today lengthy spells of unemployment

Table 5.13   **Effect of Mean Duration of Unemployment within State of Residence on Retirement Probabilities, Men Aged 50–65 and 65 and over, 1900 and 1980**

	Age 65+		Age 50–64	
	1900	1980	1900	1980
Probability retired	.3051	.7223	.0597	.1750
Mean months of unemployment for manufacturing workers by state	3.5990	2.9349	3.5923	2.9401
Probit coefficient	.3946	.2505	.0583	.2460
Standard error of coefficient	.2125	.0212	.1898	.0188
Probit derivative	.0997	.0779	.0066	.0576
Elasticity of retirement with respect to mean months of unemployment	1.1772	.3171	.3971	.9677

Note: Estimated from a probit regression where the dependent variable was equal to one if the individual was out of the labor force and 0 otherwise and the independent variables were mean months of unemployment for manufacturing workers by state, age, marital status, race, foreign birth, extent of urbanization, and region of residence (New England, South Atlantic, East North Central, West North Central, South, Border, Mountain, and West).

raise the chances of early retirement among workers age fifty to sixty-four (e.g., Diamond and Hausman 1984; Lee 1996; Margo 1993). But fifty- to sixty-four-year-old men today are far more likely to retire when faced with unemployment than their counterparts one hundred years ago. In 1900 the elasticity of retirement with respect to average months of unemployment within a state was 0.40 among men in this age group (see table 5.13). In contrast, in 1980 the elasticity with respect to months of unemployment was 0.97. Because men in 1980 now have the means to retire, they may prefer to do so rather than change industries, work at reduced pay, or migrate to a different region. Workers in 1900 may simply not have had the means to choose retirement over a lower-paying job or a job in another region. Union army veterans did, which may explain why the elasticity of retirement with respect to months of unemployment within state of residence was higher for them than for the general population.[9]

Although mean months of unemployment experienced by workers who were unemployed in the previous year was lower in 1980 than in 1900, average unemployment rates have increased over time. The decade average for unemployment was 4 percent from 1900 to 1910, 5 percent from the 1910s to the 1920s and from the 1940s to the 1960s, 6 percent in the 1970s, and 7 percent in the 1980s (Lebergott 1964, 189; and calculated from Series 631 in U.S. Bureau of the Census 1991). Widespread seasonality at the beginning of the century meant that workers in the past faced a 37 percent greater chance of becoming unemployed than their counterparts in the 1970s, but their probability of leaving unemployment once they became unemployed was 32 percent higher and, if they were sixty years of age or older, 48 percent higher. Decreases in the probability of unemployed workers leaving unemployment have increased the average unemployment spell from around four months to five (Margo 1993, 1990).

An increase of 25 percent in the average unemployment spell implies that total months of unemployment within a year has increased by at most 25 percent.[10] This, in turn, implies that older men's probability of retiring rose by approximately 33 percent and therefore explains up to 23 percent of the increase in retirement rates among men older than sixty-four since 1900. It implies that the retirement probability of a fifty- to sixty-four-year-old man rose by 11 percent and therefore explains up to 5 percent of the increase in retirement rates among this group.

Men who became unemployed could not, however, have retired unless they felt that they could afford to do so, whether because they received modest old-age pensions, charity, or contributions from children. Wentworth (1945, 19) cites cases of men who retired of their own accord in order to avoid unemployment: "Mr. S worked as a dishwasher, but his work was not steady and he felt he would be better off receiving old age assistance and old age insurance benefits, so he quit his job. Mr. S believes that he could do light work, but he has not tried to get any." Those who found that their retirement income did not

Table 5.14   **Mean Months of Unemployment and Percentage Unemployed 6 Months or More among Nonfarm Union Army Veterans in 1900**

	Monthly Pension Amount	
	≤ $12	> $12
Mean months unemployment	1.9	2.6
Good health	1.8	2.5
Poor health	2.0	2.7
% unemployed 6 months or more	16.1	24.6
Good health	15.0	22.7
Poor health	17.5	26.5

Note: The first column was adjusted to have the same age distribution as the second. All men with a BMI between 22 and 28 are considered to be in good health.

meet their needs, however modest, returned to the labor force, often on a part-time basis to ensure that their benefits would not be cut.

Factors that affect the length of unemployment spells might also indirectly affect retirement rates. These factors do not include changes in the industrial distribution, which has had a minimal effect on unemployment duration (Margo 1990), but do include rising incomes and unemployment insurance, both of which enable workers to reject the first job that becomes available. Once unemployed for a long period of time workers might develop a taste for leisure, might find that their skills had deteriorated, or might find that employers would be less willing to hire them because they had been unemployed for such a long period of time. These workers might then retire, particularly if they were older. Secularly rising incomes could therefore have had both a direct effect on the probability of retirement and an indirect effect by lengthening the duration of unemployment.

Unemployment patterns among men today and among Union army veterans suggest that the secular rise in incomes increased the length of unemployment spells. Today unemployment benefits increase the duration of unemployment by reducing exit from unemployment (e.g., Meyer 1990). Table 5.14 shows that nonfarm Union army veterans receiving higher pensions experienced more unemployment in 1900, even controlling for health.[11] If unemployment benefits and Union army pensions increased the duration of unemployment, then secularly rising family incomes probably had the same effect, thereby contributing to the increase in retirement rates among older men.

5.4   Summary

In this chapter I have investigated whether changes in labor markets such as the increased duration of unemployment spells, declines in the farm and nonfarm self-employment sectors, and fewer opportunities for part-time work have worsened the labor market prospects of older workers. Only the increased duration of unemployment spells accounted for some of the increase in retirement rates since 1900, but the unemployed would not have been able to retire unless they had some source of income. In addition, the increased duration of unemployment spells could in turn be explained by secularly rising incomes, suggesting that secularly rising incomes indirectly increase retirement rates by lengthening the duration of unemployment. Declines in part-time work, nonfarm self-employment, and farming could not explain the rise of retirement. Opportunities for part-time work have not worsened, and an increasing proportion of the older workers who remain in the labor force are part-time workers. Although opportunities for self-employment and for employment in the farm sector have declined, low retirement rates among the self-employed relative to wage and salary workers and among farmers relative to nonfarmers are modern phenomena. In the past farmers retired at the same rate as nonfarmers and the self-employed at the same rate as wage and salary workers. Any hours flexibility offered by self-employment influences retirement only in recent times, suggesting that differences in the retirement wealth of the self-employed and of wage and salary workers provide a more likely explanation for the higher propensity of the self-employed to remain in the labor force.

Notes

1. This is a slight overestimate of the true degree of persistence within an occupational class. Men with high pensions were more likely to remain within the same occupation than men with low pensions, but the effect of pensions on occupational change was not large.

2. Moen (1994) makes a similar point on the basis of slightly different estimates.

3. Unfortunately, it is not possible to obtain information on farmers' wealth. The schedules of the Census of Agriculture for the year 1900 were lost. Linkage rates to earlier schedules have proved to be too low to obtain a viable sample.

4. Among men who were farmers in 1900 and had retired by 1910, 74 percent owned their homes in 1910, compared to 76 percent of nonfarmers. Among retirees in 1900, 80 percent of the nonfarmers owned their homes, compared to 74 percent of farmers. While significantly more of the farmers owned their homes free of mortage in 1900, the difference in 1910 between farmer and nonfarmer mortage status is insignificant.

5. Calculated from the integrated 1910 census sample (Ruggles and Sobek 1995).

6. Wages of farm laborers relative to industrial workers rose 17 percent (Schultz 1945).

7. County labor force participation rates were calculated from the 1910 public-use census and linked to county-level information on the farm sector from aggregate census statistics.

8. 1900 is compared with 1980 because, in 1980, individuals were asked weeks of unemployment in the past year, thus enabling me to construct a measure of mean months of unemployment comparable to the 1900 measure. Mean months of unemployment is estimated for manufacturing workers to ensure comparability with the 1900

estimates, but the results for 1980 remain unchanged if the figure for mean months of unemployment among all workers is used instead.

9. The difference in elasticities between the national sample and Union army veterans is also partially accounted for by region of residence.

10. Total months of unemployment within a year are simply the sum of all unemployment spells within a year. Because spells that have already begun before the beginning of the year or that continue until the end of year are censored, this will be an upper-bound estimate.

11. Additional controls for socioeconomic and demographic characteristics, a measure of seasonality within occupation, and region of residence did not change the results. (Poisson regressions where the dependent variable was months of unemployment and probit equations where the dependent variable was unemployment of six months or more were run.)

6   Displacing the Family

And worse of all, my independence is gone; for now, of course, I
shall have to live with one of my children, and I don't know which
of us will hate it the most.

An old man's lament, quoted in Epstein (1922)

The living arrangements of elderly retirees have undergone profound changes
since the end of the last century. In 1880, close to half of retired men were
living with their children or other relatives. Today, only 5 percent are, suggesting that the family now plays a diminished role in old-age support.

What could have displaced the dependence of the elderly on family and
contributed to the rise in independent, retiree households? One possible explanation includes changes in social values and expectations. A common perception is that in the past, unlike today, "nobody ever thought of not taking care
of their own."[1] Alternatively, improvements in the health of the elderly and in
household technology may now enable the elderly to live alone. The leisurely
retirement lifestyle that has become the postwar ideal is often possible only by
resettlement to another community with a better climate or recreational amenities. Many of the elderly may no longer have the option of living with their
children. Declines in fertility and increases in life expectancy at older ages
have increased the ratio of aged parents to adult children, with the result that,
whereas in the past the burden of care was spread among many children, today
it is spread among few. Finally, rising incomes, including Social Security and
private pensions, may have caused more of the elderly to live by themselves.
If the elderly prefer to live by themselves rather than with their children, they
will be able to do so only if they have sufficient income. In this chapter I investigate whether social values dictated different behavior in the past than today
or whether increases in income have always been associated with an increased
demand for the privacy and autonomy provided by separate living arrangements. If the latter proves to be the case, then rising incomes have contributed
enormously to the well-being of the elderly.

First, however, I discuss trends in the living arrangements of the elderly.
Many observers, noting the sharp increase in the percentage of single, elderly
households after 1940, have argued that Social Security has displaced the fam-

ily as a means of financial support (e.g., Michael, Fuchs, and Scott 1980; Schorr 1960). But I will show that the percentage of retired men sixty-five years of age or older living either alone or with only their wives in the household has been rising since 1880. Many economists, demographers, and historians have been unaware of the trend prior to 1940 because it has been disguised in more aggregated statistics by the relatively low retirement rates that prevailed in the past and by the unchanging coresidence patterns of labor force participants. This chapter first examines the long-term trend in coresidence patterns among elderly males and then assesses explanations for the trend.

6.1   Trends in the Living Arrangements of the Elderly

The majority of older men have always headed their own households. Over three-quarters did in 1880 and close to 90 percent in 1990. However, the fraction of retired men heading their own households was low at the beginning of the century and has risen steadily since 1880. Among men still in the labor force, change came only after 1940 (see fig. 6.1).

Although whether an elderly man was a household head is a useful indicator of authority and independence, it is a poor indicator of whether he lived alone or surrounded by family members. Another indicator of living arrangements is the percentage of elderly men living in extended families, here defined as households where a family member other than the spouse was present. For the most part, these are households in which the adult children are present, but occasionally they include other relatives. Figure 6.2 shows that the decline in

Fig. 6.1   Percentage of noninstitutionalized men sixty-five or older who were household heads, by retirement status
Note: Estimated from the integrated public-use census sample (Ruggles and Sobek 1995) using the definition of gainful employment prior to 1940 and the current definition thereafter.

Fig. 6.2   Percentage of noninstitutionalized men sixty-five or older not living in extended families, by retirement status

Sources: See fig. 6.1.

Note: Living in an extended family is defined as living in a household in which family members other than the wife are present.

the percentage of men at least sixty-five years old living in extended families from 1880 to 1940 occurred among both the retired and those still in the labor force. However, part of the decline may be due, not to the elderly being less likely to live in the households of their children or other relatives, but to declines in the age at which children leave home, in declines in the propensity of the elderly to take in relatives, or declines in numbers of dependent children. Figure 6.3, therefore, subdivides the census data even further.

Figure 6.3 classifies living arrangements as (1) household head and living in an extended family, (2) household head and not living in an extended family, (3) not household head and living in an extended family, and (4) not household head and not living in an extended family. Men in this last category lived with friends or as boarders and never constituted more than 7 percent of the population. Men who were household heads and lived in an extended family lived mainly with their unmarried, adult children.[2] The third category of households, those that the elderly man did not head but in which he lived with his children, consisted primarily of households into which the children had welcomed their aged parents. Even at the beginning of the century, instances of children taking over the households of their parents were relatively few.[3]

Since 1880 the largest change in the residence arrangements of noninstitutionalized men older than 64 has arisen from the declining proportion living as household heads with children (see fig. 6.3). A narrowing age difference between spouses and declines in fertility have led to an earlier stopping of child rearing among men, making it less likely that an older man would have dependent children present in the household. The rise of college is another

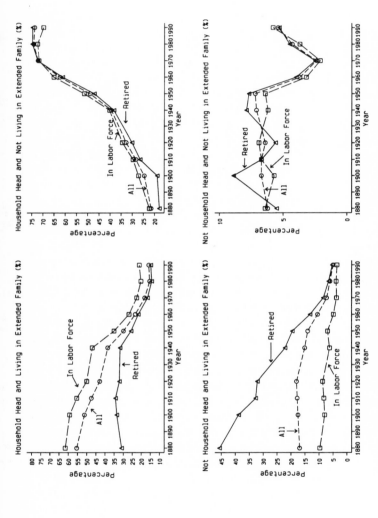

Fig. 6.3 Percentage household heads and percentage living in an extended family among noninstitutionalized men sixty-five or older, by retirement status

Sources: For sources and definitions, see figures 6.1 and 6.2.

Note: The same trends persist when all figures are reweighted to have the same age distribution as that found among retired men in 1900.

factor that may have contributed to the post-1940 decline in the age at which children leave home. The proportion living as household heads with children has been replaced by the fraction living as household heads with only a spouse. The percentage of men who were not household heads and who lived with their children or other relatives has also fallen, but the decline was not as pronounced.

Figure 6.3 shows that differences in living arrangements by retirement status were much larger in the past than they are today. Whereas at the beginning of the century the most common form of living arrangement among men older than sixty-four who were still in the labor force was as head of a household in which other family members lived, the most common form of living arrangement for the retired was coresidence with children in a household that they did not head. In contrast, the most common form of living arrangement today for both the retired and those still in the labor force is as head of a household in which only a spouse is present. For men still in the labor force, the percentage heading households in which children were present fell, and the proportion heading single, elderly households rose, suggesting that, for those still in the labor force, the largest changes in living arrangements have been caused by children leaving home. Among the retired the biggest change in living arrangements was the decline in the percentage of men living with their children, from 46 percent in 1880, to 22 percent in 1940, to 5 percent in 1990. In fact, fully 59 percent of the 1880–1990 decline in the percentage of retirees residing with their children or other relatives occurred before 1940. It is this change in coresidence among the retired that will be the focus of my subsequent empirical work. I prefer examining whether parents are in their children's households rather than whether they live in a single household to avoid controlling for differences in the age at which children leave home. Examining whether parents live in their childrens' households is also important because there has been so much change in this measure among the retired. This change is not reflected in the overall statistics because retirement rates were relatively low in the past.

The decline in the percentage of retirees residing with their children or other relatives observed in figure 6.3 occurred among the foreign and the native born, among whites and blacks, among farm and nonfarm dwellers, and in large cities and rural areas. A larger percentage of retirees lived with children or other relatives in nonmetropolitan areas in 1880 and 1900, but by 1910 the living arrangements of the retired in nonmetropolitan areas resembled those of the retired in metropolitan areas (see fig. 6.4). Early social observers noted the decline of the multigenerational family with alarm. Epstein (1922, 6) lamented that the "conditions of impotence in old age are augmented still further by the break-up of the family unit in modern society. With increasing rapidity home ties and family solidarity are being weakened and broken by the mobility so essential to modern industrial development. . . . Thousands of aged workers find themselves in a strange country without friends or relatives."

Many workers, however, still could and did depend on their families for

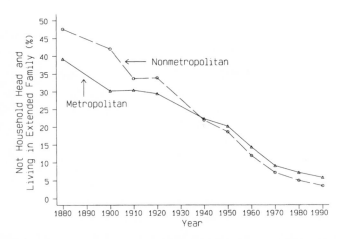

Fig. 6.4   Percentage not household heads and living in an extended family among noninstitutionalized retired men sixty-five or older, by metropolitan status
Sources: For sources and definitions, see tables 6.1 and 6.2.

support. The 1919 Ohio Commission on Health Insurance and Old Age Pensions estimated that, in Hamilton and Cincinnati, 15–25 percent of people over age fifty were dependent on relatives or friends (cited in Epstein 1928, 50).[4] The New York State Commission on Old Age Security (1930) found that, in 1925–29, half of men and women older than sixty-four were dependent on relatives and friends. Estimates for 1937 suggest that between two-fifths and half of persons age sixty-five or older were dependent on relatives or friends and that over three-quarters were at least partially dependent on children or other family members or on friends (Shearon 1938). Wentworth (1950) reported that one of the ways Social Security beneficiaries who retired in 1941 were able to live on their retirement income was by living in joint households or receiving contributions from relatives. Figure 6.3 above indicates that more than 40 percent of retired men lived with children or other relatives in 1880 and more than 30 percent in 1920. Over time, the coresidence rates of the retired fell more sharply than those of men in the labor force, with the result that, by 1990, the coresidence rates of the retired were virtually indistinguishable from those of men in the labor force. This pattern of catch-up implies that only in the past was retirement accompanied by moves into childrens' homes or children taking over their parents' households.

Loss of independence on retirement is also seen among Union army veterans. Thirty-seven percent of men who retired between 1900 and 1910 moved on retiring, generally to another town within the same county. In contrast, only 21 percent of those still remaining in the labor force moved, and, when they did move, they tended to move longer distances. When retired men did move, they lost their head-of-household status, generally to their children. Thirty percent of all retirees who moved lost head-of-household status, compared to only 9 percent of nonretirees. Retirement clearly brought with it dependence on family members.

The poor who could no longer work and had no children or family members to fall back on for support, whether because they were childless, had outlived their children, or had children too poor to support them, became dependent on private or public charity. The 1910 Massachusetts Commission on Old Age Pensions estimated that 3 percent of those age sixty-five or older received either public or private poor relief and that another 3 percent were in either almshouses or private old-age homes. In Massachusetts, 64 percent of almshouse inmates had no living children, and only 8 percent had children or other near relatives judged financially able to assist them.[5]

Relatively few of the elderly have ever been institutionalized (see fig. 6.5), never more than 6 percent of the elderly population, yet the poorhouse played a large role in the debate over old-age pensions. The majority of almshouse inmates (53 percent in 1904 and 67 percent in 1923) were above the age of sixty (Haber and Gratton 1994, 123). Advocates of pensions argued that "a pension system would take a large number of inmates out of the poor house and put them back in their homes, and would, in general greatly reduce the outlay for poor relief" (Massachusetts Commission on Old Age Pensions 1910, 254). Epstein (1922, 59) claimed that the "prospect of the poorhouse with its stigma of pauperism, so detestable to the honest wage-earner, haunts him like a dark shadow and saps every bit of his vitality." When, in *Helvering v. Davis* (1937), Supreme Court Justice Cardozo asserted the constitutionality of the Social Security Act, he wrote that "the hope behind this statute is to save men and women from the rigors of the poorhouse as well as from the haunting fear that such a lot awaits them when journey's end is near" (National Conference on Social Welfare 1985, 129). State commissions had been less sanguine. They judged 90 percent of almshouse residents sixty-five years of age or older to be physically defective and believed that residents would not be able to live on small pensions unless these were supplemented by assistance from family members—an assistance on which most inmates could not count because few had any living children (e.g., Massachusetts Commission on Old Age Pensions 1910; Pennsylvania Old Age Pension Commission 1919). Social Security did empty the almshouses, but primarily because almshouse residents were ineligible for benefits. Almshouses were merely replaced by private nursing homes in the 1930s and 1940s and by public nursing homes in the 1950s, when Social Security rules were amended. By 1940 the percentage of the elderly population that was institutionalized was higher than in 1920.

Although Social Security has not had an effect on institutionalization rates, it is widely regarded as having displaced the care of the family. In the United States today the predominant flow of monetary transfers is from the older to the younger generation (McGarry and Schoeni 1995). In contrast, in Malaysia monetary transfers flow primarily from the younger to the older generation

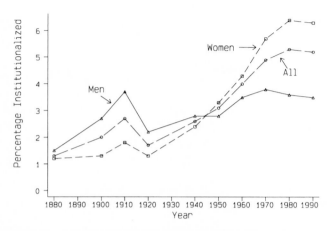

Fig. 6.5   Percentage of population age sixty-five or older currently institutionalized, men and women, 1880–1990
Note: Institutionalization rates were estimated from Ruggles and Sobek (1995).

(Lillard and Willis 1997). Malaysia was characterized by the absence of any extensive public insurance and institutional social support programs, such as Social Security, during the period of observation. Information on the extent of monetary transfers from children to parents in the United States prior to Social Security is scanty, but information on the living arrangements of the elderly provides some clues. The results of Michael, Fuchs, and Scott (1980) and Schorr (1960), suggesting that the decline in coresidence was faster among those receiving larger Social Security benefits, imply that, at the beginning of the twentieth century, the flow of transfers may have been from younger to older generations.

The likely effect of old-age pensions on the direction of the transfer of resources across generations was widely discussed even before the institution of Social Security. The 1910 Massachusetts Commission on Pensions and Annuities concluded that pensions would have a disintegrating effect on the family (cited in Epstein 1928, 227). In contrast, advocates of state-provided pensions decried the burden that dependence imposed on young and old alike and argued that both the elderly and their children would be happier if they could afford to live in separate dwellings (Epstein 1928, 144–48). They even cited the Union army pension program as building up the family because children would be more likely to find a place in their homes for parents who could partially pay their own way.[6] The old were viewed as a burden, not just on their children, but also on their children's children, who would be "doomed to undernourishment; and to a life in the midst of crowded and unsanitary quarters . . . to leave school early in life and to join the ranks of the unskilled" (Epstein 1922, 63).

The burden of the elderly should not be exaggerated. Figure 6.3 above showed that the percentage of the retired living with family members has fallen steadily since 1880. Among those individuals heading households between 1880 and 1920 and aged eighteen to forty-four, at most 9 percent of those within a ten-year age group had a parent present in the household. Contrary to the claims of social reformers, when an aged parent was present in the household, the teenage children of the household head were less likely to be gainfully employed and were more likely to be in school than if a parent was not present, controlling for household socioeconomic and demographic characteristics.[7] So few of the elderly now live with their children that, in 1990, no more than 3 percent of children cared for their parents within their own homes.

In the past, the burden of caring for elderly parents within the same household fell primarily on the wealthier members of society. Figure 6.6 shows the relative probability that a farmer, a professional or proprietor, or an artisan aged eighteen to sixty-four would have a parent present in the household, where the probability is relative to that of a laborer.[8] Relative to laborers, professionals and proprietors at the beginning of the century were much more likely to have a parent present in the household, implying that transfers from child to parent depended on the child's earnings. Social historians have argued that, in the past, wealthy families felt obligated to take in relatives with no means of support, leading to large extended families among the wealthy (e.g., Ruggles 1987). Only the wealthy could support nonproductive kin, hence the higher probability that elderly parents would reside in the homes of professionals and proprietors rather than laborers. Lillard and Willis (1997) find that, in present-day Malaysia, the child's transfers to parents depend very significantly on the child's earnings.

Over time, the income of children became a less important determinant of whether they took in their elderly parents. From 1900 to 1950 the probability that professionals and proprietors would have a parent present in the household did not rise as quickly as the absolute probability that a laborer would have a parent present. As incomes rose between 1900 and 1950, even low-wage laborers may have been able to afford to have a parent present in the household. They may have acquired houses large enough to provide for a parent in their own homes comfortably. After 1950, the probability that a parent would be present in the household fell sharply across all occupational groups, but more sharply for professionals and proprietors than for laborers. In the aggregate, the probability of a professional or proprietor having a parent present in the household relative to that of laborer narrowed from 1900 to 1980, and by 1990 professionals and proprietors were slightly less likely to have a parent present in their households than were laborers. It is this narrowing of differential probabilities that suggests that children's income now has a lessened effect on whether their parents live in their households.

The declining probability that a parent would be present in children's households regardless of children's social class has been attributed to changing social values (Ruggles 1987; Smith 1979). In the past, children may have been more

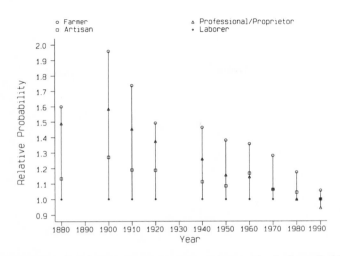

Fig. 6.6   Relative probability of having a parent present in the household, among households headed by individuals aged eighteen to sixty-four, 1880–1990

Note: All probabilities have been divided by that of laborers. Probabilities were predicted from probit regressions estimated from the integrated public-use samples and were evaluated at 1950 mean values to account for differences in household characteristics and in the age structure of the population both over time and across occupational groups.

willing to welcome their aged parents into their own homes, and more parents may have preferred to live with their children. Alternatively, rising incomes may have enabled an increasingly large fraction of the elderly to live alone. Before 1950, rising incomes and larger houses may have led more children to welcome their parents into their homes, but, after 1950, increases in retirement income, particularly among widows, who were the parents most likely to reside with children, were large enough to outweigh this effect and caused more of the elderly to live alone.

Census data provide some evidence that the elderly with higher incomes are more likely to live alone. As seen in figure 6.7, which plots the probability that an older man employed in a particular occupation would head his own household relative to the probability that a laborer would, nonlaborers have always been more likely than laborers to head their own household.[9] But, after 1950, differences in living arrangements narrowed sharply, suggesting that income is now a less important indicator not only of whether children take in their elderly parents but also of whether the employed elderly live with their children. Perhaps only those families with special needs or strong preferences for living together now do so.

It is not possible to use the early censuses to test whether rising incomes induced more of the retired elderly to establish living quarters separate from those of their children. No information is available on the incomes of the retired. But it is the rise of single households among the retired that has been the

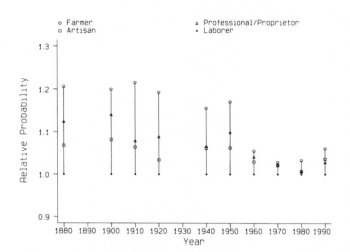

Fig. 6.7   Relative probability of heading own household, men sixty-five years of age and older and in labor force, 1880–1990
Note: All probabilities have been divided by that of laborers. Probabilities were predicted from probit regressions estimated from the integrated public-use samples and were evaluated at 1950 mean values.

ongoing, long-term process. Work using cross-sectional data from the 1960s and after suggests that income has a small effect on the propensity of the elderly to live alone (Börsch-Supan et al. 1992; Schwartz, Danziger, and Smolensky 1984; cf. Michael, Fuchs, and Scott 1980), but the applicability of these estimates to periods prior to 1940 is questionable. Fortunately, Union army pension income can be used as a test of revealed preference to determine whether coresidence or independent living was preferred by retired, elderly men at the beginning of the twentieth century.

6.2   Pensions and Living Arrangements

The living arrangements of the elderly are the outcome of a joint decision between adult children and their aged parents or relatives. A bargaining model—that is, a model in which individual, not family, resources matter—would predict that, because Union army pensions were so large, representing 30 percent of the average income of a manufacturing worker in 1910, they would enable veterans to live either on their own or with their children and thus to pick their preferred residence option. Parents who wished to live with their children may have offered them financial transfers as compensation for the children having to listen to interminable Civil War stories. In return for transfers, parents may have received free market goods and services that might otherwise have had to be provided by the pensioners themselves, their spouses, or hired help. They would also have been near their grandchildren. But elderly retirees who chose to live with their children may have been more constrained in their choice of consumption bundles. For example, they may not have been able to increase the size of their living space and therefore guarantee themselves a certain amount of privacy.

In contrast to the bargaining model, a model of altruism predicts that total family income, not individual income, determines living arrangements. Children who take their parents into their homes will be motivated, not by the prospect of financial transfers, but by the knowledge that their parents were being taken care of. The elderly who live alone do so, not because they can afford it, but because the family can afford it. Thus, children might transfer income to their parents to enable them to live on their own. Pension income would either partially or wholly displace children's transfers. If pension income is relatively small, then pension amount might have either no or very little effect on the living arrangements of the elderly. But, because Union army pensions represented over 30 percent of average yearly income, the implied substantial increase in total family income should have affected the living arrangements of the elderly.

I cannot observe the children's decision; I can observe only the veteran's decision. I subdivide this decision into two stages. The veteran first determines the best bundle of goods and household services that he can obtain under either living arrangement given his income, in the case of a bargaining model, or both his and his children's income, in the case of an altruism model. Although his income does not depend on the coresidence decision, the prices that he faces for market goods and household services such as meal preparation and personal care will vary. For some goods, he may face an infinite price under the coresidence option because he will have lost some degree of autonomy in his choice of goods. Utility when independent of family members can therefore be written as $U_i(C_i^*; Z)$ and utility when living with family members as $U_d(C_d^*; Z)$, where C^* is the consumption bundle that is chosen, and Z is a vector of demographic variables and of utility shifters such as age and ethnicity. If $U_i(C_i^*; Z) \geq U_d(C_d^*; Z)$, the veteran will maintain an independent household. Transforming the utility functions into indirect utility functions, the veteran will maintain an independent household if $V_i(p_i, y; Z) \geq V_d(p_d, y; Z)$, where p_i is the price of the bundle when independent, p_d is the price of the bundle when dependent, and y is income. Therefore, if the indirect utility functions are assumed to be linear in their arguments, the utility-maximizing individual evaluates the decision function

$$I^* = V_i(p_i, y; Z) - V_d(p_d, y; Z).$$

Although the value of I^* is not observed, several indicators of living arrangements are, such as whether an individual was a household head or whether the individual ever lived with extended family members.

Figures 6.8 and 6.9 suggest that Union army pensions determined the living

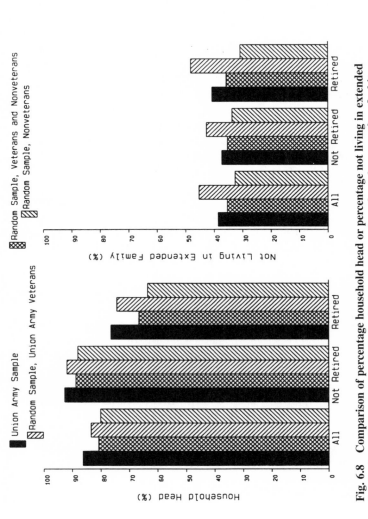

Fig. 6.8 Comparison of percentage household head or percentage not living in extended family, by retirement status, between Union army sample and random samples of white veterans and nonveterans aged sixty-seven to eighty-seven, 1910

Note: The random sample was drawn from the integrated public-use sample of the 1910 census (Ruggles and Sobek 1995) and was restricted to white, noninstitutionalized men who either were born in a Union state or, if foreign born, immigrated prior to the Civil War. Veterans and nonveterans are identified in the sample. The random sample was reweighted to have the same geographic distribution as the Union army sample. Reweighting by age would not materially change the results. The main difference between the Union army sample and the national sample of either veterans or nonveterans is rural residence, not age. Living in an extended family is defined as living in a household in which family members other than the wife are present.

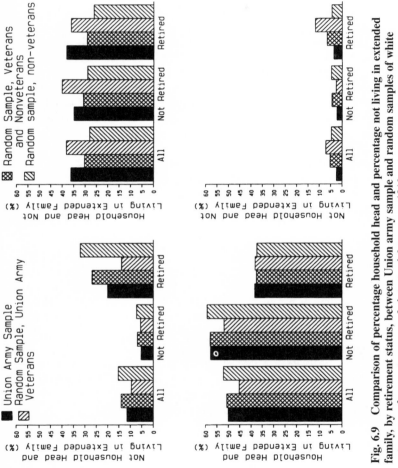

Fig. 6.9 Comparison of percentage household head and percentage not living in extended family, by retirement status, between Union army sample and random samples of white veterans and nonveterans aged sixty to eighty-seven, 1910

Sources: See table 6.8.

Note: Living in an extended family is defined as living in a household in which family members other than the wife are present.

arrangements of the elderly. Seventy-six percent of retired men in the Union army sample and 74 percent in the random sample of Union army veterans were household heads in 1910. But only 64 percent of retired nonveterans were household heads. The percentage of retired Union army veterans living with no family members other than their wives was 41 percent in the Union army sample and 48 percent in the random sample. In contrast, 31 percent of retired nonveterans in the random sample were living with no family members other than their wives. Figure 6.9 suggests that there were large differences by veteran status in the percentage of older men living without any children in the household and in the percentage of older men living as dependents in their children's homes. Thirty-eight percent of retired veterans in the Union army sample and 36 percent of retired veterans in the random sample headed families consisting only of the elderly couple. Only 26 percent of retired nonveterans did so. Twenty percent of retired veterans in the Union army sample and 14 percent in the random sample lived with a relative who was the household head. In contrast, 32 percent of retired nonveterans in the random sample did so.[10]

Figure 6.9, therefore, suggests that the probability of parents living with their children as dependents depended on the parents' income. Recall that I will be examining this variable in the subsequent empirical work. The probability of parents heading households in which there were no children present depended both on their income and on whether their children had left home. But there were no differences in the percentage of retirees heading households in which children were present, suggesting that whether children remained in a household headed by their elderly parents did not depend on their father's veteran status.

Although both figures 6.8 and 6.9 are suggestive, they are inconclusive. Veterans are a selected sample. Lower morbidity rates or higher incomes among veterans may have decreased their probability of living in their relatives' households relative to that of nonveterans. Therefore, I compare living arrangements among retired veterans controlling for characteristics such as health, previous occupation, and property ownership. Provided that I control for age and health, I will be able to identify a pension effect.

Rewriting the utility-maximizing veteran's decision function,

$$I^* = V_i(p_i, y; Z) - V_d(p_d, y; Z)$$
$$= -X'\beta + \varepsilon,$$

where ε is a standard normal error term, and X is a vector containing the vector of demographic and socioeconomic variables and of utility shifters Z, income y, and prices of consumption bundles p_i and p_d under the independent living and coresidence options, respectively. Although I cannot directly observe the prices that a veteran faces, I can observe such characteristics as marital status that will determine the price of household goods the veteran faces. Although I cannot observe household income, I can observe pension income and such proxies for other household income as past occupation. I cannot observe the children's earnings. But, if the altruism model holds, total family income determines the coresidence decision. If a bargaining model holds, children's income might determine coresidence if children give transfers to parents to avoid coresidence. In fact, figure 6.6 above showed that the probability that a child would have a parent present in the household was much greater for wealthier children, children who were either farmers or professionals or proprietors rather than laborers. Low-wage laborers may not have been able to afford to welcome their parents into their homes, nor might their parents have wanted to move into the cramped quarters of a laborer. Fortunately, omitting children's earnings from my empirical specification will not bias my estimates of the effect of pension income on the probability of coresidence. Pension income and children's earnings are unlikely to be correlated. Most individuals received pensions only after 1890, long after they had invested in their children's human capital.

The value of I^*, the difference in utilities under either residence option, is also not observed, but a discrete headship indicator is observed, given by

$$I = \begin{cases} 0 & \text{if } I^* < 0, \\ 1 & \text{otherwise,} \end{cases}$$

where 1 represents dependence and 0 independence. The probit equation that is then estimated is

$$\text{prob}(I = 1) = \text{prob}(\varepsilon < X'\beta) = \Phi(X'\beta),$$

where $\Phi(\ )$ is a standard normal cumulative distribution function. Because independent living is costly, a veteran with a high pension will have less of a need for the free market goods and household services that he can obtain with coresidence than a veteran with a low pension. Therefore, two individuals identical in all characteristics except pension income may be expected to have different living arrangements. If the individual with the low pension picks the coresidence option while the individual with the high pension does not, this suggests that independent living is preferred to coresidence. Only insufficiency of income inhibits it.

In comparing living arrangements among retired veterans controlling for characteristics, the measure of coresidence that I use as a dependent variable is a dummy variable equal to one if the veteran lived in a household that an extended family member headed. This measure is a useful indicator of dependence on family members. Recall that this measure differs across veterans and nonveterans and that the secular decline in this coresidence indicator has been ongoing since 1880.

The sample is restricted to noninstitutionalized veterans who had retired by 1910. The control variables are derived from the 1900 and 1910 censuses and the pension and surgeons' records. They include number of children, health, age, changes in marital status between 1900 and 1910, property ownership in 1900, occupation, literacy, foreign birth, extent of urbanization in county of residence, and geographic region. Foreign birth may determine social norms governing the living arrangements of the elderly. The previous chapter discussed differences in farmers' retirement and subsequent living arrangements by ethnicity. Those who are older and those who are in poor health may find it more costly to maintain their independence. Changes in marital status should matter to the residence decision because the spouse may provide a stream of household services that are not so easily or cheaply replaced by hired help but may be replaced by a daughter or daughter-in-law. More important, hired help may be a poor substitute for the companionship of family members. The number of children will matter because only those with children can be dependent on their families. Property ownership and occupation in 1900 will be proxies for wealth holdings, but property ownership might also reflect any difficulties in liquidating assets. Property ownership is known only for men who were household heads in 1900. Therefore, the lack of property is also an indicator of 1900 living arrangements, which will be correlated with 1910 living arrangements among those who had retired in 1900.

The probit results are presented in table 6.1. A $1.00 increase in monthly pension amount lowered the probability of coresidence by 0.0075. Evaluated at the pension means, the elasticity of coresidence with family members with respect to pensions was -0.77 ($= -0.0075\,[18.93/0.1847]$). No sharp changes in coresidence at specific pension amounts could be detected. Interactions of pension amount with age dummies, health, and occupation yielded coefficients that were small and insignificant. There were no sharp changes in coresidence at the ages at which Union army veterans became eligible for a larger pension. The coresidence decision of those in higher-paying occupations was less sensitive to pension income, but the effect was very small and insignificant.

Because Union army pensions represented a pure income effect, the estimated elasticity of coresidence with family members with respect to Union army pensions can be used to determine the effect of increases in income on coresidence rates. Assuming that the assets of the elderly kept pace with per capita GNP and increased by 32 percent between 1910 and 1940, the estimated elasticity implies that up to 86 percent of the decline in coresidence rates between 1910 and 1940 can be explained by increases in income.

Other important cross-sectional determinants of coresidence were age and changes in marital status. The probability of coresidence was lower at younger ages. Changes in marital status raised the probability of coresidence by the substantial amount of 0.1861. When pension amount was interacted with the dummy indicator for changes in marital status, the results were inconclusive but suggested that pensions were especially likely to affect the coresidence decisions of widowers. Pensions do not appear to have affected the remarriage decision. In a national sample, Union army veterans were not significantly

Table 6.1   **Probit of Probability of Living with Family Members as Dependent among Retirees, with Coresidence as the Dependent Variable (361 observations, pseudo R^2 = .27)**

Variable	Mean	Coef.	S.E.	$\partial P/\partial x$
Dummy = 1 if coresiding	.20			
Constant		−8.5004‡	1.3185	
Monthly pension	18.93	−.0384†	.0198	−.0075
Age in 1910	71.50	.1021‡	.0186	.0198
Number of children	3.61	.0889	.1041	.0173
Number of children squared	20.91	−.0109	.0117	−.0021
Dummy = 1 if:				
Poor health	.37	.1345	.1984	.0261
Health status unknown	.09	−.0168	.3142	−.0033
1900 occupation:				
Professional or proprietor	.16	−.0373	.2616	−.0073
Artisan	.13	−.0388	.2948	−.0075
Laborer	.20	−.1982	.2622	−.0385
Owned no property	.29	.7822‡	.1956	.1520
Illiterate	.07	−.5635	.4227	−.1095
Foreign born	.10	−.6469	.3392	−.1257
Marital status changed	.18	.9296‡	.2028	.1806
Lives in Midwest in 1910	.88	.3282	.3093	.0638
100 or more people per square mile in county residence in 1910	.20	.3653	.2224	.0710

Note: The omitted dummies are good health and farmer. The symbols *, †, and ‡ indicate that the coefficient is significantly different from zero at at least the 10 percent, 5 percent, and 1 percent levels, respectively. $\partial P/\partial x = \beta(1/n) \sum \phi (x'\beta)$, where ϕ is the standard normal density and is $\partial P/\partial x$ is in probability units.

Source: Costa (in press).

more likely to have remarried compared to their nonveteran counterparts. Although changes in marital status are an important explanation of coresidence in this cross section, the decreased probability of an older man being widowed could not explain the decrease in coresidence from 1910 to 1940. The percentage of men older than sixty-four who were married remained unchanged, at around 67 percent, between these years. However, since 1940 older men's probability of being widowed has fallen sharply. In 1990, 77 percent of men older than sixty-four were married.

The number of children, whether included linearly or as a spline, was insignificant. But the signs on the coefficients suggest that those with fewer children were less likely to coreside with their extended family as dependent relations, a finding consistent with numerous studies using recent data (e.g., Wolf 1994). The point estimates should therefore be used to investigate the effect of kin availability on coresidence. The elderly aged sixty-five or older in 1910 had on average 3.5 surviving children, those in 1940 2.2, and those in 1990 2.0.[11] The decrease in the number of surviving children between 1910 and 1940 could therefore account for a 0.03 decline in the probability of coresidence, or 30 percent of the actual decline. From 1940 to 1990 the decrease in the number of surviving children predicts only a 0.003 decline in the probability of coresidence, less than 2 percent of the actual decline.

Occupation was an insignificant predictor of coresidence. Not owning property was a significant, positive predictor, but only because those who were not households heads in 1900, and hence owned no property, were mc :e likely to coreside with family members. When the sample is restricted to men who were household heads in 1900, the coefficient on property ownership still suggests that the wealthier were less likely to reside with a family member who was a household head, but the coefficient was not statistically significant. Ethnicity remained insignificant even when the foreign born were divided into ethnic Germans and other foreign born.

Population density was not a significant predictor of the living arrangements of the elderly, but in a national sample coresidence was less likely among the retired living in a metropolitan rather than a nonmetropolitan area in 1910. Recall that figure 6.4 above showed that, by 1910, metropolitan and nonmetropolitan rates of coresidence were fairly similar and that, by 1950, coresidence rates were higher in metropolitan than in nonmetropolitan areas. Thus, the increasing urbanization of the United States is an unlikely explanation for the long-term decline in coresidence rates.

The coefficient on poor health is insignificant, but its sign implies that those in poor health were more likely to pick the coresidence option. Its insignificance is consistent with findings from recent data that most health variables—with the exception of those indicating a severe disability, such as difficulty in meal preparation, money management, and phone use—are not associated with the probability of living alone (Wolf 1990). Although the proportion of the population that is severely disabled probably has fallen, this improvement would be hard to quantify until more detailed diagnostic information becomes available.[12]

Although pensions were supposed to be awarded regardless of the veteran's financial status, employees of the Pension Bureau may have awarded higher pensions to those living with their families if they regarded coresidence as an indicator of need. Pension amount is therefore potentially endogenous. Therefore, I use whether a recruit applied under the General Law as an instrumental variable. As in chapter 3, I estimate a probit model with an endogenous explanatory variable using two-stage conditional maximum likelihood estimation (Rivers and Vuong 1988) under the assumption that the indicator variable for whether the recruit applied under the General Law is a legitimate instrument. A Hausman test for exogeneity of pension amount suggests that endogeneity is not a problem. Table 6.2 compares the derivatives of the probit estimates with those from a two-stage conditional maximum likelihood procedure among the men for whom information on the law that they applied under is available. The first-stage estimates are also presented. The change in the coef-

Table 6.2   Comparison of Derivatives from Probit and from Two-Stage Conditional Maximum Likelihood Estimates of Determinants of Coresiding with Extended Family, with Coresidence in 1910 as the Dependent Variable (352 observations)

Variable	Probit: $\partial P/\partial x$	Two-Stage Conditional Maximum Likelihood				
		First Stage: Adj. $R^2 = .36$		Second Stage: Pseudo $R^2 = .27$		
		Coef.	S.E.	Coef.	S.E.	$\partial P/\partial x$
Dummy = 1 if applied under General Law	−.0084	10.4657‡	.8234			
Constant		−4.3118	5.2133	−8.5259‡	1.3543	
Monthly pension	.0204	.3119‡	.0693	−.0407*	.0222	−.0081
Age in 1910	.0188	−.1872	.3980	.1029‡	.0190	.0203
Number of children	−.0024	.0350	.0416	.0941	.1052	.0186
Number of children squared				−.0114	.0119	−.0022
Dummy = 1 if:						
Poor health	.0226	1.0198	.8504	.1089	.2013	.0215
Health status unknown	−.0083	2.2378	1.4675	−.0573	.3271	−.0113
1900 occupation:						
Professional or proprietor	−.0082	−2.1099	1.1682	−.0400	.2620	−.0079
Artisan	−.0093	−1.0035	1.4594	−.0503	.2958	−.0099
Laborer	−.0333	−1.6120	1.1040	−1.6195	1.1044	−.0319
Owned no property	.1489	−1.9222	.9018	.7617	.2015	.1506
Illiterate	−.1138	−3.5312‡	1.6051	−.5955	.4368	−.1177
Foreign born	−.1308	−.2705	1.3243	−.6602	.3413	−.1305
Marital status changed	.1832	.8585†	1.0492	.9241‡	.2049	.1826
Lives in Midwest in 1910	.0675	−3.2096‡	1.2430	.3553	.3174	.0702
100 or more people per square mile, 1910, in county residence	.0757	1.2071	1.0453	.3818	.2237	.0755
Residuals first stage				−.0051	.0253	−.0010

Note: The first stage is a regression of pension amount on the exogenous variables and whether the veteran applied under the General Law. The second stage is a probit with the exogenous variables, pension amount, and the first-stage residuals as explanatory variables. The standard errors have been corrected. The symbols *, †, and ‡ indicate that the coefficient is significantly different from zero at least the 10 percent, 5 percent, and 1 percent levels, respectively. $\partial P/\partial x$ is in probability units. $\partial P/\partial x = \boldsymbol{\beta}(1/n)\sum \phi(\mathbf{x}'\boldsymbol{\beta})$, where ϕ is the standard normal density, and $\partial P/\partial x$ is in probability units.

ficient on pension amount is small, with the estimated mean effect of a dollar increase in monthly pension amount on the coresidence probability falling from -0.0084 when a probit is estimated to -0.0081 when two-stage conditional maximum likelihood estimation is used. The elasticity of coresidence with respect to pension amount is -0.80 ($= -0.0081$ [18.93/0.1905]).

I have shown that my estimate of the effect of Union army pensions on living arrangements is unbiased. I can therefore use the elasticity of coresidence with respect to pension income to calculate the effect of a 100 percent reduction in pension amount (from $18.93 to $0.01 per month) on average coresidence rates in both the Union army sample and the random sample of Union army veterans. This pension reduction would increase the percentage of veterans residing in households headed by a family member from 20 to 36 percent in the Union army sample and from 14 to 25 percent in the random sample of veterans. Because 32 percent of nonveterans in the random sample were living in an extended household that they did not head, 60–100 percent of the difference in coresidence rates between Union army veterans and non-veterans can therefore be attributed to pensions.

Recall from chapter 3 that another source of variation in the Union army pension program was disparate treatment by type of veteran. Confederates were ineligible. As noted in chapter 3, in 1910 Union pensioners were collecting an average pension of $171.90 per year, and about 90 percent of all Union veterans were on the pension rolls, whereas Confederates were collecting an average pension of just $47.24 per year from southern states, and fewer than 30 percent of all Confederate veterans were receiving a pension. Therefore, the difference in coresidence rates by veteran status in a southern-born sample should reflect a veteran effect, while the difference in coresidence by veteran status in a northern-born sample should reflect both a veteran and a pension effect. In fact, among retirees in the southern-born sample, there was no difference in coresidence by veteran status.[13] But, among retirees in the northern-born sample, 17 percent of veterans lived in households headed by a family member, compared to 30 percent of nonveterans.

Lower coresidence rates among Union compared to Confederate veterans persist even controlling for age, marital status, farm residence, literacy, urbanization, and region of residence (see table 6.3). Note, that in contrast to figure 6.4 above, coresidence was less common among households in rural than in urban areas. But, when the variable indicating farm residence is omitted, the coefficient on rural area implies that coresidence was more common among households in rural areas. Because farmers who retired moved to nearby, rural towns, then, controlling for farm residence, coresidence was less common in these rural areas than in urban areas.

The coefficient on Confederate veteran in the southern-born regression in table 6.3 shows that being a Confederate veteran had an insignificant, positive effect on the probability of coresidence. The coefficient on Union veteran in the northern-born regression is positive and significant, implying that Union veterans were less likely to coreside with their extended families than northern-

Table 6.3 Probit of Probability of Living with Family Members as Dependent among White, Native-Born Retirees, Aged 60–87 in 1910 (from Public-Use Sample), with Coresidence as the Dependent Variable

Variable	Northern Born (1,775 observations, pseudo R^2 = .28)				Southern Born (385 observations, pseudo R^2 = .32)			
	Mean	Parameter Est.	S.E.	$\partial P/\partial x$	Mean	Parameter Est.	S.E.	$\partial P/\partial x$
Dummy = 1 if coresiding	.26				.37			
Intercept		-1.8423‡	.4111			-.9258	.8334	
Dummy = 1 if:								
Union veteran	.27	-.2312‡	.0900	-.0201				
Confederate veteran					.37	.2000	.1674	.0193
Married	.60	-1.1607‡	.0755	-.1010	.57	-1.0647‡	.1569	-.1029
Illiterate	.04	.1288	.1724	.0112	.13	.4232*	.2269	.0409
Lives on farm	.19	1.1972‡	.0964	.1042	.38	1.5358‡	.1771	.1484
Lives in Northeast	.45				.00			
Lives in South	.11	.2405†	.1236	.0209	.80	-.0939	.2333	-.0091
Lives in Midwest	.47	.0548	.0852	.0048	.15	.0716	.3605	.0069
Lives in West	.08	-.0616	.1469	-.0054	.05	-.5437‡	.2128	-.0525
Lives in rural area	.61	-.4047‡	.0863	-.0352	.80			
Age	71.54	.0242‡	.0055	.0021	72.01	.0109	.0111	.0011

Source: Costa (in press).

Note: The sample consists of white, noninstitutionalized, native-born men aged 60–87 drawn from the 1910 census (Ruggles and Sobek 1995). Rural areas are defined as all unincorporated places and all incorporated places with fewer than 2,500 residents. The omitted dummy is residence in the East in the northern-born equation and residence in the South in the southern-born equation. The symbols *, †, and ‡ indicate that the coefficient is significantly different from zero at at least the 10 percent, 5 percent, and 1 percent levels, respectively. $\partial P/\partial x = \beta(1/n) \sum \phi \, (\mathbf{x'\beta})$, where ϕ is the standard normal density, and $\partial P/\partial x$ is in probability units.

born nonveterans. When the northern- and southern-born participation functions are used to estimate whether the difference in coresidence rates between the northern- and the southern-born samples is largely due to differences in observable characteristics or in participation behavior, the results imply that at least 10 percent of the 11 percentage point difference in coresidence rates between the northern- and the southern-born samples can be explained by differences in participation behavior and therefore Union army pensions.[14]

6.3 Implications

Union army pensions exerted a sizable, negative effect on the coresidence rates of the retired. The elasticity of coresidence with family members with respect to Union army pensions was −0.77. Union army pensions could thus explain 60–100 percent of the difference in coresidence rates between retired Union army veterans and nonveterans and at least 10 percent of the difference in coresidence rates between native-born men born in the North and those born in the South. Those findings suggest that it is not just the aged of today who prefer to live alone (University of Michigan Survey Research Center 1962) but the aged of the past as well. Social norms have not changed. Increases in income have always been associated with an increased demand for the privacy and autonomy provided by separate living arrangements. Rising incomes have therefore contributed enormously to the increase in well-being among the elderly.

Estimates of the effect of Union army pensions on coresidence rates can be used to calculate the effect of a secular increase in income on the secular decline in coresidence with family members among the retired. These imply that up to 86 percent of the decline in coresidence rates between 1910 and 1940 can be explained by increases in income. Rising incomes were therefore one of the most important factors enabling the elderly to live alone. Additional factors were the decreased probability of the elderly being widowed and the increased ratio of elderly to children. The decrease in the number of surviving children could explain up to 30 percent of the decline in coresidence from 1910 to 1940. Reductions in the probability of elderly men being widowed contributed to declining coresidence rates after 1940. Improvements in elderly health have undoubtedly played a role as well, but their effect could not be quantified from the data.

The role of rising incomes in declining coresidence rates after 1940 is less clear. Extrapolations of the regression results to the present yield nonsensical results. One explanation is that, because extrapolating to 1990 falls outside the sample range, there may be nonlinearities in living arrangements with income that I am not detecting. Michael, Fuchs, and Scott (1980) find that, among young, single men and women in the postwar period, the relation between income and coresidence is S shaped, with the probability of coresidence increasing slowly at low income levels, then rising sharply at higher income levels, before leveling off again. Although I found that pension income had a smaller effect on the coresidence decision of those in high-earning occupations, this effect was small and statistically insignificant. Nonetheless, that the average elderly man may now be wealthy enough to be unaffected by small changes in income cannot be ruled out.

Another explanation for my inability to extrapolate to the present is that the income elasticity of coresidence has fallen, and not just because we have become a richer society. Using recent data, Börsch-Supan et al. (1992) argue that increasing the income of the elderly does not raise the probability of their living alone relative to the probability of their living with their children. Schwartz, Danziger, and Smolensky (1984) also find that income has a small effect on the propensity of the elderly to live alone. Although Michael, Fuchs, and Scott (1980) find that income has a substantial effect on the coresidence propensities of the elderly, they may have estimated a high income effect because they were examining a sample of widows. Recall that my results suggested that Union army pension income had a particularly large effect on the coresidence decision of widowers, suggesting that the responsiveness of the widowed to income changes may be greater than that of the married.

The income elasticity of coresidence may have declined because, now that only 5 percent of older men live in their children's homes, those who do so are likely to have special needs or tastes. The income elasticity of coresidence may now be lower because the price of independent living fell. The income effect as I and other researchers have measured it probably incorporates some response to price changes. The appearance of single-portion food products, the growth of housing for single individuals and of retirement communities in low-cost living areas, the declining price of transport and of communication with family members, and the rise in private and state social support services have lowered the price of the elderly living alone. If independent living is now relatively inexpensive, changes in income may have a relatively small effect on coresidence rates.

Independent living may be not only cheaper than it was in the past but also much more attractive. Today, a leisurely retirement lifestyle, filled with recreational activities, including mass tourism, low-impact sports such as golf, and inexpensive entertainments, is often made possible by resettlement to a community with a better climate or other environmental amenities or to one with a low cost of living. Since 1940, the demand by the elderly for residence in an area with a warm February temperature has increased, even though the price has risen (Cragg and Kahn 1997). Such a community is not necessarily one in which children or relatives reside, but it is one with greater recreational opportunities. As recreational opportunities have expanded, independent living may have become more attractive. The increasing attractiveness of independent living may in turn have increased the attractiveness of retirement. The income elasticity of retirement is now lower than it was in 1900, implying that the retirement decision of older men is simply no longer as responsive to changes in income. One explanation is that retirement is now much more attractive. The elderly can now live independently, spending their time in recreational pursuits.

6.4 Summary

This chapter has shown that, since 1880, increasing numbers of retirees have been living by themselves. In 1880, 46 percent of all retired men age sixty-five or older were living in a household headed by children or other relatives. By 1940, this fraction had fallen to 22 percent and, by 1990, to 5 percent. In contrast, among all men age sixty-five or older and still in the labor force, the fraction living in a household headed by children or other relatives was only 10 percent in 1880, 6 percent in 1940, and 4 percent in 1990. Differences in living arrangements by retirement status have narrowed. This difference has narrowed, not because of changes in social norms, or because the ratio of aged parents to adult children has fallen, but because incomes have risen. Although retirees in the past would have preferred to lead lives independent of those of their children, they simply could not have afforded to do so. Income has now become a less important determinant of living arrangements than it was in the past, perhaps because it has become increasingly attractive for the elderly to live alone.

Appendix 6A

Table 6A.1   **Percentage of Noninstitutionalized Men 65 or Older Who Were Household Heads and Who Did Not Live in Extended Families, by Retirement Status**

	% Household Heads			% Not Living in Extended Family		
Year	Total	Retired	Not Retired	Total	Retired	Not Retired
1880	76.9	48.9	83.9	27.7	23.5	28.7
1900	75.8	52.3	86.3	31.3	27.8	32.9
1910	75.5	60.7	85.1	35.1	33.1	36.4
1920	75.6	62.3	84.4	39.1	35.8	41.3
1940	77.8	70.0	87.7	46.5	46.2	46.9
1950	78.8	72.8	86.7	56.3	54.9	58.1
1960	85.8	82.9	92.0	66.3	65.2	68.5
1970	90.4	89.0	94.3	74.8	75.1	73.9
1980	89.7	89.0	92.5	78.7	79.4	76.2
1990	89.7	89.5	90.8	79.3	80.2	75.6

Note: See figs. 6.1 and 6.2. Estimated from the integrated public-use census series (Ruggles and Sobek 1995). Living in an extended family is defined as living in a household in which family members other than the wife are present. The number of retired was calculated using the concept of gainful employment prior to 1940 and the concept of current employment in 1940 and later. The basic pattern remains unchanged if the institutionalized are included.

Table 6A.2 Percentage Household Heads and Percentage Living in an Extended Family among Noninstitutionalized Men 65 or Older Household, by Retirement Status

Year	% Household Heads and Living in Extended Family (1)			% Household Heads and Not Living in Extended Family (2)			% Not Household Heads and Living in Extended Family (3)			% Not Household Heads and Not Living in Extended Family (4)		
	Total	Retired	Not Retired	Total	Retired	Not Retired	Total	Retired	Not Retired	Total	Retired	Not Retired
1880	55.4	30.9	61.6	21.5	17.8	22.3	16.9	45.6	9.7	6.2	5.5	6.4
1900	51.2	33.5	59.2	24.6	18.8	27.2	17.5	38.8	8.0	6.7	8.9	5.7
1910	47.4	34.2	55.4	28.4	26.5	29.7	17.8	32.7	8.3	6.7	6.7	6.7
1920	42.9	32.1	50.0	32.8	30.2	34.5	18.0	32.1	8.7	6.4	5.6	6.9
1940	38.4	31.7	46.9	39.4	38.3	40.7	15.1	22.1	6.2	7.1	7.9	6.2
1950	29.7	25.6	35.0	49.1	47.2	51.7	14.0	19.5	6.9	7.2	7.7	6.4
1960	23.3	21.6	26.7	62.5	61.3	65.2	10.5	13.2	4.8	3.7	4.0	3.2
1970	18.0	16.5	22.4	72.4	72.5	71.9	7.2	8.5	3.7	2.4	2.5	2.1
1980	15.3	14.2	20.0	74.4	74.9	72.5	6.0	6.5	3.8	4.3	4.5	3.7
1990	15.8	14.7	21.0	73.9	74.8	69.8	4.9	5.2	3.5	5.4	5.3	5.8

Source: Costa (in press).

Note: See fig. 6.3. See previous table for sources.

Notes

1. The phrase of an elderly Bostonian interviewed by Gratton (1986, 59).

2. In 1900 only 14 percent of these households contained married children. Although by 1950 this figure had risen to 30 percent, in 1990 it was down to 9 percent. (Estimated from the integrated public-use census series.) Because a child who was well established financially would most likely be married, transfers across family members within these households probably went from parents to children, not the other way around.

3. The longitudinal data described in the next section shows that 53 percent of the men who in 1910 were not household heads and who lived with their children, but whose living arrangements in 1900 differed, had moved to a different town. Of those who had moved to another town, approximately 80 percent changed residences.

4. The fraction was probably lower among men.

5. Similar findings are reported in Ohio Health and Old Age Insurance Commission (1919) and Pennsylvania Old Age Pension Commission (1919).

6. Dissenting opinion in Massachusetts Commission on Old Age Pensions (1910).

7. Estimated from the integrated public-use census sample (Ruggles and Sobek 1995). Probit regressions showed that the presence of an aged parent in the household, whether male or female, working or retired, was a positive predictor of a teenage child being in school and a negative predictor being employed. This relation may exist because the presence of an aged parent may have been an indicator that the household was well off.

8. The probabilities used in constructing fig. 6.6 were predicted probabilities evaluated at 1950 mean values to account for differences in household characteristics and in the age structure of the population both over time and across occupational groups. The probit regressions that were estimated included as control variables the age of the household head, the number of children in the household, race, foreign birth, occupation (including none), region of residence, and extent of urbanization.

9. These probabilities are predicted and evaluated at 1950 mean values. Probit regressions were estimated in which the dependent variables were age, marital status, occupation, race, extent of urbanization, and region of residence.

10. The percentage of men who were not household heads and lived with extended family members was greater in the Union army sample than in the random sample of Union army veterans, perhaps because residing with nonrelatives was not an option in rural areas.

11. The 1910 census asked women the number of children ever born and the number of children surviving. Among women sixty-five years of age or older the respective averages were 5.5 and 3.5. Later censuses asked women only the number of children ever born. The average woman age sixty-five or older in 1940 had borne 3.8 and one in 1990 2.5 children. Assuming that a 1900 life table represents the mortality experience of children born to women age sixty-five or older in 1940 and a 1940 life table that of children born to women age sixty-five or older in 1990, the number of surviving children would be 2.2 and 2.0, respectively.

12. Alternatively, the insignificance of the coefficient on poor health might suggest that the health variable that I use might be a poor proxy for true health. If it is indeed a poor proxy, then, because those with higher pensions are less healthy, the effect of pension income on coresidence will be overstated. One solution would be to use another health proxy as an instrument for poor health. When I used subsequent mortality as an instrument for poor health, the sign of the coefficient on poor health reversed but was still insignificant, and the coefficient on pension amount remained unchanged.

13. Thirty-six percent of retired southern-born nonveterans in 1910 were living in households headed by a family member, compared to 38 percent of veterans. The difference is not statistically significant.

14. The absolute value of the actual difference in coresidence rates is 10.2.

7   The Rise of the Leisured Class

> Increased means and increased leisure are the two civilizers of man.
>
> Disraeli (1872)

> Youth for work and age for leisure.
>
> Slogan of the Townsend movement

Increasing numbers of retirees are citing a preference for leisure as their main motivation for leaving the labor force. Among men who began collecting Social Security benefits at age sixty-five, in 1941 and in 1951 only 3 percent stated that they had retired because they preferred leisure to work, and these tended to be the beneficiaries with the highest incomes (Stecker 1955; Wentworth 1945). By 1963 the figure was 17 percent and by 1982 48 percent. Among men who began collecting Social Security benefits at ages sixty-two to sixty-four, in 1968 17 percent stated that they had retired because they had wanted to and in 1982 38 percent (Palmore 1964; Sherman 1985). Morse and Gray (1980, 75) found that cohorts retiring in the late 1970s were more likely to state that they had worked long enough as an explanation for retirement, compared to cohorts retiring in the late 1960s, even though they felt less financially secure on retirement.

An increased proportion of men may be expressing a desire to retire to enjoy leisure, not because their numbers are actually increasing, but because it has become socially acceptable to do so. Alternatively, demand for leisure may now be greater because incomes are larger, because there are more forms of leisure from which to choose, or because the cost of recreational goods has fallen. In chapter 3 I showed that the elasticity of retirement has declined since 1900, speculating that this decline was driven in part by an increased demand for leisure fueled by rising incomes and by the increase in the variety of low-cost leisure-time activities. Leisure may now be attractive and inexpensive enough that a decrease in income will not lead to a huge increase in labor force participation rates. Conversely, an increase in income will not lead to a huge decrease in labor force participation rates because income is no longer such an important input to the enjoyment of leisure. This chapter investigates whether income has become a less important input to the enjoyment of leisure. If it has, then the typical worker is increasingly more likely to look forward to retirement.

7.1   Trends in Leisure Consumption

Most social scientists define leisure as the time spent in activities unrelated to employment, housework, or maintenance of self. Leisure is thus defined purely in terms of free time and may be either interesting or dull, depending on the activities carried out within that time. When the activity is pleasurable, it is considered recreation. Recreational activities may, therefore, consist of daydreaming, walking in city parks, socializing with neighbors, reading, watching television, or skiing. Some activities, such as daydreaming, require relatively few expenditures, whereas others, such as skiing, may require considerable outlays. The ability to engage in recreational activities depends, therefore, on the availability of both time and money.

The time available for recreational activities has increased dramatically. Not only have labor force participation rates of older men been decreasing since 1880, but, since the end of the nineteenth century, the average workweek has fallen, and paid vacations, holidays, sick days, and personal leave have increased. Between 1900 and 1920 ten hours were eliminated from the average workweek, and by 1940 the forty-hour workweek had been put in place. Although the decline in hours decelerated after 1940, paid vacations, holidays, and sick leave increased. In the 1910s fewer than 30 percent of male wage earners reported having a vacation, and that was not paid (Bevans 1913; and U.S. Bureau of Labor Statistics 1986). By 1940 25 percent of union workers received a paid vacation and by 1957 92 percent. Today, 96 percent of both union and nonunion workers receive a paid vacation that has grown in length from the one week received in 1940 (Owen 1969; Wiatrowski 1994). This trend has continued in recent times. Among employed males aged eighteen to sixty-four total hours of work declined by 14 percent between 1965 and 1985 and hours spent at work, including commute time and work breaks, declined by 17 percent. Although increasing participation rates among women have increased women's average paid market time, total work hours of couples still has fallen (estimated from Converse and Robinson 1980; and Robinson 1993).

Around 1910, fifty-five-hour workweeks were the norm for manufacturing workers, their wives worked even longer in nonmarket activities, and only the rich had both the time and the money to pursue pleasure.[1] In fact, one possible interpretation of the strongly backward-bending labor supply curve of early twentieth-century workers is that, because workers had so little nonwork time, any increases in income were automatically used to purchase increased leisure (Whaples 1990). The diminution of the degree to which the labor supply curve is backward bending suggests that workers today are no longer so time constrained. Early surveys indicate that, at the turn of the century, workers earning low wages spent little time on recreation relative to better-paid workers (e.g.,

Bevans 1913). Such was the contrast between rich and poor that in 1899 Veblen was able to argue that, throughout history, the possession and use of leisure defined ruling classes (see Veblen 1994). Today, it is the rich who work the longest hours. The loss of leisure by the upper strata was noted more than thirty years ago by Wilensky (1963), who argued that the longer vacations and shorter work lives (because of delayed entry and often earlier retirement) of professionals and proprietors did not offset their longer work weeks and year-round employment. Using census data, Coleman and Pencavel (1993) found that, since 1940, the average hours of work for men in the labor force have remained roughly constant but that they have been rising for the well educated and declining for those with little schooling. Although time-use surveys, which provide a more accurate indication of hours worked than census data, show that the average workweek has grown shorter in the recent past, the workweek of men in a very broadly defined upper strata has grown longer relative to the workweek of men in the lower strata. In 1965, the work hours of employed men in the upper 35 percent of the household income distribution were the same as the hours of men in the bottom 10 percent of the income distribution, whereas in 1985 the work hours of men in the top 35 percentile of the income distribution were 1.2 times greater than those of men in the bottom 10 percentile (calculated from Converse and Robinson 1980; and Robinson 1993).[2]

Another measure of the importance of income to the enjoyment of recreation is the fraction of people within an income class engaging in a given recreational activity. Although numbers are almost impossible to obtain, specific cases can be cited. Automobile touring was initially an exclusive prerogative of the rich, largely because of the expense of upkeep and operation. As president of Princeton University, Woodrow Wilson decried the motorist as "a picture of the arrogance of wealth, with all its independence and carelessness," and warned that "nothing has spread socialistic feeling in this country more than the use of the automobile" (quoted in Dulles 1965, 313–14). But automobiles diffused rapidly to the general population, and by the 1940s half of all households owned an automobile. Innovations in recreational vehicles followed those in automobiles. Before World War I, only the wealthy toured the countryside in custom-built "house cars," whereas, by the 1930s, fully furnished house trailers became available to the middle class, and, from the 1950s on, the production of recreational vehicles developed into a major industry. Like the car, golf also began as a prerogative of the rich. Club memberships, caddy fees, clubs, and balls were all expensive, but the growth of public recreational facilities, which almost tripled the number of golf courses from 1921 to 1930, led authors to write of "the democracy of golf" (Grantland Rice in *Collier's,* cited in Dulles 1965, 359) as early as 1928. Similar changes were witnessed in other sports as well. The number of public swimming pools more than tripled, and the number of baseball diamonds more than doubled, from 1921 to 1930 (Series H 849–861, U.S. Bureau of the Census 1975, 398). The increasing homogenization of leisure has been noted before. Listening to the radio was the most popular amusement in every pre–World War II study of leisure-time activities. Today, television is the dominant activity, and the percentage of spare time spent on television is fairly constant across income groups.[3]

Examining trends in the fraction of individuals engaged in a given recreational activity will underestimate the extent to which recreational activities have become affordable to individuals even in the lowest income groups. Technology and a mass market have made entertainment "superstars" available to all (Rosen 1981). Sports events that could barely be seen from stadiums can now be seen from many angles in living rooms at virtually no cost. Music is no longer provided mainly by such musical instruments as guitars or the family piano, an expensive piece of furniture; rather, it comes from a noted artist on a relatively inexpensive stereo. Entertainment through technology has been increasingly available for many decades. In the 1930s, the manager of a chain of theaters in Kentucky commented, "Radio is successfully competing with the theatre. Hard times have added millions of persons to the radio audience. You can get Eddie Cantor on the air for nothing. It costs you 50 cents or more to get him at the theatre" (quoted in Braden 1988, 119). If the more elusive nature of entertainment goods, such as the possibility of hearing a noted artist, could be quantified, then the price of entertainment has fallen tremendously and access increased enormously.

Finally, expenditures on recreational goods indicate whether recreation is affordable to all. In the late 1880s, less than 2 percent of household expenditures were devoted to recreation, approximately 75 percent going to food, shelter, and clothing. By 1917, the budget share for food, shelter, and clothing had fallen to less than 70 percent, and the share for recreation had risen to 3 percent. The former continued to decline—to less than 60 percent by the mid-1930s and to less than 40 percent by 1991—while the latter, however, continued to rise, reaching 5 percent in 1972 and 6 percent in 1991 (see table 7.1).[4] Estimates of the budget share of recreational expenditures based on the market value of purchases of goods and services by individuals and nonprofits are higher but follow the same trend (see fig. 7.1).[5]

Whether recreation is the prerogative of the rich can therefore be measured by the relative expenditure share of rich and poor households devoted to recreational goods. If a good takes up a larger share of the budget of better-off households, then access to recreational goods is limited to higher-income households. A good that takes up a larger share of the budget of better-off households is defined as a luxury. The best way to determine whether a good is a luxury is to estimate expenditure elasticities or Engel curves. These are readily calculated from the surveys of family income and expenditures that have been available since 1888. Provided that recreational expenditures and retirement are complements, the decline in retirement elasticities should be accompanied by a decline in recreational expenditure elasticities. I will show that recreational expenditure elasticities have declined and will argue that sev-

Table 7.1   Budget Shares for Specific Items (%)

Item	1888–90	1917–19	1934–36	1950	1972–73	1991
Food	44.5	39.2	34.7	30.7	20.7	14.4
Shelter	13.7	13.6	10.9	10.6	16.2	17.5
Apparel	16.7	16.2	10.9	11.5	5.7	5.9
Utilities	6.0	5.4	7.4	4.2	5.5	6.7
Furniture and equipment	3.2	3.9	4.1	7.1	3.8	4.1
Transportation		3.0	8.5	13.8	16.1	17.4
Health	3.3	4.5	4.0	5.1	5.8	5.2
Education		0.4	0.5	0.4	0.7	1.5
Recreation	1.9	3.2	3.5	4.5	4.6	5.6
Other	10.7	10.6	15.5	12.1	20.9	21.7
Number of observations	6,716	12,817	14,469	7,007	19,975	97,918

Note: Estimated from the Department of Labor's Cost of Living of Industrial Workers in the United States and Europe, 1888–1890 (U.S. Department of Labor 1986); the Bureau of Labor Statistics's Cost of Living in the United States, 1917–19 (U.S. Department of Labor, Bureau of Labor Statistics 1986); the Survey of Money Disbursements of Wage Earners and Clerical Workers, 1934–1936 (Williams 1941), covering families of employed workers in cities of 50,000 or more; the Study of Consumer Expenditures, Incomes, and Savings (U.S. Bureau of Labor Statistics 1956), covering wage-earner and clerical worker families in cities of 2,500 or more; the Survey of Consumer Expenditures, 1972–1973 (U.S. Department of Labor, Bureau of Labor Statistics 1987); and Consumer Expenditures in 1991 (U.S. Department of Labor 1992). The shelter category includes only rent in 1888–90. Reading materials are included in the recreation budget share.

eral factors account for this change, including the secular increase in income, the increasing public provision of the complements of recreational goods, and technologically driven price declines.

Expenditures are, of course, a very narrow measure of recreational consumption. Many of the retirees interviewed in the late 1930s as part of the WPA Life Histories Collection reported that they spent their time "visiting friends," an activity that requires relatively few expenditures. Nonetheless, growing evidence of the complementarity of recreational goods with leisure (Abbott and Ashenfelter 1976; Owen 1969) suggests that the value of leisure depends on the goods enjoyed during leisure.

Expenditures on recreational goods reflect some very important aspects of the recreational experience, including "relief in unconsidered muscular action," such as the possibility of chasing or swatting balls, and the ability to experience illusions.[6] Physical activity has been stimulated by the provision of public recreational facilities and the development of the automobile, which brought recreational facilities within easy reach. Technological improvements have enabled the creation of better illusions. In 1791, a London bookseller who traveled across America remarked that the "poorer sort of farmers, and even the poor country people in general, who before . . . spent their winter evenings in relating stories of witches, ghosts, hobgoblins, etc. now shorten the winter

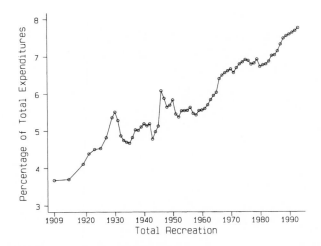

Fig. 7.1 Recreational budget share, 1909–93
Source: Calculated from Dewhurst and Associates (1995) and U.S. Department of Commerce (1966, 1995).

night by hearing their sons and daughters read tales" (cited in Braden 1988, 77). A founder of Luna Park, one of the turn-of-the-century Coney Island amusement parks, described his attempt to create "a different world—a dream world, perhaps a nightmare world—where all is bizarre and fantastic—crazier than the craziest part of Paris—gayer and more different from the everyday world" (cited in Kasson 1978, 66–69). Luna Park re-created such disasters as house burnings, the destruction of Pompeii, the 1902 devastation of Martinique by a volcano, the Johnstown flood of 1899, and the Galveston flood of 1900. New goods soon provided better and cheaper illusions. A Coney Island resident remarked, "Once upon a time Coney Island was the greatest amusement park in the world. The radio and the movies killed it" (cited in Kasson 1978, 112). Television, described as "the radio with eyes, . . . the press without the travail of printing, . . . movies without the physical limitations of mechanical reproduction and projection" (John Houseman in the May 1950 *Harper's,* cited in Braden 1988, 120), was able to provide even better illusions.

7.2 Engel Curves

The relation between income and budget share is given by Engel curves. These relate the demand for a commodity to income or total expenditures at constant prices. At a specific time t the budget share of good i is therefore related to total expenditures through a functional form, $w_{it} = f_{it}(z)$, where prices have been absorbed into the functional form. Engel curves for the years 1888–90, 1917–19, 1935–36, 1972–73, and 1991 are shown in figure 7.2. These

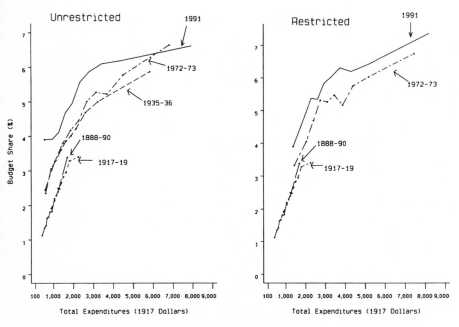

Fig. 7.2   Budget share of recreation and total expenditures in 1917 dollars, 1888–90, 1917–19, 1935–36, 1973–73, and 1991

Note: Estimated from Consumer Expenditure Surveys for 1888–90, 1917–19, 1935–36, 1972–73, and 1991. In the right-hand-side panel households in 1973–73 and 1991 were restricted to those in the labor force, at neither extreme of the income distribution, and under age sixty-five to ensure comparability with earlier surveys. The curves were estimated by taking averages within each decile of total expenditures.

curves show that, if only income were to change over time, consumers would remain on the same Engel curve but might be at either a steeper or a flatter part of the curve. But more than income has changed. Recreation is a time-intensive activity, and wages have increased. Prices have also changed, whether because of technological change or the public provision of complementary goods. Not only have technological advances lowered the price of existing products, but they have also introduced new products that have lowered the price of elusive goods, such as listening to a piece of music or watching a comic skit. The price for a quality-adjusted quantity has fallen, and the variety of recreational goods has increased. Consumers have therefore moved to Engel curves with both different intercepts and different slopes. At a single point in time, the Engel curve therefore indicates how egalitarian consumption is, but it does not accurately portray how consumption would change over time.

   In a single cross section budget shares can be related to total expenditures under the assumption that all consumers face the same price. Becker (1965) argues that, when households combine time and market goods to produce commodities that they value, they face different commodity prices because their earnings differ. Thus, because recreational goods are time intensive, their high relative price will lead consumers to substitute away from them, and the effect of income on these goods will be understated. If the time costs of the wealthy have increased relative to those of the poor, then, because the wealthy are no longer consuming as much recreation as they would have if their time costs had remained the same, we will observe that Engel curves have become less steep over time. I will return to this issue when I discuss explanations of changes in the steepness of Engel curves.

The slope of Engel curves may also be affected by the shift from nonmarket recreational goods, such as baseball leagues and libraries, to market recreational goods, such as private gyms and paperback books. If the shift from nonmarket to market goods has occurred disproportionately among those with lower incomes, then Engel curves estimated using market goods will become less steep over time, but the slope of the "true" Engel curves may remain unchanged. This issue will also be addressed later.

Figure 7.2 shows that, at the beginning of the century, when the slope of Engel curves was very steep, the recreational budget share rose sharply with income, whereas today the rise is more gentle. The distribution of budget shares was less egalitarian, and recreational goods were luxuries, their consumption limited to the wealthy few with sufficient income to purchase them. Whether a good is a luxury is measured by the expenditure elasticity, defined as $e_i = \partial \log f_i(z)/\partial \log (z)$, with an expenditure elasticity greater than one indicating that the good is a luxury. The greater the expenditure elasticity, the more of a luxury the good is. I will estimate recreational expenditure elasticities for 1888–90, 1917–19, 1935–36, 1972–73, and 1991 using the surveys described in the remainder of this section.

The surveys examined in this chapter are the Department of Labor's Cost of Living of Industrial Workers in the United States and Europe, 1888–1890 (U.S. Department of Labor 1986); the Bureau of Labor Statistic's Cost of Living in the United States, 1917–19 (U.S. Department of Labor, Bureau of Labor Statistics 1986); the Department of Labor's Family Income and Expenditures, Consumer Purchases Study, 1935–1936 (U.S. Department of Labor, Bureau of Labor Statistics, Works Progress Administration 1941); and the Consumer Expenditure Surveys for 1972–73 and 1991 (U.S. Bureau of Labor Statistics 1973, 1991). Only the published results are available for 1935–36. Micro data are available for all other years. The surveys are described in more detail in appendix 7A.

Compared to subsequent surveys, coverage in the early surveys was limited; the early surveys were often restricted to husband-and-wife families with one or more children present, included only the currently employed, and excluded both the very rich and the very poor. To ensure a comparable age and income distribution across years, families found in the 1972–73 and 1991 Consumer Expenditure Surveys were restricted to husband-and-wife families above the poverty line in which at least one spouse was employed and in which the husband was under sixty-five. Results from the full samples are presented for comparison. Although elderly households are excluded from the analysis, the 1972–73 and 1991 surveys suggest that expenditure elasticities are similar for both elderly and nonelderly households. One should therefore be able to generalize the results to the elderly.

The questions asked about recreational expenditures grew more detailed with each subsequent survey. In 1888–90 only two questions were asked about recreational expenditures, one about expenditures on books and newspapers, the other about expenditures on amusements and vacations. By 1917–19, recreation played a more important role in families' lives. Families were asked about the total cost of purchased musical instruments, records, and rolls (used for mechanical instruments) and of toys, sleds, and carts and the individual cost of movies, plays, dances, pool, excursions (e.g., to amusement parks), vacations, books, and newspapers. In 1935–36 families were asked even more questions about recreational expenditures, specifically expenditures on books, newspapers, games or sports equipment, radio purchase, radio maintenance, musical instruments, movies, the combined category of plays, concerts, and lectures, spectator sports, the combined category of dances, circuses, and fairs, sheet music and records, photographic equipment, toys, pets, entertainment, and social and recreational club dues. By 1972, the individual categories are too extensive to itemize, and the questions that were asked suggest that the scope of recreation increased over time. But did recreation become increasingly affordable to all?

7.3 Less of a Luxury

Economic theory gives no general guidance in the specification of Engel curves, and many functional forms have been explored in the literature. One extremely common form is that developed by Working (1943) and Leser (1963), in which budget shares are related linearly to the logarithm of expenditures,

$$w = \alpha + \beta \log(z),$$

where w is the budget share, and α and β are parameters to be estimated. Recent work suggests that this simple specification should be generalized to higher-order terms (Hausman, Newey, and Powell 1995). Therefore, the specification that was estimated was

$$w = \alpha + \beta_1 \log(z) + \beta_2 \log^2(z) + \beta_3 \log^3(z),$$

where w is the budget share of recreation, and z is total expenditures.[7] A test of this specification is provided by economic theory and is given in appendix 7B.

Engel curves that include demographic variables were also estimated. Age and age squared of the husband were included to account for life-cycle effects, the number of children and the number of children squared to account for differences in household size, and the extent of urbanization to account for differences in recreational opportunities. Engel curves were also estimated for the more recent data that included the total hours worked by both husband and wife. Although the recreational share was negatively related to total hours worked, the relation was not statistically significant, and the inclusion of this variable did not affect the estimated expenditure elasticities. Using the more recent data, separate Engel curves were also estimated for families with and without children and for families where the household head was older and younger than sixty-five. The resulting elasticities were very similar, suggesting that changes in demographic characteristics cannot explain the secular pattern in expenditure elasticities. Because total expenditure is likely to be measured with error, I tested whether the OLS estimates were close to the IV estimates by restricting the sample to households still in the labor force and using household income as an instrumental variable. The resulting IV estimates were reasonably close to the OLS estimates, and both accurately estimated the elasticities. Because household income was a poor instrument for total expenditures when nonworking households were included in the sample, only the OLS estimates are reported.[8]

Table 7.2 shows that there has been a sharp decline in expenditure elasticities since the beginning of the century. (Elasticity estimates are reported at three quartiles so that the shape of the Engel curves can be compared.)[9] For 1917–19, two different definitions of *recreation* were used—with and without expenditures for vacations and excursions. The first definition is more comparable to that used in 1888–90, the second to that used in subsequent surveys. However, both yield similar elasticities. Expenditure elasticities ranged from about two or greater at the beginning of the century but fell to about 1.5 by the mid-1930s and to about 1.3 by 1991. Expenditure elasticities in 1991 were even lower when no restrictions were imposed on the data. These estimates imply that, at the beginning of the century, a 1 percent increase or decrease in total household expenditures led to a 2 percent increase or decrease in recreational expenditures, whereas in 1991 a 1 percent change in total expenditures produced only a 1.3 percent change in recreational expenditures. Income is therefore a less important determinant of recreational expenditures now than it was in the past. Demographic variables exerted a significant influence on expenditure shares in all years, but the expenditure elasticities are affected only in the early years (upward). Although elasticities fall somewhat at higher percentiles, secular increases in income alone cannot explain the secular decline in expenditure elasticities. When expenditure elasticities are evaluated at 1917–19 inflation-adjusted means and percentiles, they still decline between 1917 and 1991, although not continuously.

The observed decline in expenditure elasticities may be an artifact of the way recreation is defined. No distinction can be made between reading for educational purposes and reading for pleasure. Recreation was also narrowly defined. Alcohol and tobacco can be thought of as adult forms of entertainment. In the 1880s and 1890s, the saloon was the primary recreational diver-

Table 7.2 Recreation Expenditure Elasticity Estimates

Year	Without Demographic Variables (Percentile)			With Demographic Variables (Percentile)			Evaluated at Means 1917 Demographic Variables and at 1917 (Percentile)		
	25	50	75	25	50	75	25	50	75
1888–90	1.59	1.63	1.80	2.40	2.25	2.15	2.07	2.05	2.02
	(.02)	(.05)	(.02)	(.03)	(.04)	(.02)	(.01)	(.01)	(.04)
1917–19	2.04	1.92	1.71	2.25	2.10	1.87	2.25	2.10	1.87
	(.03)	(.07)	(.06)	(.01)	(.05)	(.04)	(.01)	(.05)	(.04)
1917–19	1.91	1.81	1.62	2.06	1.95	1.76	2.06	1.95	1.76
	(.03)	(.07)	(.06)	(.00)	(.05)	(.04)	(.00)	(.05)	(.04)
1935–36	1.47	1.47	1.46	1.46	1.46	1.46	1.46	1.46	1.46
	(.01)	(.02)	(.02)	(.19)	(.19)	(.19)	(.19)	(.19)	(.19)
1972–73 (restricted)	1.47	1.39	1.32	1.55	1.47	1.40	1.81	1.74	1.67
	(.01)	(.02)	(.01)	(.01)	(.01)	(.01)	(.20)	(.11)	(.04)
1991 (restricted)	1.35	1.31	1.23	1.38	1.33	1.25	1.34	1.37	1.39
	(.01)	(.04)	(.04)	(.01)	(.02)	(.03)	(.16)	(.07)	(.00)
1972–73 (unrestricted)	1.50	1.42	1.36	1.60	1.50	1.42	1.62	1.60	1.57
	(.01)	(.01)	(.00)	(.01)	(.00)	(.00)	(.02)	(.00)	(.01)
1991 (unrestricted)	1.19	1.20	1.22	1.16	1.17	1.20	1.30	1.29	1.27
	(.02)	(.03)	(.01)	(.01)	(.01)	(.00)	(.01)	(.00)	(.01)

Note: Expenditure elasticities were calculated for 1917–19 under two different definitions of recreational expenses. The first definition includes expenditures for vacations and excursions. The second does not. The first definition is more comparable to that for 1888–90. The second definition is more comparable to that for 1935–36. Demographic variables included in the specifications for 1888–90, 1917–19, 1972–73, and 1991 were age and age squared of the husband, the number of children and the number of children squared, and extent of urbanization. City fixed effects were included in the 1935–36 demographic specification. Adjustments for inflation were made in calculating elasticities at 1917 percentiles. Standard errors are in parentheses. Expenditure elasticities labeled *restricted* were estimated for individuals in the labor force, at neither extreme of the income distribution, and below age 65.

sion of working-class men, and only in the first decade of the century did it begin to be displaced by commercial amusement (Rosenzweig 1983). Another form of adult recreation is eating out. Although today it is likely to be a form of recreation for working couples, in the past it was more likely to be the recreation of the male household head.[10]

The effect of differing definitions of *recreation* can be assessed from table 7.3. The basic results remain unchanged. When reading is excluded, there are sharp falls in recreational expenditure elasticities from 1888–90, to 1917–19, to 1935–36, to 1972–73. There is a smaller decline from 1972–73 to 1991. When alcohol and tobacco or food eaten away from home are included as recreational expenditures, the decline in expenditure elasticities is fairly continuous.

A potentially even more important omission is transportation expenditures. Middletown wives interviewed by the Lynds in 1925 valued automobile ownership ahead of home ownership, stating, "The car is the only pleasure that we have," and, "I'll go without food before I give up the car" (Lynd and Lynd 1929, 256). The share of budget expenditures devoted to transportation rose from 3 percent in 1917, to 9 percent in the mid-1930s, and to 14 percent in 1950 (see table 7.1 above). The number of registered automobiles rose from eight thousand in 1900, to 8 million in 1920, and to 23 million in 1930. The percentage of families owning a car rose from 54 percent in 1948 to 82 percent in 1970 (Series Q 148–162 and Series Q 175–186, U.S. Bureau of the Census 1975, 716–17). Steiner (1933) estimated that, in 1930, total travel represented 64 percent of the annual cost of recreation and automobile touring within the United States. At the same time progress in highway construction decreased travel costs. The automobile has made possible visits to national parks as well as short recreational trips within the community to beaches, outlying parks, and golf courses. In 1930, 92 percent of visitors to national forests and 85 percent of visitors to national parks entered using automobiles (Steiner 1933). More widespread car ownership contributed to a thirtyfold increase in visits to national parks from 1904 to 1930 and to an eightyfold increase since 1930 (Series H 836–848, U.S. Bureau of the Census 1975, 398; and table 314, U.S. Bureau of the Census 1993, 244).

Some idea of the effect of vacation travel on expenditure elasticities can be obtained from the 1972–73 survey, which specifically identifies vacation travel. When vacation travel is included as a recreational expense and demographic variables are included in the specification, the expenditure elasticities at the twenty-fifth, fiftieth, and seventy-fifth percentiles are 1.30, 1.23, and 1.16 in the restricted data and 1.39, 1.27, and 1.16 in the unrestricted data, respectively. Recall that, when vacation travel was excluded as a recreational expense, the expenditure elasticities at the twenty-fifth, fiftieth, and seventy-fifth percentiles were 1.55, 1.47, and 1.40 in the restricted data and 1.60, 1.50, and 1.42 in the unrestricted data. The inclusion of vacation travel thus lowers expenditure elasticities in 1972–73. Since recreational expenditure elasticities were 2.25,

Table 7.3   Recreation Expenditure Elasticity Estimates under Alternate Definitions of Recreation, Estimated Using Demographic Variables

Year	Without Reading Materials (Percentile)			Including Tobacco and Alcohol (Percentile)			Including Transportation (Percentile)			Including Restaurants (Percentile)		
	25	50	75	25	50	75	25	50	75	25	50	75
1888–90	4.09	3.33	2.81	1.52	1.72	1.82						
	(.03)	(.04)	(.02)	(.03)	(.04)	(.02)						
1917–19	2.66	2.38	2.06	1.59	1.58	1.51	2.26	2.11	1.88	2.09	2.00	1.85
	(.02)	(.01)	(.01)	(.00)	(.02)	(.01)	(.01)	(.01)	(.01)	(.02)	(.00)	(.03)
1917–19	2.50	2.27	1.98	1.42	1.43	1.38	2.08	1.98	1.79	1.94	1.88	1.77
	(.02)	(.01)	(.01)	(.00)	(.01)	(.01)	(.00)	(.01)	(.01)	(.01)	(.00)	(.00)
1935–36	2.66	2.25	2.00									
	(.63)	(.55)	(.46)									
1972–73 (restricted)	1.61	1.51	1.43	1.15	1.15	1.15	1.52	1.44	1.34	1.46	1.38	1.30
	(.01)	(.00)	(.00)	(.00)	(.01)	(.01)	(.00)	(.00)	(.00)	(.00)	(.01)	(.00)
1991 (restricted)	1.41	1.37	1.29	1.01	1.02	1.00	1.30	1.56	1.68	1.26	1.30	1.24
	(.02)	(.02)	(.03)	(.01)	(.04)	(.04)	(.01)	(.00)	(.00)	(.01)	(.01)	(.01)
1972–73 (unrestricted)	1.69	1.56	1.46	1.14	1.15	1.15	1.54	1.47	1.35	1.63	1.47	1.35
	(.01)	(.00)	(.00)	(.00)	(.01)	(.00)	(.00)	(.01)	(.01)	(.00)	(.00)	(.00)
1991 (unrestricted)	1.17	1.19	1.24	.94	.95	.99	1.21	1.34	1.49	1.16	1.16	1.13
	(.01)	(.01)	(.00)	(.01)	(.02)	(.01)	(.00)	(.00)	(.01)	(.01)	(.01)	(.00)

Note: Expenditure elasticities were calculated for 1917–19 under two different definitions of recreational expenses. The first definition includes expenditures for vacations and excursions. The second does not. The first definition is more comparable to that for 1888–90. The second definition is more comparable to that for 1935–36. Demographic variables included in the specifications for 1888–90, 1917–19, 1972–73, and 1991 were age and age squared of the husband, the number of children and the number of children squared, and extent of urbanization. City fixed effects were included in the 1935–36 demographic specification. Standard errors are in parentheses. Expenditure elasticities labeled *restricted* were estimated for individuals in the labor force, at neither extreme of the income distribution, and below age 65.

2.10, and 1.87 in 1917–19, when excursions are included in the definition of *recreation,* the decline in expenditure elasticities is substantial. When recreational expenditures and transportation expenditures are combined, expenditure elasticities fall from 1917–19 to 1972–73, rising slightly between 1972–73 and 1991 (see table 7.3).

Although only expenditure elasticities across households in which the husband was younger than sixty-five years of age were compared because early consumption expenditure studies did not survey the elderly, recreational expenditure elasticities for the elderly appear to have declined as well. Many of the innovations in recreational activities such as movies, radio, and television or low-impact sports such as golf do not require a high degree of physical exertion and are thus easily accessible to the elderly. They are also accessible financially as well. In recent consumption expenditure surveys, there is no difference between recreational elasticities calculated from a sample restricted to the elderly population and those calculated from a younger sample (see table 7.4). This suggests that the elderly as well now need less income to enjoy recreational activities during their retirement years.

The observed decline in recreational expenditure elasticities—a decline that suggests that the additional amount of income needed to enjoy recreation has fallen—is consistent with the decline in the income elasticity of retirement over the course of this century described in chapter 3. The income elasticity of retirement fell from 0.47 in 1910 to 0.25–0.42 by 1950. By the 1970s, the retirement elasticity was 0.23–0. Recreational expenditure elasticities were around 2 at the beginning of the century but around 1.5 by the 1970s. The decline in recreational expenditure elasticities may have occurred by 1935, but, given that aggregated data were used to estimate the 1935 expenditure elasticity, there is some uncertainty attached to this estimate.

7.4   Explaining the Decline

Potential explanations for the decline in recreational expenditure elasticities include rising incomes, an increase in the time costs of the wealthy relative to

Table 7.4   **Recreational Expenditure Elasticities by Age**

Year	Husband or Reference Person < 65 (Percentile)			Husband or Reference Person ≥ 65 (Percentile)		
	25	50	75	25	50	75
1972–72	1.66	1.51	1.42	1.63	1.58	1.50
	(.02)	(.00)	(.00)	(.04)	(.02)	(.04)
1991	1.19	1.23	1.27	1.44	1.31	1.15
	(.01)	(.01)	(.01)	(.27)	(.10)	(.08)

Note: No restrictions on income were imposed on the sample. Demographic variables were included in the specification. Standard errors are in parentheses.

the poor that has led the wealthy to substitute away from recreational goods, a shift from nonmarket to market goods accompanied by a disproportionate increase in the consumption of market recreation by poorer individuals, the public provision of the complements of recreational goods, and declining prices of recreational goods. Table 7.2 above showed that secular increases in income alone cannot explain the secular decline in expenditure elasticities. Recall that, when the 1991 expenditure elasticities were evaluated at the 1917–19 inflation-adjusted means and percentiles, they remained unchanged. However, the 1972–73 expenditure elasticities did rise, producing a decline of only 17 percent between 1917–19 and 1972–73 rather than one of 30 percent. Thus, at most half the decline in recreational expenditure elasticities from the beginning of the century to recent times could be accounted for by rising incomes.

Rising time costs of the wealthy relative to the poor are an unlikely explanation. The distribution of total household income in 1972–73 and in 1991 lay between that found in 1888–90 and 1917–19. When those households earning more than $36,000 per year in 1972–73 were deleted from the restricted sample, recreational expenditure elasticities at the twenty-fifth, fiftieth, and seventy-fifth percentiles rose slightly from 1.55, 1.47, and 1.40 to 1.63, 1.58, and 1.50, respectively. They remained virtually unchanged at 1.44, 1.31, and 1.15 when households earning more than $100,000 were omitted from the 1991 restricted sample.[11] Furthermore, trends in wage inequality do not coincide with trends in expenditure elasticities. Inequality in wage ratios between the skilled and the unskilled is now at pre–World War II levels. The premium to education fell from the 1890s to the late 1920s and leveled off during the 1930s (Goldin and Katz 1995). Thus, the large differences in expenditure elasticities at the beginning of the century and at its end cannot be explained by the rising time costs of the wealthy inducing them to substitute away from recreational goods.

Differences in expenditure elasticities by city size in 1917 provide some clues to the effect of a shift from market to nonmarket recreational goods. In the past, differences in recreational opportunities between rural and urban areas were much greater than they are today. Rural areas and small cities simply did not have a large enough population to support many market forms of activity such as permanent theaters or dance halls. But table 7.5 shows that elasticities were fairly similar between cities with a population of more than 1 million and those with a population of less than twenty-five thousand, suggesting that the shift from nonmarket to market goods has not had a large effect on the slope of Engel curves. However, there is a tendency for elasticities at the seventy-fifth percentile to be smaller in smaller cities. Perhaps there were so few recreational opportunities in small cities that, after a given level of income had been reached, money could buy very little additional recreation.

It is virtually impossible to obtain direct evidence that declining prices or investments in public recreational facilities have lowered expenditure elasticities. Information on recreation prices in the first half of this century is limited. Owen (1969) has pieced together an index of recreation prices, but this index

Table 7.5   **Recreational Expenditure Elasticities in 1917–19 by City Size**

| | City Population Is: | | | | | |
| | ≥ 1,000,000 (Percentile) | | | ≤ 25,000 (Percentile) | | |
Sample	25	50	75	25	50	75
Excludes vacations and excursions	2.12	2.04	1.88	2.15	1.90	1.61
	(.10)	(.00)	(.04)	(.01)	(.05)	(.04)
Includes vacations and excursions	2.29	2.17	1.99	2.19	1.94	1.68
	(.12)	(.01)	(.04)	(.02)	(.04)	(.04)

Note: Estimated using the mean demographic variables and percentiles of the entire sample. Standard errors are in parentheses.

Table 7.6   **Changes in the Recreational Budget, 1888–1991**

| | % Recreational Expenditures Spent on: | | | |
Year	Reading Materials	Movies and Live Entertainment	Home Entertainment	Sporting Equipment
1888–90	65.5			
1817–1919	38.9	22.9	10.4	
1935–36	27.2	23.8	12.6	8.5
1972–73	21.0	15.3	30.4	7.0
1991	20.9	7.1	37.1	4.0

Note: Home entertainment includes expenditures on musical instruments, sheet music, movie rentals, cable television, and the purchase, repair, or rental of radios, televisions, stereos, and videocassette recorders.

cannot account for the "price" changes that result from the introduction of a new product, previously unavailable to consumers. Although Hausman (1997) demonstrates how a price index that incorporates the demand for new goods could be estimated, the data requirements are extensive. I therefore provide only indirect evidence. I divide recreational goods into broad categories (reading materials, movies and live entertainment, home entertainment, and sporting equipment) and equate changes in expenditure elasticities with the introduction of new products, price declines in existing products, and the provision of public recreational goods.

Trends in the percentage of recreational expenditures devoted to these four broad recreational categories are described in table 7.6. The share of reading materials has fallen from 66 percent in 1888 to 39 percent in 1917 and has remained at about 21 percent in the last twenty years. The share of movies and live entertainment fell from 21 percent in 1917 to 7 percent in 1991. The share of home entertainment (everything from musical instruments to television) rose from 10 percent in 1917 to 37 percent by 1991. In contrast, recreational expenditures on sporting equipment have fallen from 9 to 4 percent between 1935 and 1991. Other categories of recreation (not given) that have declined in importance include club memberships and toys, the former falling from 8 to 6 percent between 1917 and 1991 and the latter from 17 to 4 percent.

Table 7.7 shows that expenditure elasticities for reading materials fell between 1888–90 and 1917–19, precisely when the price of newsprint fell, pulp magazines, rotary presses, and speedy typesetting machinery were introduced, advertising increasingly began to subsidize the cost of a newspaper, and publishers built circulation through deep discounting and promotional gifts and prizes. Circulation rose rapidly from 0.5 newspapers per household to more than 1.3 by 1915, and immediately after World War I more than nine in ten low- and medium-income urban families took a paper (Leonard 1995, 60, 163–64, 178–79). A particularly important innovation after World War I that brought reading to even more people was the mass manufacture of paperback books, which began in the 1930s.

Expenditure elasticities for movies and live entertainment fell between 1917 and 1935. Early social investigators noted that, among lower-income households, the "usual attitude toward any expenditure for pleasure is that it is a luxury which cannot be afforded" (More 1907, 142). In fact, in the first decade of the century, vaudeville prices ranged from ten cents to one dollar, with most seats costing twenty-five to fifty cents. But, by 1905, moving picture tickets cost only five to ten cents (Peiss 1986, 144). Expenditures for pleasure thus became an affordable luxury, and, by 1910, almost three-quarters of all moviegoers were working class, and weekly attendance was 10 million (Owen 1969; Peiss 1986, 146). The increasing diversity in types of pictures produced attracted the patrons of popular melodrama, variety, and burlesque and forced the closing of the "people's" theaters in the 1920s. Although movie prices rose within this time period, the quality-adjusted price probably fell. For example, sound was introduced in 1927, and, by 1936, over 90 percent of movie theaters could reproduce sound. The increasing popularity of movies is evident in the attendance figures, which registered a ninefold increase between 1910 and 1930 (Owen 1969, 89–90).

Elasticities for home entertainment fell sharply between 1917–19 and 1935–36, when the radio and the phonograph replaced musical instruments as the main form of home entertainment. In 1867, an article in the *Atlantic Monthly* claimed that "almost every couple that sets up house-keeping on a respectable scale considers a piano only less indispensable than a kitchen range" (quoted in Braden 1988, 110). It was indispensable because it provided amusement. An article appearing in *Home Amusements* in 1881 stated, "The family circle which has learned three or four instruments is to be envied. They can never suffer from a dull evening"—at the same time admitting that "the necessity of practicing . . . is a home torture" (cited in Braden 1988, 111). Player pianos, offering "perfection without practice" and in 1919 outnumbering standard pianos, and the phonograph, introduced in the 1890s and thereafter steadily im-

Table 7.7   **Expenditure Elasticity Estimates for Specific Recreational Goods, Estimated Using Demographic Variables**

Year	Reading Materials (Percentile)			Movies and Live Entertainment (Percentile)			Home Entertainment (Percentile)			Sporting Equipment (Percentile)		
	25	50	75	25	50	75	25	50	75	25	50	75
1888–90	1.54	1.34	1.23									
	(.01)	(.03)	(.02)									
1917–19	1.18	1.15	1.07	2.20	2.02	1.85	4.10	3.28	2.57			
	(.01)	(.02)	(.02)	(.01)	(.02)	(.02)	(.38)	(.13)	(.04)			
1935–36	1.00	.87	.79	1.43	1.45	1.29	1.13	.96	.96	2.66	2.55	2.00
	(.00)	(.01)	(.02)	(.66)	(.69)	(.63)	(.24)	(.07)	(.06)	(11.54)	(8.08)	(5.55)
1972–73 (restricted)	1.15	1.06	1.00	1.49	1.39	1.26	.97	.90	.86	1.37	1.23	1.16
	(.03)	(.01)	(.01)	(.04)	(.04)	(.05)	(.04)	(.07)	(.10)	(.05)	(.06)	(.06)
1991 (restricted)	1.15	1.06	1.00	1.63	1.35	1.15	.96	.83	.70	1.98	1.50	1.29
	(.00)	(.04)	(.04)	(.04)	(.06)	(.07)	(.01)	(.04)	(.05)	(.27)	(.05)	(.12)
1972–73 (unrestricted)	1.18	1.10	1.04	1.51	1.43	1.30	1.01	.94	.90	1.69	1.45	1.30
	(.08)	(5.32)	(2.19)	(.00)	(.00)	(.00)	(.13)	(.28)	(.52)	(.77)	(1.55)	(3.46)
1991 (unrestricted)	1.06	1.03	.91	1.10	1.34	1.33	1.01	.88	.74	2.40	1.86	1.53
	(.02)	(.03)	(.02)	(.04)	(.04)	(.02)	(.02)	(.03)	(.01)	(.18)	(.04)	(.01)

Note: Home entertainment includes expenditures on musical instruments, sheet music, movie rentals, cable television, and the purchase, repair, or rental of radios, televisions, stereos, and videocassette recorders. Demographic variables used in estimation were age and age squared of the husband or the reference person, the number of children and the number of children squared, and the extent of urbanization. Standard errors are in parentheses. Expenditure elasticities labeled *restricted* were estimated for individuals in the labor force, at neither extreme of the income distribution, and below age 65.

proving in quality, were the first products to make music in the home relatively easily obtained by most households. Phonograph sales reached a peak in the 1920s before plummeting in the early 1930s, displaced by the comparatively free entertainment provided by the radio. Although radio sales were insignificant in 1919, when radio ownership was limited to hobbyists listening to ship transmissions and to each other, the popularity among radio enthusiasts of a music broadcast from a Westinghouse plant led to regular program transmissions. Falling radio prices and the growth of broadcasting produced an eightfold rise in radio sales from 1923 to 1929. The number of families owning radios continued to rise even during the depression (Owen 1969), suggesting that, if radios were a luxury, they were an affordable one. Elasticities have continued to trend downward, perhaps because compact discs, televisions, and VCRs continued to lower the price of entertainment. These are all inexpensive forms of entertainment. Their marginal cost is close to zero, and the fixed cost is small when amortized. The fall in elasticities has not been sharper because these forms of entertainment often merely replaced the radio, which was already widely diffused. Those who were children when television was first introduced later wrote, "Once television arrived, my whole life changed. I don't think that I ever listened to the *The Lone Ranger* or *Straight Arrow* on the radio again. They just didn't stand a chance against the likes of *Six-Gun Playhouse, Howdy Doody,* or *Beat the Clock*" (quotation from Braden 1988, 121).

Elasticities for sporting equipment fell sharply between 1935–36 and 1972–73. After World War II the popularity of sports boomed, in part because technical advances made by the armed forces in outdoor equipment during World War II became available to consumers (Dewhurst et al. 1955, 346–47) in the form of waterproof clothing, portable boats, tents, cooking equipment, and nylon and plastics, and in part because recreational facilities were expanded. Boating, which in the nineteenth century was almost wholly limited to the wealthy, grew somewhat slowly in the 1920s and 1930s but then expanded explosively in the postwar years, stimulated by the development of artificial lakes and reservoirs. Whereas at the beginning of the century there were only a few thousand pleasure craft registered throughout the country, in the 1960s they numbered in the millions. Golf, tennis, and particularly skiing also experienced large postwar increases in participation, the expansion of the first two sports aided by increases in land availability resulting from suburbanization. Bowling, whose participants probably numbered about 8 million in the 1930s, gained 22 million more adherents by the 1960s (Dulles 1965, 357–62). Table 7.7 thus suggests that price declines and product improvements arising from technological change and the creation of a mass market and the public provision of recreational facilities have turned recreation into less of a luxury.

7.5   Who Has Benefited?

This chapter has emphasized that income no longer limits recreational activities as sharply as it did in the past. By lowering the price of entertainment, technological change has made recreation affordable to all and has improved the standard of living of those in the lower deciles of the income distribution. The increase in public recreational facilities has had the same effect. Estimated expenditure elasticities for recreational goods have fallen from slightly more than two in the 1880s to slightly more than one in this decade. Expenditure elasticities have continued to fall even during the last two decades, when income inequality increased. Leisure is now less of a luxury. Investments in public goods, technological change, and the lack of leisure becoming an identifying feature of the upper rather than the lower classes have made entertainment inexpensive and readily available to rich and poor alike.

The group that has benefited the most has been the elderly. The retired have become the true leisured class. A man aged twenty in 1880 would expect to spend only 2.3 years, or less than 6 percent of his life, in retirement. In contrast, a man aged twenty in 1990 may expect to spend up to a third of his life in retirement (Lee 1996), much of it engaged in leisure activities. The amount of time spent on recreational activities increases at older ages.[12] Recall that recreational expenditure elasticities for elderly households were similar to those for younger households, suggesting that, among the elderly as well, income is no longer as important a determinant of recreational expenditures as it once was. In fact, activities that individuals found to be of interest before retirement remain of interest or become increasingly attractive after retirement (Morse and Gray 1980, 58).

The variety of recreational activities available to the elderly today is much greater than that available to the elderly of the past. Technological change has permitted producers to satisfy increasingly narrow segments of the market. Dulles (1965, 307–9) recounted how movies led to the rapid demise of traveling theater companies, thereby leading to the concentration of the theater in a few cities and therefore limiting the legitimate theater to the more sophisticated audiences of metropolitan centers, thus indirectly encouraging theatrical producers to present more serious plays rather than those that appealed to the largest possible nationwide audience. More recently, the growth of cable television with its nonstop sports, weather, news, and arts channels has satisfied a wide variety of tastes. Leisure may have become more uniform in that watching television is now the most common form of entertainment, but the variety of television programming has increased.

Technological change has also broken the link between the consumption of entertainment and location, thereby increasing the recreational possibilities of the elderly living in rural areas and perhaps inducing more of the elderly to migrate to areas with a lower cost of living. Although the early consumer expenditure surveys provide no information on rural populations, we know that rural-urban differentials are no longer as pronounced as at the beginning of the century. Commercial amusements played a relatively unimportant part in rural life prior to the advent of the movie theater and the automobile. First the radio and then television brought commercial recreation directly into the rural home. National clubs replaced the Grange and fraternal societies and linked the recreational habits of rural people more closely with those of the rest of country. Walter Damrosch, who in the 1920s conducted weekly radio concerts with the New York Symphony Orchestra, recounted, "As the majority of these people, living far away from the centres of musical culture, had never heard the kind of music which I gave them, and as even the names of Mozart, Beethoven, and Wagner were unknown to them, it was a joy to cultivate such a virgin field and to find out how easy it was to make willing converts of my listeners" (quoted in Braden 1988, 177).

More leisure may now be consumed because its price has fallen. An increase in variety may have caused the marginal utility of leisure to fall less rapidly, leading to the consumption of more leisure.[13] Owen (1969) has argued that recreational goods and leisure are complements and that the fall in the relative price of recreational goods can explain much of the decline in work hours in the first forty years of this century, but relatively little thereafter. His index of the price of recreation shows little change after 1940. But surely a quality-adjusted index would. For example, not only were the first radios and televisions of poor sound and quality, but program choices and broadcasting hours were limited as well. Only 104 operating broadcast stations existed in 1950, but by 1970 881 did and by 1990 1,442 (United States Bureau of the Census 1975, 1993). Adjusting for quality, a price index of television sets fell from 159.7 in 1950, to 99.5 in 1972, and to 95.3 in 1984 (Gordon 1990, 306). Were it possible to construct a quality-adjusted index of the price of seeing and hearing a comic skit, one would no doubt find that the introduction of new goods, such as television, has lowered the price tremendously.

But why is so much of modern recreation taken at older ages rather than being spread more evenly over the life cycle? Many of the innovations in home entertainment may have disproportionately benefited the elderly because these activities are not physically demanding. Improvements in health now enable the elderly to enjoy activities that the elderly of the past could not. In the 1880s, bean bakes followed by dances were often sponsored by the Union army veterans' organization, the Grand Army of the Republic (GAR), but an observer recounted that, by 1910, when the mean age of veterans was sixty-nine, the popularity of these events had dwindled because "most of the old men left in the GAR were too feeble to dance" (quoted in Braden 1988, 37–38). In contrast, many of the retirees interviewed by Morse and Gray (1980) filled their time with square dancing. But it appears unlikely that the growing attractiveness of leisure alone could explain why so much leisure is now taken at older ages.[14]

An alternative explanation for why so much of recreation is taken at older ages lies in the tax structure of the U.S. economy. Although the progressive nature of income taxes suggests that workers should reduce hours of work and instead work more years, pensions provide another solution to the problem of reducing the lifetime burden of taxation. Because pension earnings are tax exempt, pensions make savings for retirement less costly than savings otherwise would be. In addition, most pensions provide the incentives to retire described in chapter 2.

Finally, another explanation for the leisure-age pattern must lie in the contract that the firm is willing to offer and the worker to accept. Leisure could be spread more evenly over the life cycle, but only at a level of compensation most workers are unwilling to accept. Workers reaching retirement age have considerable assets compared to the elderly of the past. Although declines in the workweek mean that they also have more time, there are still only twenty-four hours in the day. Furthermore, the pursuit of recreation requires not only part-time but also part-year work. One of the retirees interviewed by Morse and Gray (1980, 94) wrote, "I now feel an ideal situation would be to have a one-day-a-week job (with pay), provided it would be both pleasant and stimulating—and it would have to be with freedom to leave for long periods of travels." This retiree did acknowledge that "such a job is not easy to find." In fact, Hurd and McGarry (1993) find that at most 24 percent of workers had the option to reduce hours of work.

Morse and Gray (1980, 60) found that retirees who said that they traveled frequently before retirement increased from 13 percent before retirement to 37 percent after retirement. It was not just the frequency of trips that increased but also their length. One interviewee, who retired at sixty years of age, reported,

> My wife and I have completely changed our lifestyle since retirement. For the first couple of years we traveled around the country to see sights and country (historical and scenic) I wanted to see. Then we joined the Wally Byam Caravan Club International and have greatly enjoyed new friends and a new lifestyle. We live in a 31-foot AIRSTREAM trailer—spend seven months in winter in a park in Melbourne, FL, where we have every kind of activity. We dance and square dance and party all winter. Then in summer we travel about—stop and spend some days with children and grandchildren and rest of time traveling to rallies in caravans and sightseeing from Canada through 48 states and Mexico. My goal in trying to retire early was to be able to do just this kind of thing before either my wife, who is older, or I become ill or unable to physically do as we have been doing for six years now. (p. 59)

Another retiree, who retired at age sixty-one, wrote,

> We planned on traveling. Since retirement we sold our home and moved into an apartment for one year. We then put our things in storage and moved into our travel trailer for seven and a half years. During this time we toured 17 European countries, Canada (east to west, including Newfoundland and Prince Edward), Mexico, and all of the Central American countries to the Panama Canal and end of Pan American Highway. After another year in an apartment we are back in our trailer, full time again. As long as our health continues we plan on being on the road or on a travel trailer lot we own in Florida. (p. 61).

Job requirements would clearly impinge on this sort of extended travel. These retirees' comments also show that workers may be willing to take most of their leisure when they retire only if their health still permits them to enjoy their retirement.

In the 1950s, community leaders lamented the inability of Americans to enjoy doing nothing, which made retirement so difficult, and proposed a national effort to educate people into leisure (Graebner 1980, 228). Leisure became a subject of study among sociologists (e.g., Kaplan 1960; Smigel 1963) concerned that the retired did not know how to use leisure. Scitovsky (1976, 235) wrote, "When people retire they are suddenly deprived of the stimulus satisfaction their work has given them, and, naturally they try to fall back on the other sources of stimulation available to them. If they are unskilled consumers, they soon find their sources of stimulation inadequate; the result is the heartrending spectacle of elderly people desperately trying to keep themselves busy and amused but not knowing how to do so." Although it is true that some individuals face great difficulties adapting to retirement, the majority of men interviewed by Morse and Gray (1980) expressed satisfaction with retirement. The more educated tended to be happier, but in general dissatisfaction was related to financial difficulties and poor health. As one retiree emphasized, "Retirement is *wonderful*" (Morse and Gray 1980, 105). The majority of the elderly appear to be satisfied enough with their leisure to continue to retire.

7.6 Summary

In this chapter I have shown that income has become a less important input to the enjoyment of leisure. The expenditure elasticity of recreational goods has fallen from more than two at the beginning of the century to slightly more than one today. Expenditure elasticities fell not only because people have grown richer but also because technological change has lowered the price of recreation and because the public provision of goods, such as recreational facilities, that are complementary to recreational goods has increased. At the same time the increase in the variety of recreational activities has made leisure more attractive. The findings imply that the elderly may be well off enough and that recreation may now be attractive and inexpensive enough that decreases in income will not lead to substantial increases in labor force participation rates. Conversely, increases in income will not produce substantial decreases in labor force participation rates. These results are consistent with the observed decline in the income elasticity of retirement since the beginning of the century.

Appendix 7A
Consumer Expenditure Surveys

Compared to subsequent surveys, coverage in 1888–90 was restricted. The sample was limited to workers in nine protected industries (bar iron, pig iron, steel, bituminous coal, coke, iron ore, cotton textiles, woolens, and glass) and appears to have been stratified by the proportions employed in each industry. Twenty-three states were covered, none of them in the West. Sample families were selected from employer records and were limited to families of two or more persons. For greater comparability with the 1917–19 and 1935–36 surveys, the sample was restricted to husband-and-wife families.[15] Total sample size is 6,716. Only two questions were asked about recreational expenditures. One was about expenditures on books and newspapers, and the other was about expenditures on amusements and vacations.

Families from the 1917–19 study were also selected from employer records and were restricted to those where both spouses and one or more children were present, where salaried workers did not earn more than $2,000 a year, where families had resided in the same community for a year prior to the survey, where families did not take in more than three boarders, where families were not classified as either slum or charity, and where non-English-speaking families had been in the United States five or more years. Ninety-nine cities in forty-two states were covered. The sample contains 12,817 families, 849 of whom were black. Families were asked about the total cost of purchased musical instruments, records, and rolls and toys, sleds, and carts and the individual cost of movies, plays, dances, pool, excursions, vacations, books, and newspapers.

The 1935–36 Consumer Purchases Study was limited to native-born husband-and-wife families in metropolises, white families in large cities with a minimum income of at least $500, and families in other cities with an income of at least $250. The communities covered by the study included fifty-one cities, 140 villages, and sixty farm counties, representing thirty states. More than a million families were interviewed. Questions were asked about family expenditures on books, newspapers, games or sports equipment, radio purchase, radio maintenance, musical instruments, movies, the combined category of plays, concerts, and lectures, spectator sports, the combined category of dances, circuses, and fairs, sheet music and records, photographic equipment, toys, pets, entertainment, and social and recreational club dues. Vacation expenditures were not explicitly identified. The published tabulations give average total expenditures and average expenditures on specific recreational items by expenditure class for the seven major cities and for eight aggregated smaller city categories. Information on black families is available for two of the major cities and two of the aggregated smaller city categories. These average values are used in the analysis.[16]

By 1972, the consumer expenditure surveys are representative of the entire population, and questions asked about specific recreational items range from country club memberships to electrical equipment to music lessons to swimming pool maintenance. Vacation expenditures were explicitly identified in 1972–73 but in 1991 were classified as expenditures on such items as transportation or shelter. Because neither the 1935–36 nor the 1991 survey categorized vacation expenditures as recreation, I do not include vacation expenditures in the 1972–73 definition of recreation.

With the exception of 1991, when five quarters of data are given, covering the end of 1990, 1991, and the beginning of 1992, all data are annual. Only data for the second quarter of 1991 were used in regression estimates because households are surveyed more than one quarter and combining quarters would have led to heteroscedasticity.[17] The restrictions imposed on the 1972–73 and 1991 Consumer Expenditure Surveys produce an income distribution slightly wider than that found in the 1917–19 data but similar to that found in the 1888–90 data. The 1935–36 distribution is much wider but is comparable to the income distributions in the unrestricted 1972–73 and 1991 data. When total expenditures rather than income are considered, the restricted 1972–73 and 1991 distributions are wider than those in 1888–90 and 1917–19. Despite the widening observed in the restricted income distribution, the distribution of recreational expenditure shares has narrowed over time. That is, the share of recreational expenditures no longer rises so sharply as household expenditure increases.[18]

Appendix 7B
Engel Curve Specification

Economic theory provides a test of the Engel curve specification of polynominal degree three used in the estimation. Gorman (1981) showed that, provided that the polynomial functions that contain expenditures do not depend on price in the demand curve specification, then, when several budget share items are considered, the rank of the matrix of coefficients for the polynomial terms in income is at most three. For the specification of polynomial degree three, the restriction takes the form that the ratio of the coefficient of the quadratic term to the coefficient of the cubic term will be constant across budget share equa-

Table 7B.1   **Ratio of β_2 to β_3 for Specification without Demographic Variables**

	1888–90	1917–19	1973–73	1991
Recreation	−31.89	−21.52	−27.45	−22.57
	(.31)	(.12)	(.86)	(1.54)
Food	−31.25	−20.98	−25.99	−24.86
	(.30)	(.43)	(.72)	(.54)
Shelter		−21.60	−26.02	−22.13
		(.08)	(.12)	(3.05)
Clothing	−32.55	−20.26	−25.91	−23.46
	(.68)	(.85)	(.13)	(.82)

Note: Standard errors are in parentheses. Engel curves for housing were not estimated for 1888–90 because information is available only for renters. The estimates for 1972–73 and 1991 are based on the unrestricted data.

tions (Hausman, Newey, and Powell 1995). This rank restriction is tested in table 7B.1, which reports the ratio of β_2 to β_3 for recreation, food, shelter, and clothing when demographic variables are excluded from the specification. The estimated ratios are similar, suggesting that the Gorman rank condition is satisfied. These results remain unchanged when demographic variables are added to the specification.

Notes

1. If the long hours of domestic servants are any indication (seventy-two hours a week in 1900, compared to the sixty hours of nonfarm workers), housewives worked even longer hours than manufacturing workers (Lebergott 1993, 67).

2. Breakdowns by the wage rate are possible for 1985. Among labor force participants, those in the bottom 10 percent of the wage-rate distribution worked forty-four hours a week and spent thirty hours a week on recreation. The number of hours worked then falls with an increasing wage rate before reaching the top 15 percent of the wage-rate distribution. Those in the top 15 percent worked fifty hours a week and spent twenty-nine hours a week on recreational activities.

3. Forty-seven percent of all time devoted to recreational activities in 1985 was spent watching television among those with household incomes of under $15,000, $15,000–$25,000, and $25,000–$35,000. Those earning $35,000 or more spent 43 percent of all recreational time watching television (calculated from Robinson 1993).

4. Reading has been included in the recreation budget share. The increase in budget share since 1917–19 is underestimated because earlier definitions of recreation included the amount spent on vacations and excursions. Travel and lodging were not included in 1934–36, 1950, 1972–73, and 1991.

5. Definitions are consistent across time.

6. George Tilyou, the founder of Steeplechase, an amusement park in which customers were twirled and spun around, said that "what attracts the crowd is the wearied mind's demand for relief in unconsidered muscular action. . . . We Americans want either to be thrilled or amused, and we are ready to pay well for either sensation" (cited in Kasson 1978, 58).

7. The use of the alternative specifications

$$w = \alpha + \beta_1 \log(z) + \beta_2 \log^2(z)$$

and

$$w = \alpha + \beta_1 \log(z) + \beta_2 z \log^2(z)$$

does not alter the basic conclusions, but the fit is much worse.

8. Hausman, Newey, and Powell (1995) find that, when previous quarter's expenditures are used for current quarter's expenditures, both the IV and the OLS estimates accurately estimate the elasticities.

9. The expenditure elasticity is equal to $1 + \partial \hat{w} / \partial \log(z) \, \hat{w}^{-1}$, where $\hat{w}$ is predicted at one of the percentiles. Polynomial coefficient estimates are not reported because they are relatively uninformative.

10. For example, in one of the families surveyed by the New York State Factory Investigating Commission in 1914, the husband would go out for a meal on Sundays (see New York State Factory Investigating Commission 1915).

11. The specifications used included demographic variables.

12. Recall that approximately 19 percent of the time of twenty-five- to fifty-four-year-olds in 1985 was spent on recreation. In contrast, fifty-five- to sixty-four-year-olds spend 24 percent of their time on recreation and those over sixty-five years of age 28 percent (see table 2.1 above).

13. In contrast, Linder (1970) has emphasized that the acquisition of goods that increase the intensity of pleasure requires work effort and therefore has argued that work time has increased. Also, if an increase in the attractiveness of leisure increases the marginal utility of leisure, then the first-order conditions imply that less leisure and more goods may be consumed. But hours of work have fallen since the beginning of the century, and work time has decreased even over the last two decades.

14. In a simple life-cycle model, the rate of change in hours of labor is inversely related to the substitution effect times the rate of change in the wage rate and positively related to the income effect times the difference between the rate of time preference and the interest rate. Chapter 3 showed that the income effect has fallen since the beginning of the century. Either a rising substitution effect or a positive difference between the rate of time preference and the interest rate could lead hours of work to fall more sharply at older ages. But the outcome is ambiguous even under these conditions.

15. Since relatively few sample households were not husband-and-wife families, the results remain unchanged when the entire sample is used.

16. For more details about the coverage and methodology of the 1888–90, 1917–19, and 1935–36 surveys, see Lamale (1959).

17. The results remain unchanged when another quarter of data is used.

18. Of course, the distribution of other goods may have widened over time. In fact, the poor now spend disproportionately more on shelter and the rich disproportionately more on education, perhaps because of the increasing public provision of education.

8   Pensions and Politics

> In general, the art of government consists of taking as much
> money as possible from one class of citizens to give to the other.
>
> Voltaire (1764)

> People who think the mighty in Washington can be persuaded, or
> corrupted, if you will, by anything less than votes just don't under-
> stand what it's all about and never will. They don't know what
> Washington juice is made of.
>
> George E. Allen (1950)

The elderly of today are much wealthier than the elderly of the past, not just because rising compensation has made financing retirement consumption easier, but also because the elderly have benefited from a redistribution of public-sector resources. Total public-sector expenditures have increased in real dollar terms, and the fraction of those expenditures consumed by the elderly has increased. Although programs aimed at the elderly greatly mitigated old-age poverty and therefore have obvious merits, these programs have rapidly become extremely expensive and have displaced other expenditures, including education.

This chapter investigates the growth of three different programs aimed at the aged: the Union army pension program, state old-age assistance programs, and Social Security Old Age Insurance. These programs share certain common features: they grew rapidly from very modest beginnings; their growth was spurred in part by increasingly well-organized pressure groups; and their growth was made possible by the availability of revenue sources that could be tapped to finance them. By examining the history of these programs we can learn what the political pressures facing Social Security in the future are likely to be.

8.1   Union Army Pensions

At the beginning of the century Union army pensions were the most widespread form of assistance to the elderly. In 1910 an estimated 25 percent of the population older than sixty-four benefited from the program, receiving either veterans' or widows' benefits.[1] In contrast, a relatively small percentage of the population older than sixty-four received either public or private assistance. In Massachusetts, only 3 percent of those older than sixty-four received either public or private poor relief, and another 3 percent were in almshouses or private homes. Although the relative size of the elderly population was increasing—from 3 percent in 1880 to 4 percent in 1910—unlike Union army veterans the elderly were not a well-organized group. Unlike the group of men who had defended the Union they did not elicit as much public sympathy.

The Union army pension program was originally a modest undertaking, serving only severely disabled soldiers and the dependents of soldiers who had died from wartime causes. When the program was instituted in 1862, the most that an enlisted man could receive for total disability was $8.00 per month, an amount equivalent to 30 percent of the earnings of an unskilled laborer. The program was soon liberalized. Congress raised the pension for total disability to $20.00 per month in 1866 and to $24.00 in 1872, the latter a sum that replaced 76 percent of the monthly earnings of an unskilled laborer. The definition of *total disability* was liberalized as well. The sum of $24.00 was given to those unfit for any manual labor, even lighter kinds. Another disability category was therefore created, and by 1873 those who were so disabled as to require the regular aid and attendance of another person received $31.25 per month. The sums of $31.25 and $24.00 per month were soon increased and by 1883 had risen to $72.00 and $30.00 per month, respectively. When the rate of $30.00 per month was established, it almost completely replaced the income of a laborer. Veterans and their dependents also greatly benefited from the passage of the Arrears Act of 1879, which permitted those who had failed to file a pension claim to collect back payments in a lump sum.[2]

With the act of 27 June 1890 the number of beneficiaries increased dramatically. Any disability, even one not related to military service, now entitled a veteran to a pension of $6.00–$12.00 per month. Interpreting old age as a disability, the Pension Bureau granted the maximum rate to those seventy-five years of age or older and the minimum rate to those at least sixty-five years of age. Dependents of a veteran who had died from any cause became eligible for pensions. The number of pensioners on the rolls almost doubled between 1889 and 1892. In 1904 old-age provisions were further liberalized, with the Pension Bureau granting applicants pensions of $6.00, $8.00, $10.00, and $12.00 per month at ages sixty-two, sixty-five, sixty-eight, and seventy, respectively. Age-based pension amounts were increased once more in 1907, when Congress granted pensions of $12.00 per month to those aged sixty-two to sixty-nine, $15.00 per month to those aged seventy to seventy-four, and $20.00 per month to those older than seventy-four. The next major pension law, that of 11 May 1912, established a system in which rates rose with both age and length of service. Pension ratings for age and service were increased automatically after 1912.

8.1.1   Politics

The increasing generosity of the Union army pension program was extremely costly. Total real costs of the program rose sharply with the passage of the Arrears Act of 1879, which permitted veterans and their dependents who neglected to file a pension claim to collect a lump-sum pension in back payments. Real costs and the total number of pensioners then skyrocketed with the passage of the 1890 law, and in 1893 Union army pensions consumed 43 percent of all federal expenditures. That such a large fraction of outlays should be spent on a single program is unusual. The Social Security program today consumes only 21 percent of all federal outlays. Although the total number of pensioners began to decline after 1906, the passage of the 1907 and 1912 laws increased the costs of the programs and kept them high (see fig. 8.1).

The federal government was able to finance a program of this magnitude because, between 1866 and 1920, the federal budget registered a budget surplus for thirty-seven years. This surplus was distributed to veterans and their dependents. James Tanner, a disabled veteran appointed commissioner of pensions in 1888, reportedly stated, "I will drive a six-mule team through the Treasury," and, "God help the surplus" (quoted in Glasson 1918a, 226).

High tariffs on imports produced the federal budget surplus. The high tariffs of the Civil War years were never effectively lowered and were kept high by the passage of the McKinley Tariff Act in 1890 and the Dingley Tariff Act in 1897, which raised customs duties above 50 percent. Between 1866 and the passage in 1913 of the constitutional amendment granting Congress the power to tax incomes, close to half of all federal revenues came from tariffs. The other half originated from excise taxes. Veterans lobbied vigorously to maintain tariffs at high levels. Assuming that tariffs would have been lower in the absence of such lobbying, then, because tariffs were a regressive tax, the costs of the program were borne by the poor and by groups who did not benefit from the Union army pension program, such as southerners, recent immigrants, and younger cohorts. This was well recognized by contemporaries. Glasson (1918a, 238) wrote, "To a large extent the necessities and comforts of the poor were taxed and the resulting funds paid out in gratuities to persons who were better off than a large proportion of the taxpayers."

Behind the enactment of this large-scale redistributive program was a major lobbying effort on the part of veterans, pension lawyers, and tariff interests. Soon after the war's end, the survivors of the war organized the Grand Army of the Republic (GAR). GAR outposts were present in most counties, and after 1881 the GAR was regularly represented in Washington during the sessions of Congress. After 1883, the commander in chief of the GAR would appoint annually a committee of five known as the Committee on Pensions to lobby Congress. Pension attorneys, who earned a fixed fee each time a veteran filed for a pension, were allied with the GAR. George E. Lemon, a leading pension lawyer, started his pro–pension program newspaper, the *National Tribune,* in 1877. The newspaper experienced a rapid growth in circulation, and Lemon was still publishing it in 1916. In addition to printing articles of a historical and literary nature and advertisements for Lemon's business, the newspaper ran editorials championing the expansion of the pension program. Other claims agents printed their own newspapers. Claims agents were also active in sending out

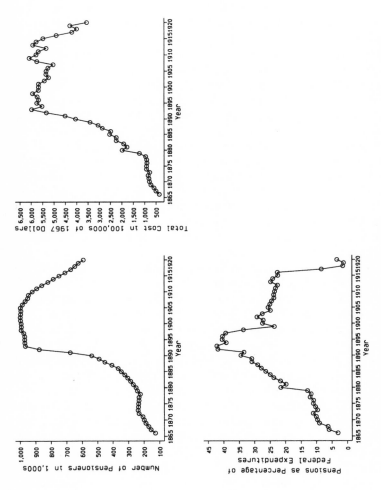

Fig. 8.1 Total number of pensioners, real costs of pension program, and pension program as percentage of all federal expenditures, 1865–1920

Note: Compiled from Glasson (1918a: 273), the U.S. Bureau of Pensions 1920 *Report of the Commissioner of Pensions*, and table Y 335-338 in U.S. Bureau of the Census (1975, 1104).

literature and letters throughout the country on behalf of new pension bills. The newspapers of claims agents gave their editorial space freely to arguments that ex-soldiers ought to fight the proposals of the Free Traders to lower tariffs because otherwise there would be no surplus available for pensions.

Pensions were a very important political issue. Each major political party included Civil War pension proposals in their national party platforms. At an 1888 meeting of the Grand Army of the Republic, when that organization was lobbying for a disability pension program, a member of Congress recounted how he had won his seat: "The gallant General Harvey of Indiana, Captain White of Fort Wayne, and myself represent three districts in Indiana, and in each of those districts the majority against us is from twelve to fifteen hundred. We held a council of war. We declared in favor of universal pension. Our opponents were foolish enough to fall into the trap and opposed it. Harvey carried his district by fourteen hundred majority, Captain White carried his by over twelve hundred, and I carried mine by eleven hundred and fifty." At the same meeting another speaker said, "We have a presidential election, and I tell you that there is a power behind that. I am no prophet, but I would predict that a President who will again veto a disability Pension Bill can never be reelected President of the United States" (both quoted in Glasson 1918a, 205, 206). In fact, Grover Cleveland, who as president had vetoed a pension bill that would have given pensions to disabled, needy veterans, lost in 1888 to Benjamin Harrison, who promptly signed the 1890 act providing pensions to all disabled soldiers.

Both Republicans and Democrats used the pension system to gain political support. For example, the commissioner of pensions in the first Cleveland administration was charged with filling the Pension Bureau with Democrats and increasing pension allowances and payments in areas with either a strong core of Democratic support or a concentration of veterans (Glasson 1918a, 224). Logue's (1992) statistical analysis shows that, in the mid-1880s, the more Democratic the county, the greater the proportion of pensioners, whereas in the early 1880s, under a Republican administration, the more Republican the county, the greater the proportion of pensioners.

After 1895, the administration of pensions grew more professional. The pension laws' increasing generosity made the granting of political favors through the pension system almost impossible. Almost everyone was already on the rolls. In the pension records used in this research there is no statistical evidence that pension amount varied according to the strength of either the Republican or the Democratic Party in the county of the pensioner's residence (Costa 1993). Pensions did, however, still remain a political issue. Although the pension system could no longer benefit specific subgroups of the elderly, veteran population, elderly veterans as a group could still benefit.

8.1.2   A Lasting Legacy?

The first experiment with a disability and old-age pension program in the United States died with the last Union army veterans and their widows. It had been the hope of social reformers that Union army pensions would prove to be "a very important entering wedge for a national system of old age pensions." According to their calculations the rapid decline in the number of surviving veterans meant that, "a large appropriation will, therefore automatically become available, which will permit the establishment of a national old age pension scheme without even any material disturbance" (Rubinow 1916, 409). This was not to be. Although the federal government ran a budget surplus from 1920 to 1930, the few state-provided old-age pensions that were established were set up by individual states, not the federal government. A question that scholars have tried to answer is why the Union army pension program did not lead to national old-age pensions.

It has sometimes been argued that the revulsion of the elite and of the middle class against Union army pensions retarded the growth of a national old-age pension scheme until the New Deal.[3] According to this view, one part of the legacy of the Union army pension program was the fear that individual cases would be decided on the basis of fraudulent documents or political cronyism and a distrust of government administration of any pension program. But all social programs, including the old outdoor poor relief system and the present Social Security retirement and disability system, have been criticized on the grounds of abuse. It should, therefore, come as no surprise that Civil War pensions were criticized as well. Some fraud undoubtedly did exist, but, by the time most old-age programs were being debated, the Civil War pension system had already been professionalized. As discussed in appendix A at the end of the book, the pension records themselves provide no evidence that corruption was common. Demographic and socioeconomic characteristics predicted neither pension amount nor the ratings of the examining surgeons. Those who were in worse health, as measured by such objective criteria as the BMI or subsequent mortality, received higher pensions.

If perceived corruption was on such a grand scale as to inspire widespread disgust, why did social reformers at the beginning of the century deliberately draw analogies between Civil War and old-age pensions? They boldly asked, "The nation and the states have already declared it to be our duty to shelter the aged and wounded soldier, why should the victims of the 'army of labor' be neglected? They have also served their country in occupations even more dangerous and destructive than war, and quite as useful" (Henderson 1909, 286). At the end of the 1920s, when interest in old-age pensions had revived, social reformers were still writing about Union army pensions, pointing out that our experience with them showed that old-age pensions did not corrupt the recipients and their families (Epstein 1928, 184).

It is true that the Union army pension program did not immediately serve as an entering wedge for a system of national old-age pensions. This is more likely to have resulted from factors other than widespread disgust with Union army pensions. One of these must be the lack of political organization on the part of the elderly. Without organization, their numbers were simply too few for them to be an effective voting block. In contrast, countries where the elderly represented a larger share of the population had greater expenditures on pensions (Lindert 1994). Another factor must be that a system of national old-age pensions would have been far more costly than the Union army pension program. Total expenditures on Union army pensions to veterans, widows, and their dependents equaled $150,959,327 in 1910. Had this amount been redistributed to all men and women age sixty-five or older, each individual would have only received $38.00 per year, whereas the average payment to veterans, wives, widows, and other dependents over age sixty-four was $152 per year. One possibility would have been to redistribute the money to the poorest 25 percent of the elderly population, but this may not have been feasible politically. In a country such as the United States, where the middle class is more closely allied, economically and spiritually, with the upper than the lower classes, the poorest 25 percent of the elderly would not necessarily elicit the compassion needed to give them special claims on the public purse.

8.2 Pensions and the States

The first universal old-age pensions were state, not federal, programs.[4] One of the first bills introduced in a state legislature was in Massachusetts in 1903, but, like so many old-age pension bills, it was not passed. In 1915 both Arizona and Alaska enacted old-age pension laws, but the Arizona law was declared unconstitutional. No further laws were enacted until 1923, when old-age pension laws were passed in Nevada, Montana, and Pennsylvania. The Pennsylvania law was found unconstitutional, and only in 1931 did that state pass a constitutional amendment permitting the enactment of old-age pension laws. In 1923 the residents of Ohio defeated a state referendum proposing the institution of old-age pensions. From 1925 to 1926 old-age pension laws were passed in Wisconsin, Kentucky, Maryland, and Colorado. A California pension law was passed by the state legislature in 1925 but vetoed by the governor. California, together with Wisconsin, enacted the first statewide mandatory laws in 1929. Utah enacted an old-age pension law in 1929 as well, but in that year legislation failed to win approval in either house of thirteen state legislatures. States that had pension programs by 1929 were nonsouthern and tended to have relatively small elderly populations. In 1930 old-age pension laws were passed in Massachusetts and New York. In 1931 old-age pension bills were pending in thirty-eight states and were passed in Delaware, Idaho, New Hampshire, New Jersey, and West Virginia. Pension laws were enacted in Arizona, Indiana, Maine, Michigan, Nebraska, North Dakota, Ohio, Oregon, Pennsylvania, Washington, and Hawaii in 1933, far more than had been passed in any previous year. In 1934, Iowa passed an old-age pension law, and the laws of Maryland, Washington, and Minnesota were made mandatory. By the end of 1934 twenty-eight states and two territories had established old-age pension laws. Those states that established pension programs between 1930 and 1934 were again nonsouthern but this time tended to have relatively large elderly populations.

The typical state old-age pension program was of limited scope. Although some states provided pensions to those age sixty-five or older, most provided pensions only to those age seventy or older. The maximum annual pension was generally between $300 and $365 per year, or 32 percent of average 1933 earnings of full-time employees, but was as low as $150 in North Dakota and as high as $420 in Alaska. Only those who had resided in the state for a long period of time, generally fifteen years, were eligible. The recipient was prohibited from earning more than a given amount per year, generally between $300 and $365. He was also usually prohibited from owning property worth $3,000 or more and was required to have the value of all pensions deducted from his estate on death. Pensions could be denied to those who had financially responsible relatives, failed to work when judged capable, had deserted their families, were tramps or beggars, disposed of their property to qualify for a pension, were recipients of other government pensions, or were inmates. Given these strict requirements, the proportion of pensioners to persons of eligible age in 1933 varied from less than 1 percent in Maryland to 22 percent in Arizona.

Although these programs were passed by state legislatures, they were not always statewide. Of the thirty states and territories having old-age pension programs, in eleven the participation of a county in the program was optional. Even among those states that did have mandatory county participation, the state would often establish only broad conditions on eligibility, determine the maximum condition payable, and leave the funding and administration to the county.

Old-age pensions began to emerge as a political issue in the 1920s. The social insurance leadership launched systematic campaigns using grassroots legislative pressure exerted by local clubs. For example, the Fraternal Order of Eagles' Old Age Pension Commission cooperated with state federations of labor and with the National Old Age Pension Committee of the United Mine Workers. They sponsored citywide public meetings to discuss old-age pensions. They organized an old-age pension club in every Indiana community with an "aerie." They prepared old-age pension legislation for introduction in states such as Rhode Island and Ohio. Nonetheless, they were not as well organized as Union army veterans, and relatively few states passed old-age pension laws before 1929. Among those that did, passage was rarely smooth. For example, the Pennsylvania bill enacted in 1923, after having been defeated in 1921, was declared unconstitutional in 1924. Although the 1925 legislature adopted a joint resolution to amend the constitution, two successive legislatures had to approve the constitutional amendment, and the resolution failed in 1927. Groups opposed to the Pennsylvania old-age pension scheme included the National Civic Association, the Pennsylvania State Chamber of Commerce, and the Pennsylvania Manufacturers Association. The latter argued that an old-age pension plan would necessitate either a tax on manufacturers, an income tax, or both. While the opposition to old-age pensions gathered, the proponents of old-age pensions were divided by personal and organizational rivalries. At the end of the 1920s, Abraham Epstein, one of the leaders of the old-age pension movement, declared that "the leadership of the movement was silenced and interest waned" (quoted in Weaver 1982, 56).

The Great Depression revived the old-age pension movement and eroded opposition to old-age pensions among employers, trade unions, and the general population. Older workers were more likely to be unemployed than their younger counterparts. Long periods of unemployment wiped out people's savings. Many private and trade union pension plans were discontinued; others curtailed benefits. Unemployed children and relatives could no longer shoulder the burden of caring for the elderly. The middle-class elderly risked becoming dependent on outdoor relief or on the almshouse, an institution increasingly regarded as inhumane and more costly than old-age pensions. As public sympathy for the elderly increased, many politicians became convinced that there was broadly based support for old-age pensions. While governor of New York, Franklin Delano Roosevelt noted, "Judging by the number of letters I am receiving, there is a more widespread popular interest . . . than most of us people in public life had realized" (cited in Haber and Gratton 1994, 137). Whereas only eleven states and territories passed old-age pension bills between 1915 and 1929, after 1929 nineteen states and territories did. Compared to the bills passed before 1930, those passed after 1929 were more likely to be mandatory, to be administered by the state, and to use state funds, sometimes in combination with county funds.

The year 1933 marks the creation of popular, grassroots old-age pension movements. The elderly began to wield some of the political might of Union army veterans. In 1933 Upton Sinclair, the socialist author, proposed a glorified barter scheme as a solution to the depression, in which he also advocated giving pensions of $50.00 per month to all needy persons who had lived in California for at least three years. This proposal would have reduced the minimum pensionable age by ten years, raised the average monthly grant by nearly $30.00 to 58 percent of the average earnings of full-time employees, lowered the residence requirement by twelve years, and eliminated citizenship and character requirements. At the same time Dr. Townsend, a California physician, proposed another economic cure in which $200 per month, more than twice the earnings of full-time employees, would be given to every person in the United States sixty years of age or older, provided the person spent the money within a month of receiving it. The plan would be financed by a transactions tax. Townsend described one of the advantages of his plan as giving the elderly "time to enjoy life and gain the full advantage from recreation, political, and civil life, and have time to travel and get fresh viewpoints without keeping their noses to the grindstone" (quoted in Putnam 1970, 53).

Both plans achieved political popularity. Upton Sinclair won the Democratic nomination for governor, and the Democratic party platform was an abbreviated version of his program. However, Sinclair was soon deserted by influential Democrats, and he never pushed the old-age pension issue in the campaign on the grounds that Roosevelt had promised to recommend passage of a national social insurance law at the next session of Congress. What is more, he labeled the Townsend plan a complete delusion. In contrast, Governor Merriam, the Republican candidate, summoned a special session of the legislature, in which he secured passage of a resolution memorializing Congress to pass a national old-age pension law and recommending that the Townsend plan be studied by the federal government. He won the support of the Townsend press. Haight, a progressive Republican and a candidate of the Commonwealth Party, said of the Townsend plan, "The best way to see whether it's any good is to try it" (quoted in Putnam 1970, 41). On election day, Merriam won 48 percent of the vote, to Sinclair's 37 percent and Haight's 13 percent. The Sinclair movement survived, but it shifted its focus to pensions and continued to nominate or endorse candidates for office until 1947.

The Townsend movement had an impressive grassroots organization. Townsend clubs were rapidly organized, in part because district organizers were allowed to keep 20–40 percent of the twenty-five-cent enrolling fee of all new members. The Townsend *National Weekly* had a circulation of 300,000. A 1936 Gallup poll found that 14 percent of California voters favored payments of $200 per month to the aged, and George Gallup concluded that the Townsendites probably did hold the balance of power between the Republican and the Democratic parties in the state (Putnam 1970, 57). The Townsend organization used its power mainly to induce the California legislature to send memorials to Congress requesting passage of Townsend's legislation. They flooded anti-Townsend legislators with letters and telegrams until a memorial resolution was passed. Once it was passed, Townsendism ceased to be a decisive political factor in California. A new Townsend party was launched in 1938 whose main purpose was to elect California congressmen sympathetic to the plan, but in 1942 the party failed to receive the minimum vote necessary to remain on the ballot.

Despite pressures from the elderly and other citizens for the passage of more generous old-age pension laws, there was little that state legislatures could do. Because the depression was shrinking the tax base, they could not finance new or expanded relief programs. In California, fifty-six hundred persons were drawing state pensions in 1930, but by 1934 the number had risen to eighteen thousand. Increased demand for pensions led to benefit cuts. Whereas the average monthly pension in June 1933 was $22.00, the average monthly pension in June 1934 was $20.00. Other states cut benefits as well, refused to take on new pensioners, and sometimes suspended pension payments until their funding situation improved.

The financial difficulties of the states led to demands for federal participation in state old-age pension programs, and assistance for the elderly poor became a major election-year issue in 1934. But federal subsidies for old-age assistance became available only with the Social Security Act of 1935. By insisting that old-age assistance be part of a comprehensive Social Security Insurance package, Roosevelt was able to use old-age assistance, as well as unemployment insurance, as a bargaining chip to ensure the passage of Old

Age Insurance. States were promised that the federal government would pay 50 percent of any Old Age Assistance pension that was $30.00 per month or less. Witte, a member of the Committee on Economic Security, doubted "whether any part of the social security program other than the old-age assistance title would have been enacted into law but for the fact that the President throughout insisted that the entire program must be kept together. Had the measure been represented in separate bills, it is quite possible that the old-age assistance title might have become law much earlier" (quoted in Weaver 1982, 77). The Great Depression provided social reformers with a unique political opportunity to enact comprehensive social legislation.

Twelve months after the passage of the Social Security Act, thirty-six states and the District of Columbia had developed plans for old-age assistance programs and were receiving money. Even before the act was passed, the California legislature had passed a bill empowering the governor to accept federal funds if offered and liberalizing the conditions for the receipt of a pension. The primary beneficiaries of federal subsidization of old-age assistance programs were nonsouthern states, particularly those with large proportions of dependent aged. Only the nonsouthern states already had old-age pension programs, and expenditures were disproportionately concentrated within certain states. In 1933 California, Indiana, Massachusetts, New Jersey, New York, and Ohio accounted for 90 percent of all state expenditures on old-age pensions and housed 83 percent of all pensioners. Injections of federal money rapidly increased total expenditures. In California fewer than seventeen thousand elderly individuals were receiving pensions in June 1934, but by December 1938 more than 125,000 were. In 1934–35 total expenditures for old-age pensions in the state were less than $5 million, but by 1938–39 they were over $49 million. Much of the increase in expenditures was accounted for by larger individual pensions. The average pension rose from $20.00 per month in June to $32.43 per month in December 1938.

The infusion of federal funds did not fully resolve the recurrent financial crises that led to temporary suspensions in pension payments, particularly in those states that depended wholly or in part on county funding. For example, in California the average monthly pension rose from $31.46 to $33.40 between July and September 1937 but by May 1938 was down to $32.30. Old-age pensions therefore still remained a political issue. The California Ham and Eggs movement, which promised thirty one-dollar warrants to be issued every week to unemployed Californians age fifty or over, was able to collect enough votes to put an amendment on the 1938 ballot and gained electoral success when Democratic candidates who supported the amendment won the election for governor, lieutenant governor, and the U.S. Senate. Although Ham and Eggs ballot initiatives were twice voted down by the electorate, in 1940 California had the second highest average monthly pension in the nation and, thanks to the efforts of new lobbying groups, the highest average monthly pension in the nation in 1950.

Figures 8.2 and 8.3 illustrate the national pattern in 1940 and 1950. In 1940 states such as California, Massachusetts, and New York, which had the highest old-age pensions in 1933, were still among the states with the highest Old Age Assistance payments. The southern states, who had no old-age programs in 1933, uniformly had the lowest pensions of all. Although average wage earnings in the South were lower than the national average, lower earnings cannot explain the pattern, which persists even when payments are adjusted for state cost of living. Quadagno (1988, 125–51) argues that southern states kept average pensions low out of fear that old-age pensions might subsidize whole black families, thereby raising labor costs in cotton agriculture. In 1946, when the formula determining subsidization of Old Age Assistance was changed so that the federal government began to subsidize 80 percent of the first $25.00 per month and 50 percent of all amounts above $25.00 up to $30.00 per month, the southern states responded by increasing the average number of recipients rather than the average payment. Often payments that had formerly been given jointly to husbands and wives were now split between the two. For example, Georgia increased the fraction of all beneficiaries from 18 percent of the elderly population to 46 percent between 1940 and 1950, when the 1950 national average was only 22 percent. In contrast, northern states raised the average payment. As seen in figure 8.3, southern payments were still low in 1950. Louisiana, with its Populist politics, and Florida, with its unusually large elderly population, were the exceptions.

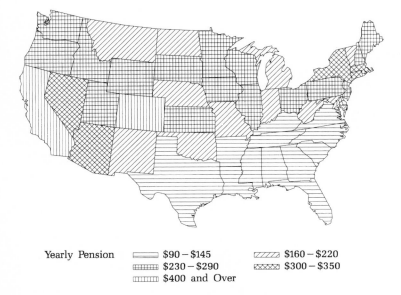

Yearly Pension   ▭ $90 – $145   ▨ $160 – $220
                 ▦ $230 – $290   ▧ $300 – $350
                 ▥ $400 and Over

Fig. 8.2   Average yearly old-age assistance payment, 1940
Note: Average pension values are from Friedberg (1996).

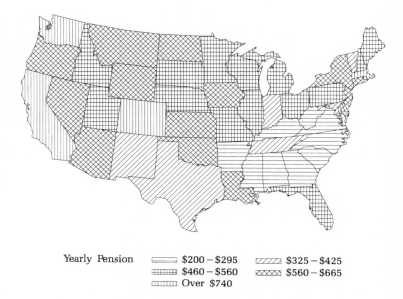

Yearly Pension $200 – $295 $325 – $425
                              $460 – $560 $560 – $665
                              Over $740

Fig. 8.3   Average yearly old-age assistance payment, 1950
Note: Average pension values are from Friedberg (1996).

The proportion of elderly within a state partially accounts for the pattern in state payments. Together, region of residence and the percentage of the population older than sixty-four account for 50 and 60 percent of the state variation in Old Age Assistance payments in 1940 and 1950, respectively. The average pension payment rose with the relative size of the elderly population, but increases were more rapid at low percentages. Had the elderly constituted 20 percent of a state's population, old-age payments probably would have fallen with further increases in the size of the elderly population, although this is impossible to determine with certainty because the elderly never represented more than 10 percent of a state's population.

The Old Age Assistance program was at its peak in 1950. Twenty-eight million Americans, or 22 percent of the elderly population, received Old Age Assistance benefits. By the end of 1950 the liberalization of Old Age and Survivors Insurance had already led to declines in the number of Old Age Assistance recipients. By 1960 only 14 percent of the elderly population were collecting Old Age Assistance benefits, and by 1988, when Old Age Assistance had become Supplemental Security Income, less than 7 percent were (Myers 1993, 819–22). Quadagno (1988, 146) argues that, faced with a changing economy, one no longer as heavily dependent on cotton agriculture, southern congressmen played a critical role in effecting transformation from Old Age Assistance to Old Age and Survivors Insurance. Liberalization of Old Age and Survivors Insurance enabled states to shift the rising burden of caring for the elderly onto the federal government. Between 1940 and 1950 combined federal and state real expenditures on Old Age Assistance rose by 84 percent. Combined real expenditures rose by only 3 percent between 1950 and 1960 even though the average Old Age Assistance payment became more generous. Between 1950 and 1960 the total number of state pensioners fell from 22 to 14 percent of the elderly population, but the percentage of the elderly receiving Social Security Old Age Insurance payments rose from 17 to 62 percent.

8.3 Social Security

As enacted in 1935, Social Security Old Age Insurance was a simple program of limited scope that resembled private insurance. It covered all employees under age sixty-five in industry and commerce other than railroad workers, thus excluding agricultural workers, government workers, domestic workers, and the self-employed. Only about 43 percent of the labor force was covered. Monthly benefits were payable only to retired workers when they reached age sixty-five. If a worker died before reaching age sixty-five or attained age sixty-five without meeting the eligibility criteria, he received a "money-back guarantee" equal to the contributions he had paid into the system plus interest. The benefit formula was based on cumulative wage credits and slightly favored lower-income workers. An individual was to be ineligible to receive benefits in any month in which he received covered wages. The combined employer-employee tax rate was to rise in three-year steps of 1 percent each from 2 percent on the first $3,000 in earnings in 1937–39 to 6 percent in 1949 and thereafter. Benefits would not be paid until 1942. While taxes would be paid into the system, a large fund would accumulate, and by 1949 interest earnings and tax revenues would support the system indefinitely.

As enacted in 1935, Social Security Old Age Insurance sought to be actuarially fair across generations. According to the U.S. Committee on Economic Security (1935), Old Age Assistance would "meet the problem of millions of persons who are already superannuated or shortly will be so and are without sufficient income for a decent subsistence." Old Age Insurance was to be for younger workers and was necessary because without "a contributory system the cost of pensions, would, in the future, be overwhelming" (p. 25). Secretary of the Treasury Henry Morgenthau argued before the Committee on Ways and Means in 1935, "There are some who believe that we can meet this problem as we go by borrowing from the future to pay the costs. . . . They would place all confidence in the taxing power of the future to meet the needs as they arise. We do not share this view. We cannot safely expect future generations to continue to divert such large sums to the support of the aged unless we lighten the burden upon the future in other directions. . . . We desire to establish this system on such sound foundations that it can be continued indefinitely in the future" (quoted in Weaver 1982, 85).

The actuarial principles underlying Old Age Insurance were abandoned even before benefits began to be paid. The 1939 amendments to the Social Security Act replaced the "money-back guarantee" with monthly benefits for survivors and dependents, modified the basis of the benefit formula in favor of cohorts approaching retirement, and modified the benefit formula to favor lower-income workers and to favor workers with larger families while reducing benefits to single retirees, workers who died without an eligible survivor, and workers who would not eventually become eligible for benefits. Workers could now earn up to $15.00 per week without losing their benefits. Benefits were now to be paid in 1940, and the 1 percentage point increase in the payroll tax that was scheduled to take place in 1940 was repealed.

By abandoning actuarial principles the Social Security Board was able to ensure the survival of its program. Old Age Insurance faced several challenges in the early years of its existence. It was a major political issue in the 1936 election, and the Republican platform called for replacing Old Age Insurance with a greatly expanded old-age assistance program based on need and financed by both federal and state governments using a broadly based tax. The Townsend movement denounced the program, and Senator Long's scheme to provide pensions for the poor elderly through taxes of 100 percent on large incomes, inheritances, and property was gaining attention. The unspent surplus soon became a liability for Social Security supporters. It was created with money taken from workers during a depression and would provide the government with an unprecedented degree of control over investment in the private economy. Because it provided the government with an easy market for its debt, it would encourage other types of government spending. Detractors also argued that surpluses would encourage program liberalization and thus defeat all efforts at planning for the future. According to Senator Vandenburg (a Michigan Republican), "Such a treasure—all in one place and conveniently eligible for Congressional raids throughout the years—is an utterly naive conception" (quoted Berkowitz 1991, 41). A pay-as-you-go system would have none of these problems.

Subsequent liberalization of eligibility requirements and benefit increases without matching payroll tax increases effectively turned Old Age Insurance into a pay-as-you-go system and won it widespread political support. The history of the subsequent amendments and the politics surrounding them is relatively well known, and accounts can be found in Achenbaum (1986), Berkowitz (1991), Myers (1993), and Weaver (1982), among others. Therefore, I summarize the changes only briefly, highlighting the salient features.

Between 1950 and 1960 Social Security expanded rapidly, particularly during election years. Figure 8.4 illustrates some of the changes. The average real benefit paid to retired workers rose by 46 percent, after having fallen in the previous decade. Coverage increased sharply between 1949 and 1954, from 55 percent of the labor force to 71 percent. By 1960 almost 80 percent of the labor force was covered. This increase in program coverage provided revenue that translated to benefit increases for current beneficiaries. Revenue was also pro-

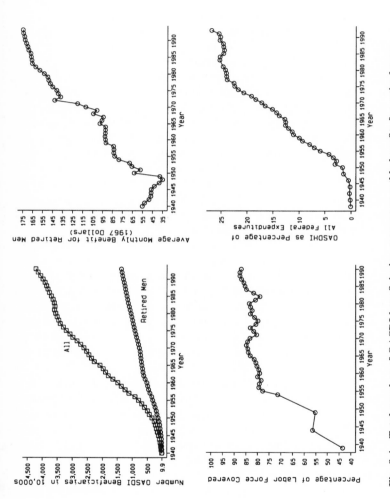

Fig. 8.4   Total number of OASDI beneficiaries, average monthly benefits for retired men, percentage of labor force covered, OASDHI as percentage all federal expenditures, 1937–93

Note: Compiled from tables 5.A4, 5.B5, and 5.C2 in *Social Security Bulletin, Annual Statistical Supplement* (1994, 197, 208, 214); Series H 48-56 in Kurian (1994, 131); Series Y 605-637 in U.S. Bureau of the Census (1975, 1124); and various issues of *Government Finances.*

vided by increases in the payroll tax. Combined employee-employer taxes rose from 3 to 6 percent, no more than originally planned, but now the taxes were to finance much more generous benefits. Taxes on the self-employed rose from zero in 1950, when they were not covered, to 4.5 percent in 1960. The program that in 1950 had represented less than 2 percent of total federal expenditures represented 11 percent in 1960.

The expansion of Social Security between 1950 and 1960 arose in part from the lobbying efforts of trade unions and of such groups as Americans for Democratic Action and in part from congressmen's desire to ease welfare burdens in their home states. In House hearings on the extension of Social Security to farmworkers, the public welfare commissioner of Alabama testified, "We have larger and larger numbers of needy old people and correspondingly smaller numbers within the population who can earn and pay taxes. Not only do we have an increasing number of old people, but we are a state with an unusually high proportion of children. . . . Our rate of application for aid also continues to be as high, and there is less and less demand for unskilled and older workers" (Quadagno 1988, 147). California and New York, two politically powerful states, and Rhode Island and New Jersey established state-run temporary disability programs in the 1940s. The real costs of these programs grew by close to 240 percent from 1950 until 1956, when federal disability insurance was enacted (estimated from Merriam and Skolnick 1968, 207–9, tables 2-1 and 2-2).

The expansion of Social Security continued until 1973. In 1961 age sixty-two was adopted as an early retirement age, with reduced benefits. As seen in figure 8.4, the average real benefit for retired men rose by almost 50 percent between 1960 and 1973, with half the increase occurring between 1970 and 1973. A retired worker and his wife who had paid less than $30.00 per month in taxes before 1970 might in 1973 be collecting Social Security benefits of $800 per month. Many of the amendments that increased Social Security benefits also increased state aid for Old Age Assistance, which in 1974 became incorporated into Supplemental Security Income. Medicare, a program for those older than sixty-four consisting of a hospital insurance component financed by compulsory taxes and a voluntary supplementary medical insurance program subsidized out of general revenues, was enacted in 1965. The net result was that Old Age and Survivors, Disability, and Hospital Insurance combined almost doubled its share of all federal expenditures from 11 percent in 1960 to 21 percent in 1973.

Prior to the enactment of Medicare, the health insurance issue dominated all others in the early 1960s. Of course, the health insurance debates have an even longer history. In the 1910s there were campaigns at the state level for compulsory health insurance for wage earners. During the New Deal, and during the Truman years, both national and state health insurance plans were defeated, but less comprehensive forms of assistance were enacted. In the 1940s some state legislatures began to make appropriations for pensioners in county medical institutions and to cover private medical care of many kinds. The 1950 amendments to the Social Security Act permitted welfare departments to use federal matching funds for cash assistance to negotiate for care with pre-payment and insurance plans. A 1955 California report declared, "The medical needs of Old-Age Security recipients and the manner of meeting them constitute a problem which is increasingly predominant" (quoted in Putnam 1970, 134). In real terms state and local expenditures on vendor medical payments rose by almost 130 percent between 1950 and 1956. In 1956 additional federal funds became available for medical vendor payments on a 50 percent federal matching basis up to a specific per capita limit. But these did not begin to pay for the cost of medical payments in states with more generous programs. Real state expenditures on vendor medical payments rose by an additional 22 percent between 1956 and 1960 (estimated from Merriam and Skolnick 1968, 207–9, tables 2-1 and 2-2). In 1960 further relief became available to the states when the Kerr-Mills program specified that the federal government would pay between 50 and 80 percent (with higher percentages going to poorer states) of the costs of welfare medicine programs aimed at the aged poor. State and local expenditures on medical assistance for the aged rose by more than 1,000 percent between 1960 and 1965 (estimated from Merriam and Skolnick 1968, 207–9, tables 2-1 and 2-2).

State governments were not the only ones lobbying for an expanded federal role in providing the aged with medical care. Unlike previous legislative battles over amendments to the Social Security Act, the battle over Medicare turned the elderly into active campaigners. When a Senate subcommittee on aging held hearings around the country in 1959, one staff member later recalled, "The old folks lined up by the dozen everyplace we went. . . . And they didn't talk much about housing or recreational centers or part-time work. They talked about medical care" (cited in Starr 1982, 368). Within two years congressmen were reporting more mail on the subject than on any other pending legislation (Starr 1982, 368).

By the end of the 1960s, the elderly had become a well-organized group. The director of a senior center in New York City (cited in Pratt 1976, 72) reported, "Ten years ago [the mid-1950s] we couldn't get politicians from the major parties to come talk to our people. They weren't interested. . . . But in 1960, things began to change. They began to make an effort to come when invited. And today [1966] we frequently have to throw them out when they come—as they frequently do—uninvited, to campaign and distribute literature. Politicians now realize that the elderly represent a large number of votes, that they do vote, and that they have needs and desires." Senior citizen centers, like the local chapters of the Union army veterans' organization, thus served to organize the elderly in a voting bloc. Many senior citizen groups gained access to key policy makers. One staff member of the American Association of Retired Persons (AARP) interviewed by Pratt (1976, 147–48) reported, "During President's Nixon's first term in office [1969–73] the White House had a staff man, Evans was his name, assigned to dealing with old-age problems. He kept us informally apprised of White House thinking, and they wouldn't make a move on a major old-age issue without first consulting AARP."

The final large legislated increase in the Social Security Act came in 1972, when Congress raised benefits across the board by 20 percent and adopted automatic cost-of-living adjustments for Social Security benefits. This increase was enacted when both parties were trying to reduce national spending and when nationally prominent actuaries, such as Robert Myers, former chief actuary of the Social Security system, warned that the proposed changes would burden future generations. But a large trust fund surplus combined with the political pressure exerted by senior citizen groups led to large benefit increases. According to a staff member of the House Ways and Means Committee interviewed by Pratt (1976, 160), "The trust fund allowed a large increase and there's no doubt about that. . . . But the increase which was finally proposed would not have been as high if the NCSC [National Council of Senior Citizens] and other senior-citizen groups hadn't pushed for it on the Hill and the [White House] conference [on aging]." By adopting automatic cost-of-living adjustments, congressmen may have hoped to lessen the constant pressure from senior citizen groups to increase benefits.

Liberalization of Social Security from 1960 to 1973 was financed both out of the trust fund and by increasing tax rates and the ceiling on taxable earnings. The combined employer-employee tax rate rose from 6 to 9.7 percent, with payments toward Hospital Insurance bringing the total tax to 11.7 percent (see fig. 8.5). After 1967 increasing the ceiling on taxable earnings became the most common way of financing program expansion. The ceiling on taxable earnings had remained $3,000 from 1935 to 1951 and in real terms exceeded the 1938 level only in 1968. But from 1966 to 1976 the ceiling on taxable earnings increased by 34 percent in real terms (see fig. 8.5). Weaver (1982, 160) argues that, because by 1965 compulsory coverage had been extended to the higher-paid, self-employed professionals, increases in the ceiling on taxable earnings after 1965 financed benefit increases for current beneficiaries without burdening the average taxpayer and the near elderly.

Although Social Security did not unfold as originally planned by the Committee on Economic Security, current coverage levels and benefits would have come as no surprise to the original planners. Miron and Weil (1998) estimate that, under the 1939 amendments to the Social Security Act, a same-age couple retiring in 1990 in which the husband had annual wages of $1,000 per year and a continuous work history would have 60 percent of earnings replaced by Social Security benefits and would have earned a 4 percent rate of return. In 1990 the actual replacement rate for such a couple was 61 percent and their rate of return 6 percent. Of course, if the value of Medicare benefits were included, the replacement rate would be much higher. But the members of the Committee on Economic Security had hoped that a system of national health insurance would be enacted at a later date. What would have come as a surprise to the Commit-

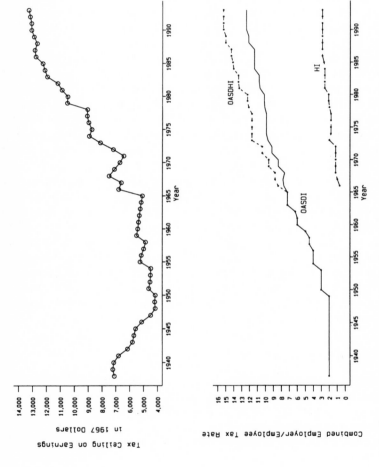

Fig. 8.5 Tax ceiling on earnings (in 1967 dollars) and combined employer-employee tax rate, 1937–93

Note: From Myers (1993, 131–32).

tee on Economic Security is the current level of the combined employer-employee tax rate. Had there been no changes to the Social Security system after the 1939 amendments, the tax rate in 1990 would have been 6 percent. Instead, it was more than 11 percent, largely because until 1960 the tax rate was much lower than projected by the committee. Increases in benefits were financed, not by increasing the tax rate, but by depleting the trust fund.

The rapid expansion of Social Security between 1960 and 1973 produced the first financial crisis facing Social Security. These problems were compounded by the use of a benefit formula that overadjusted for inflation. This indexation problem was fixed in 1977, cutting the Social Security wealth of younger relative to older cohorts by 13 percent. But this was not enough, and by late 1982 it was unclear whether the Old Age and Survivors Insurance program would be able to meet benefit payments. This short-range financing problem was resolved by implementing scheduled tax increases earlier than originally planned, by including more fringe benefits (such as deferred compensation) as covered wages, by taxing the benefits of upper-income Social Security recipients with taxes going directly to the Social Security trust fund, and by modifying the cost-of-living adjustment formula. At the same time, the age at which full benefits are received was to increase incrementally from sixty-five to sixty-seven between 2005 and 2025. This solution, however, maintains the system's fiscal solvency only until at most 2029, at which point the large numbers of the retired elderly relative to workers will have consumed the trust fund. Financing the Social Security retirement and disability system thereafter with incoming tax revenues alone would require taxes greater than 17 percent of taxable payroll. An additional 7 percent of taxable payroll would be needed to finance Hospital Insurance. Expenditures on Old Age and Survivors Disability Insurance and Hospital Insurance combined would be greater than 10 percent of GDP. Further reforms are therefore needed to maintain the system's solvency.

8.4   Fixing Social Security

The 1910 Massachusetts Commission on Old Age Pensions predicted that, if old-age pensions were passed, "There would be constant political pressure to increase the amount of pensions, to lower the age limit, to make the administration laxer" (p. 238). The history of the Union army pension program, of state old-age pension programs, and of Social Security old-age insurance proves that the commission's expectation was realistic. All programs began modestly, covering only a limited group of individuals, and the Social Security old-age insurance program was even based on sound actuarial principles. All became enormous undertakings far removed from actuarial principles. Although some of their growth was spurred by well-organized pressure groups, such tactics were effective only when revenue sources were available. Had the federal government not been running a surplus, it is unlikely that the Union army pension program would have been so generous. States showed no inclination to develop generous programs until they were able to obtain federal financing for their activities. The existence of a large trust fund and the possibility of financing current benefits by increasing revenue through increases in program coverage, tax increases, and increases in the tax ceiling permitted the federal government to finance an extremely generous Social Security program.

The growth of Social Security crowded out other forms of social spending. Politicians, responsive to the pressure of both interest groups and voting taxpayers, need to compare the costs and benefits in votes or campaign donations of increasing the total tax burden with raising new tax revenue to redistribute to a given group. Interest groups are therefore competing for public-sector resources. Poterba (1996) finds that an increasing proportion of the elderly within a state jurisdiction is associated with a reduction in per child educational spending. Lindert (1994) concludes from cross-country evidence that a similar pattern held in the past as well.

As the Social Security trust fund becomes depleted, it is unlikely that in the future the program will be as generous. Although recent polls suggest that individuals favor raising taxes to maintain benefits, as the proportion of the elderly to taxpayers increases, although they may still be willing to finance a system that protects the elderly against hardships, taxpayers may be less willing to finance a system that provides for a long and, for many, a recreation-filled retirement. Social reformers at the beginning of the century believed that old-age pensions would provide for "a few years before death when they [wage earners] will no longer be able to earn wages" (Ohio Health and Old Age Insurance Commission 1919, 201). In a 1938 radio address President Roosevelt stated, "The [Social Security] Act does not offer anyone, either individually or collectively, an easy life—nor was it ever intended so to do. None of the sums of money paid out to individuals in assistance or insurance will spell anything approaching abundance. But they will furnish that minimum necessary to keep a foothold; and that is the kind of protection Americans want" (National Conference on Social Welfare 1985, 148).

Social Security alone has never provided individuals with an abundant retirement. But it has provided individuals with an income sufficient to meet modest needs. As the population grew richer and healthier, Social Security, when combined with pensions and other savings, began to provide for both a lengthy and a comfortable retirement. The living standards of the elderly have improved substantially. Whereas in 1960 those older than sixty-four were twice as likely to be living below the poverty line as the rest of the adult population, today they are no more likely (Hurd 1994). When Social Security was first established, a twenty-year-old could expect to spend 12 percent of his remaining life in retirement. Because of unexpected increases in life expectancy, he spent 22 percent of his life in retirement, part of it in recreational activities. If improvements in life expectancy continue, a twenty-year-old today will spend one-third of his remaining life in retirement (Lee 1996). Even with no changes in the basic structure of Social Security, some combination of tax increases and benefits is therefore likely, but even more fundamental reforms have been proposed, including the complete privatization of Social Security.

The idea that Social Security should be privatized, or, more accurately, transformed into a system of individual mandatory savings accounts, has recently attracted the attention of economists and has been implemented in Chile. A scheme similar to that implemented in Chile would consist of mandatory savings plans supplemented by minimum pension guarantees for those with sufficient years of coverage. During the transition period in Chile, savings flowed into the new individual retirement accounts rather than into the old pay-as-you-go social insurance system. Payments to retirees were met out of government revenue. Active workers received explicit government debt on account of past contributions.

One advantage of a system of individual mandatory savings accounts would be that this new pension system would be insulated from political action to increase benefits without direct financing. Although awareness of long-term trust fund problems is currently very high, the trust fund will be generating large, temporary surpluses on the order of over $1 trillion between 2005 and 2020 (U.S. Board of Trustees of the Federal Old-Age and Survivors Insurance and Disability Insurance Trust Funds 1996) at the same time that the Hospital Insurance trust fund may be facing continued difficulties. It may, therefore, be tempting to finance Medicare through the Old Age and Survivors Disability Insurance trust fund. Other temptations may arise in the more distant future as well.

Political pressure would not disappear completely under a system of mandatory savings accounts. Because the government will have the decisive say in determining when and how accumulations can be converted into retirement annuities, voters might seek to reconfigure the system to meet their immediate needs. Because government restrictions on the portfolio holdings of retirement accounts are likely, there will be some political risk associated with leaving the government to pick and choose among different sectors and firms in the capital market.

A disadvantage of replacing the current system with individual savings accounts would be the higher administrative costs resulting from the costs of soliciting and managing very small individual retirement accounts. An additional disadvantage would the poorer provision of insurance over varying lengths of the working life (see Diamond 1996). Unless an individual received an annuity based on the value of his contributions, he might run out of money if he lived longer than expected. Minimum pension guarantees would alleviate some of these problems, as would better estimates of life expectancy.

The largest political hurdle to moving toward a system of individual savings accounts is financing the transition. Will one generation bear the brunt of the transition cost? The Chilean transition was financed out of a government surplus, and the country's rapid growth rates have produced a high return on individual retirement accounts (Diamond 1996). Kotlikoff (1996) argues that, because Social Security affects work incentives, whether all generations in the United States can gain from the privatization of Social Security depends on the initial tax structure, the linkage between Social Security benefits and taxes, and the type of tax used to finance the transition. Assuming that older generations are fully compensated, then, under favorable circumstances, future generations benefit as well, but, under unfavorable ones, they suffer a welfare decline.[5] Feldstein (1996) argues that much of the gain from privatization would result from an increase in the rate of return. The transition would be financed by a bond issue that, while politically difficult to implement, would leave all generations better off.

An alternative scenario to the immediate adoption of individual savings accounts is a gradual one. As both retirement and health benefits are cut, individuals who desire a long retirement will need either to save more or to work longer. But, if they wish to save more, they will do so only if they are certain that the state will not provide for a lengthy retirement once they reach old age. Bernheim (1995) finds that individuals who expect to receive no Social Security benefits save substantially more than individuals who expect to receive reduced benefits, who in turn save more than those who expect to receive the same benefits as current retirees. He also finds that individuals' decisions of how much to save are determined not by quantitative perceptions of financial need but by vague and unquantified senses of security and urgency. The retirement of well-to-do individuals is already privatized. For these individuals, pension income, not Social Security payments, constitutes their primary source of retirement income. The immediate adoption of a system of individual accounts would serve a psychological function by breaking the link between the state and retirement. It would make individuals aware that the tax revenue to finance a lengthy retirement will not be forthcoming and that a lengthy retirement will be possible only if they provide for it.

8.5   Summary

In this chapter I have examined three different programs aimed at the elderly: the Union army pension program, the state old-age pension programs that later became Old Age Assistance, and Old Age and Survivors Insurance. All experienced rapid growth partially because well-organized lobby groups were able to tap new sources of revenue and thus redistribute program costs. The South, the young, and recent immigrants bore the costs of a pension program benefiting Union army veterans. Property owners bore the costs of state old-age pension programs, and some states were able to redistribute the costs of Old Age Assistance to others. The costs of Old Age and Survivors Insurance and of Hospital Insurance have been borne by cohorts who have paid sizable Social Security taxes all their lives.[6] The tax revenue necessary to finance a lengthy retirement for the growing numbers of elderly is unlikely to be forthcoming. In the future, the provision for a lengthy retirement will lie with individuals.

Appendix 8A

Table 8A.1   **Total Number of Union Army Pensioners, Costs of Pension Program, and Pension Program as Percentage of All Federal Expenditures, 1865–1920**

Year	Number of Pensioners	Total Costs Current $	Total Costs 1967 $	Costs as % of All Federal Expenditures
1866	126,722	15,857,710	36,040,260	3.04
1867	155,474	21,275,770	50,656,590	5.95
1868	169,643	23,654,530	59,136,320	6.27
1869	187,963	29,077,770	72,694,430	9.01
1870	198,686	29,952,490	78,822,330	9.67
1871	207,495	29,381,870	81,616,310	10.06
1872	232,229	30,704,000	85,288,890	11.08
1873	238,411	27,985,260	77,736,850	9.64
1874	236,241	31,173,570	91,686,980	10.30
1875	234,821	30,253,100	91,676,060	11.02
1876	232,137	28,951,290	90,472,780	10.92
1877	232,104	29,217,280	91,304,010	12.11
1878	223,998	27,818,510	95,925,900	11.74
1879	242,755	34,502,160	123,222,000	12.92
1880	250,802	57,624,260	198,704,300	21.53
1881	268,830	51,655,460	178,122,300	19.81
1882	285,697	55,779,410	192,342,800	21.62
1883	303,658	63,019,230	225,068,700	23.74
1884	322,756	60,747,570	224,991,000	24.88
1885	345,125	68,564,510	253,942,700	26.35
1886	365,783	67,336,160	249,393,200	27.77
1887	406,007	77,506,400	287,060,700	28.93
1888	452,557	82,465,560	305,428,000	30.78
1889	489,725	92,309,690	341,887,700	30.84
1890	537,944	109,620,200	406,000,900	34.47
1891	676,160	122,013,300	451,901,200	33.36
1892	876,068	144,292,800	534,417,800	41.82
1893	966,012	161,774,400	599,164,400	42.19
1894	969,544	143,950,700	553,656,600	39.17
1895	970,524	144,150,300	576,601,300	40.47
1896	970,678	142,212,100	568,848,300	40.38
1897	976,014	143,937,500	575,750,000	39.35
1898	993,714	148,766,000	595,063,900	33.55
1899	991,519	142,502,600	570,010,300	23.55
1900	993,714	142,303,900	569,215,600	27.32
1901	997,735	142,400,300	569,601,100	27.14

Table 8A.1 (continued)

Year	Number of Pensioners	Total Costs		Costs as % of All Federal Expenditures
		Current $	1967 $	
1902	999,446	141,335,600	543,598,600	29.13
1903	996,545	141,752,900	525,010,600	27.42
1904	994,762	144,942,900	536,825,700	24.83
1905	998,441	144,864,700	536,535,900	25.54
1906	985,971	142,523,500	527,865,000	25.00
1907	967,371	141,464,500	505,230,500	24.43
1908	951,687	155,894,000	577,385,400	23.65
1909	946,194	164,826,300	610,467,700	23.76
1910	921,083	162,631,700	580,827,600	23.45
1911	892,098	159,842,300	570,865,300	23.13
1912	860,294	155,435,300	535,983,800	22.53
1913	820,200	176,714,900	594,999,700	24.72
1914	785,239	174,484,000	579,681,200	24.05
1915	748,147	167,298,100	550,322,800	22.42
1916	709,572	160,811,800	491,779,200	22.56
1917	673,111	162,457,900	423,067,400	8.31
1918	646,895	181,362,900	402,135,100	1.43
1919	624,427	223,592,500	431,645,800	1.21
1920	592,190	214,690,300	357,817,200	3.38

Source: See fig. 8.1. Compiled from Glasson (1918a, 273), the U.S. Bureau of Pensions 1920 *Report of the Commissioner of Pensions,* and table Y 335-338 in U.S. Bureau of the Census (1975, 1104).

Table 8A.2   **Total Number of OASDI Beneficiaries, Average Monthly Benefits for Retired Men, Percentage of Labor Force Covered by OASDI, OASDHI as Percentage of All Federal Expenditures, 1937–93**

Year	Number Beneficiaries in 1,000s		Average Monthly Benefit, Retired Men		% Labor Force Covered	OASDHI as % All Federal Expenditures
	All	Retired Men	Current $	1967 $		
1938						.06
1939					43.5	
1940	222	99	23.17	55.17		.16
1941	434	175	23.32	52.88		
1942	598	224	23.71	48.59		.31
1943	748	261	24.17	46.66		
1944	955	323	24.48	46.45	56.41	.18
1945	1,288	447	24.94	46.27		
1946	1,642	610	25.30	43.25		.48
1947	1,978	756	25.68	38.37		
1948	2,315	900	25.21	34.97		1.44
1949	2,743	1,100	26.92	37.70	55.23	
1950	3,477	1,469	45.67	63.34		1.62
1951	4,379	1,819	44.44	57.12		3.06

(continued)

Table 8A.2 (continued)

| Year | Number Beneficiaries in 1,000s | | Average Monthly Benefit, Retired Men | | % Labor Force Covered | OASDHI as % All Federal Expenditures |
	All	Retired Men	Current $	1967 $		
1952	5,026	2,052	52.16	65.61		2.77
1953	5,981	2,438	54.46	68.00		3.41
1954	6,886	2,803	63.34	78.68	71.34	4.22
1955	7,961	3,252	66.40	82.79	77.78	5.90
1956	9,128	3,572	68.23	83.82	79.40	7.05
1957	11,128	4,198	70.47	83.59	79.20	7.97
1958	12,430	4,617	72.74	84.00	78.41	9.35
1959	13,703	4,937	80.11	91.76	79.94	9.98
1960	14,845	5,217	81.87	92.30	79.01	11.10
1961	16,495	5,765	83.13	92.78	79.46	11.34
1962	18,053	6,244	83.79	92.48	80.25	12.05
1963	19,035	6,497	84.69	92.36	80.69	12.64
1964	19,800	6,657	85.58	92.12	81.44	12.57
1965	20,867	6,825	92.59	97.98	83.07	12.78
1966	22,767	7,034	93.26	95.95	83.96	13.84
1967	23,705	7,160	94.49	94.49	84.12	14.34
1968	24,560	7,309	109.08	104.68	84.83	15.15
1969	25,314	7,459	110.96	101.06	84.28	16.55
1970	26,229	7,688	130.53	112.24	83.17	17.21
1971	27,292	7,952	146.13	120.38	80.32	18.36
1972	28,476	8,231	179.44	143.22	81.57	19.18
1973	29,868	8,610	182.60	137.21	83.08	20.67
1974	30,853	8,832	206.56	139.78	80.69	21.76
1975	32,085	9,163	227.75	141.23	79.77	22.43
1976	33,021	9,420	247.70	145.23	81.24	22.58
1977	34,077	9,714	268.40	147.76	83.00	23.88
1978	34,586	9,928	291.60	149.21	82.26	23.99
1979	35,125	10,192	326.80	150.17	82.92	24.04
1980	35,585	10,461	380.20	153.93	83.54	24.22
1981	36,006	10,767	431.10	158.22	80.85	24.68
1982	35,839	11,030	469.60	162.35	78.88	25.01
1983	36,085	11,358	495.00	165.81	81.67	25.33
1984	36,479	11,573	517.80	166.26	84.70	25.27
1985	37,058	11,817	538.40	166.93	85.36	24.57
1986	37,703	12,080	549.80	167.36	85.89	24.44
1987	38,190	12,295	577.50	169.60	86.89	24.57
1988	38,627	12,483	604.90	170.59	87.56	24.65
1989	39,151	12,718	638.90	171.90	87.59	25.30
1990	39,832	12,985	679.30	173.40	87.00	25.15
1991	40,592	13,227	709.30	173.74		25.48
1992	41,507	13,474	735.50	174.89		26.90
1993	42,246	13,649	759.30	175.31		

Source: See fig. 8.4. Compiled from tables 5.A4, 5.B5, and 5.C2 in *Social Security Bulletin: Annual Statistical Supplement* (1994, 197, 208, 214); Series H 48-56 in Kurian (1994, 131); Series Y 605-637 in U.S. Bureau of the Census (1975, 1124); and various issues of *Government Finances.*

Notes

1. The total number of veterans on the rolls in 1910 was 562,615, of which 80 percent (450,092) were older than sixty-four. Sixty-three percent of the wives of veterans were age sixty-five or older, suggesting that 354,447 women older than sixty-four benefited from the Union army program. In addition, if 63 percent of widows were older than sixty-four, an additional 183,590 women older than sixty-four benefited. All mothers and parents can be assumed to be sixty-five years of age or older. Therefore, the total number of elderly benefiting from the pension program is 990,888, of an elderly population of 3,949,524. (Estimated from the 1910 census and the U.S. Bureau of Pensions 1910 *Report of the Commissioner of Pensions.*)

2. There was no mention of interest payments in the act.

3. For details, see Skocpol (1992), among others.

4. For more detailed discussions, see Achenbaum (1983), Lubove (1968), Putnam (1970), Quadagno (1988), and Weaver (1982).

5. Because Kotlikoff does not account for the value of Social Security insurance in his calculations, the benefits of moving to a privatized system may be lower than estimated.

6. In theory, these cohorts may have increased bequests or transfers to their children to compensate them for the high Social Security taxes that they were paying, but we have no empirical evidence that this occurred.

9   Looking to the Future

O! I could prophesy. . . .

Henry IV, Part 1

We can't even predict the next drip from a dripping tap when it gets irregular. Each drop sets up the conditions for the next, the smallest variation blows prediction apart, and the weather is unpredictable the same way, will always be unpredictable. . . . The future is disorder.

Tom Stoppard, *Arcadia*

Many Americans now look forward to retirement. Most enjoy the health and the income needed to pursue the good life. Previous generations were not as lucky. At the beginning of this century few men could afford to retire. Many of those who retired did so because of poor health or employment prospects and became dependent either on charity or on their family. Rising incomes have enabled more men to withdraw from the labor force. Now income, health, and employment prospects are not the important determinants of the retirement decision they once were. A bit of income and the relatively inexpensive amusements provided by mass tourism and mass entertainment have made retirement both common and highly valued. Will the number of years spent in retirement continue to increase, either because the trend toward earlier retirement continues or because longevity increases even further? Will we be faced with both an aging population and a population of retirees? While I cannot prophesy, I believe that the past provides insight. The demographic and economic processes that have produced an aging population and rising retirement rates have been ongoing for more than a century.

9.1 An Aging Population

The population of the United States has been aging for over a century, slowly at first, rapidly in recent times. Figure 9.1 shows that, in 1850, less than 3 percent of the population was older than sixty-four and in 1910 only 4 percent. By 1940 the figure was 7 percent and by 1990 13 percent. By 2050 the figure is projected to rise to least 20 percent.

Both increases in longevity and declines in the number of live births account for increases in the relative size of the elderly population. The effect of these two phenomena on the age distribution of the population can be seen in figures 9.2 and 9.3. These plots show that, whereas the age distribution of the popula-

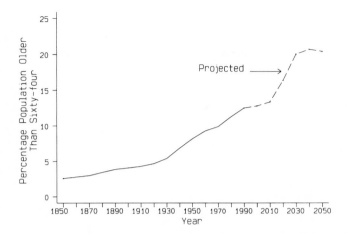

Fig. 9.1   Percentage population older than 64 (actual and projected), 1850–2050
Note: The percentage of the population older than sixty-four in 1850 was estimated from the integrated public-use census sample (Ruggles and Sobek 1995). The percentage for 1860 was interpolated. All other actual percentages are from Series A 119-134 in U.S. Bureau of the Census (1975, 15) and from table 14 in U.S. Bureau of the Census (1993, 15). The projections are from Day (1993) and are the Census Bureau's middle series.

tion could be represented by a pyramid in the nineteenth century, the base of the pyramid was narrower in 1910 and 1940. Fertility declined steadily throughout the nineteenth century and then so sharply during the 1920s and early 1930s that not enough women were born during the depression to replace the women then leaving childbearing age. By 1940 a decline in both fertility and mortality led to 7 percent of the population being older than sixty-four.

Population aging was even more pronounced after 1940, with some notable exceptions. The birthrate increased at an unprecedented rate between 1946 and 1964, reaching a peak in 1957, when more than 4.3 million babies were born. At the same time life expectancy at birth rose by almost four years, largely because of declining childhood mortality. Figure 9.3 shows that in 1970 the age distribution narrowed at young adult ages both because so few children were born in the 1930s and because the baby boom of the 1950s widened the age distribution during the teen years. Because the baby boom was followed by a baby bust, during which fertility dropped to its lowest levels in American history, the baby-boom generation has produced a "pig-in-a-python" bulge in the age distribution. Thus, in 1995 the age distribution was very narrow at young ages, bulged at ages thirty to forty-nine, and again narrowed sharply when the depression cohort reached ages fifty-five to sixty-five.

The aging of the baby-boom generation will dramatically raise the proportion of the population older than sixty-four. In 2025, when the baby-boom generation will be between ages sixty and eighty, 18 percent of the population is expected to be older than sixty-four years of age. In 2050 8 percent of the

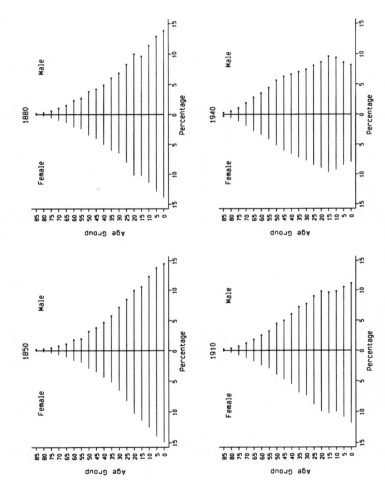

Fig. 9.2 Age distribution of the population, 1850–1940

Note: The distributions were calculated from the integrated public-use census samples (Ruggles and Sobek 1995).

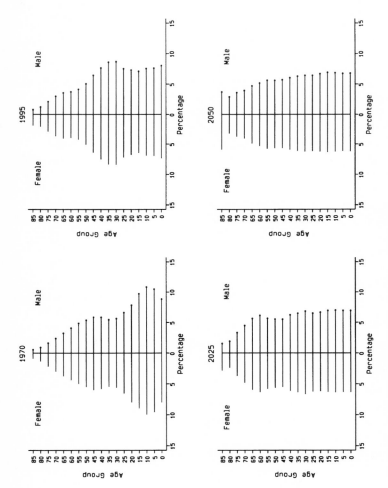

Fig. 9.3   Age distribution of the population, 1970–2050

Note: The distribution for 1970 was calculated from the integrated public-use census samples (Ruggles and Sobek 1995). The distributions for 1995, 2025, and 2050 are from Day (1993) and are the Census Bureau's middle-series projections.

population will be older than seventy-nine and 5 percent older than eighty-four.

If life expectancies increase faster than expected, the percentage of the population older than sixty-four in 2025 and in 2050 may be even greater than the 18 and 20 percent, respectively, predicted by the intermediate projections of the Census Bureau and reproduced in figure 9.3. Since 1970 about half the increases in life expectancy can be attributed to improved older-age mortality.[1] Because 80 percent of all individuals now survive to age sixty-five, any substantial improvements in future life expectancy are therefore likely to result from declining mortality above age sixty-five.

Whether future increases in life expectancy are possible depends on whether as a species we have reached a genetically programmed limit to life expectancy. Although the debate continues over whether the life span is genetically fixed, recent research suggests that it is not or that, if it is, the limit is well above the age of eighty-five, as originally postulated by Fries (1980, 1989). Vaupel (1991) has argued that children alive today may live ninety or even a hundred years on average. If there were well-defined limits on the length of the life span, then, when chronic conditions do not strike prematurely, mortality rates should accelerate rapidly at older ages. But the probability of survivorship after age eighty has increased sharply, and survivorship curves of the population aged eighty or older do not indicate an increase in age-specific mortality (Manton and Vaupel 1995). These findings suggest that, although genetics may affect vulnerability to environmental factors, absolute life spans are not necessarily rigidly determined by genetics.

Just how long are the baby boomers likely to live? Kannisto (1994) has found that the decline in older-age mortality in developing countries since 1950 has proceeded at widely varying speeds, sometimes sluggish, sometimes rapid, and that there have even been occasional short periods of mortality increases. Unfortunately, we do not yet know how to incorporate changes in socioeconomic conditions, medical technology, and the other factors that have led to mortality declines into our forecasts. One promising line of recent research is to use knowledge of early life conditions to better inform our predictions. Studies of Britain, France, and Italy conclude that the mortality experience of a cohort is largely determined by the first fifteen years of life, with improvements in adult mortality following mortality declines in the first fifteen years of life, while declines in infant mortality lagged behind until maternal health improved (Caselli and Capocaccia 1989; Kermack, McKendrick, and McKinlay 1934a, 1934b; Preston and van de Walle 1978). Buck and Simpson (1982) found a high correlation in the United States between diarrheal deaths from birth to age twenty in 1917–21 and death rates from arteriosclerotic heart disease at ages forty to forty-four and fifty to fifty-four. Many of the degenerative conditions of old age, such as coronary heart disease, hypertension, stroke, non-insulin-dependent diabetes, and autoimmune thyroiditis, have been linked to exposure to infectious disease, malnutrition, and other types of biomedical and socioeconomic stress early in life (Barker 1992, 1994). In their review of the literature on early life conditions and older-age mortality, Elo and Preston

(1992, 204) concluded, "Results from many empirical studies support the notion that childhood conditions play a major role in adult mortality."

Relative to their predecessors, the baby boomers have, indeed, been fortunate. Between 1920 and 1950 mortality rates from birth until age five fell sharply. Whereas only 83 percent of individuals reached age five in 1920, by 1950 97 percent did. The four-centimeter increase in adult height for cohorts born between 1920 and 1950, documented in this book, also implies that early life conditions improved. The baby boomers were the first generation born in the age of antibiotics, when it became possible to cure the infectious diseases of infancy and early childhood before they led to large reductions in the rate of growth or damaged developing organs. The early baby boomers have not yet reached age sixty-five. They will not begin to reach age ninety until 2035. As pointed out by Preston (1993), those who would reach ninety in 1996 were born in 1906, when life expectancy at birth was only fifty years, one of twelve children did not survive infancy, and the burden of infectious diseases was exceptionally heavy. Nonetheless, they were born at a time when life expectancy at birth had improved. In fact, improvements in the disease environment that resulted in the development of better physiques and less scarring by the sequelae of infectious disease may explain the increase in the size of the "old-old" population since the 1970s. The marked improvement in early life conditions between 1920 and 1950 suggests that the life expectancies of the elderly will increase rapidly at least twenty years into the future and that the increase may be more rapid than that observed over the last twenty years. Census and Social Security Bureau projections of the size of the elderly population, projections that are based on recent mortality declines, are therefore likely to be off the mark.

9.2   A Retired Population

When the baby boomers begin to retire in 2010, the strain on the Social Security retirement system, even under the Social Security Board's intermediate projections, is expected to be substantial. The number of beneficiaries is expected to increase much more rapidly than the number of covered workers. Under the intermediate projections of the Social Security Board of Trustees, trust funds for Old Age and Survivors Insurance and for Disability Insurance will be depleted in 2029. Financing the Social Security retirement and disability program with incoming tax revenues alone implies that the combined employer-employee tax rate plus income taxes on benefits would have to rise to 17 percent of taxable payroll from 13 percent today. After 2029, taxes would have to be even higher (Board of Trustees of the Federal Old-Age and Survivors Insurance and Disability Trust Funds 1996). If, as is likely, the baby boomers' life expectancies exceed those assumed by the intermediate projections of the Social Security Board, the strain on the Social Security retirement system will be even greater.

Another major transfer program affecting the elderly is Medicare, providing coverage to virtually all those age sixty-five or older (Congressional Budget Office 1993). Like Social Security and Disability Insurance, Medicare is not adequately financed either, and depletion of Medicare funds is expected by the year 2001 (Board of Trustees of the Federal Hospital Insurance Trust Fund 1996). Assuming that the deficit is met by increasing taxes, expected increases in the size of the elderly population under the intermediate projects of the Hospital Insurance Board of Trustees imply that outlays on federal Hospital Insurance alone will consume 3 percent of GDP by 2020 and 4½ percent by 2050, up sharply from the 1½ percent consumed today (Board of Trustees of the Federal Hospital Insurance Trust Fund 1996). Of particular concern are increases in the size of the oldest-old population. Those eighty-five years of age or older are almost twice as likely as those aged sixty-five to seventy-four to enter a short-stay hospital, and their stays there are 11 percent longer. They are almost four times as likely to enter a skilled nursing facility, and their stays there are 18 percent longer. Total Medicare program payments to those older than eighty-four are 60 percent higher.[2]

The crisis in Social Security is likely to be deeper than predicted by the intermediate projections of the Social Security Board. The American population has been growing healthier since the end of the nineteenth century. Men are no longer dangerously thin, and they no longer face the childhood disease and poor nutrition that may stunt their growth. This book has shown that chronic disease rates among the elderly have declined across a century. Disability rates among the elderly have also declined recently (Manton, Corder, and Stallard 1993). Trends in adult height and early life conditions suggest that the baby boomers will enjoy a particularly healthy and long-lived old age. But we cannot expect that, because the baby boomers will enjoy better health in their old age compared to past generations, health care costs will fall. Kim (1996) finds that the improvement in health will not be large enough completely to relieve the health care burden caused by an elderly population that will be larger both in terms of absolute numbers and as a proportion of the population. Innovations in medical technology combined with rising incomes may produce further increases in the demand for medical care.

Ballooning pension and health care costs have led to a shift in government policy from the promotion of retirement to the promotion of elderly labor force participation. By increasing the labor supply of the elderly, the government could raise tax revenue that could help finance Social Security pension and health care costs. Most of the members of the 1994–95 Technical Panel on Trends and Issues in Retirement Savings of the Social Security Advisory Council favored further increases in the age at which full benefits are to be received and agreed that the age should eventually be indexed to life expectancy. Most panel members also believed that the early entitlement age for Social Security benefits should be raised as well from sixty-two to sixty-four or sixty-five. In addition to cutting benefits by increasing entitlement ages, many policy makers have proposed abolishing the earnings test, whereby Social Security benefits are reduced for each dollar in excess of the earnings threshold.

How will the baby boomers fare if Social Security benefits are reduced? The proposed changes to the Social Security system would give households enough time to increase their savings rate to maintain their retirement income. The higher working income of baby boomers relative to that of their parents might foreshadow a higher private retirement income. Baby boomers have both significantly higher real incomes and greater accumulated wealth than their parents did at comparable ages (Cantor and Yuengert 1994; Congressional Budget Office 1993; Easterlin, Schaeffer, and Macunovich 1993), but baby-boomer households are not saving enough to maintain their current living standard into retirement (Bernheim and Scholz 1993). The problem is particularly acute for lower-income households. These are households that might well expect Social Security to replace their income adequately. Because the Social Security benefits of low-income households are not taxed, an individual who has had average earnings during his entire working life and who retires at age sixty-five with a dependent spouse now receives benefits that replace more than 80 percent of peak preretirement net-of-tax income (Feldstein 1996). These are the households that are most likely to be affected if Social Security benefits are reduced, not the well-to-do, much of whose retirement is financed by private pension plans.

Will this tinkering with the Social Security system be enough to slow down or reverse the trend toward earlier retirement? The threshold above which Social Security benefits are reduced for every dollar in earnings is already so high that it does not affect the participation decision (Friedberg 1996). Under currently legislated changes, workers will still be able to collect actuarially reduced benefits at age sixty-two. Even if the early retirement age is raised, workers will still be able to apply for Social Security disability benefits and to receive these benefits without having to accept any actuarial reduction in retirement benefits. Krueger and Pischke (1992) found that, when a legislative change substantially and unexpectedly reduced benefits to individuals who were born after 1916, a change that led to a worker who retired at age sixty-five after a career of earning the average wage to receive Social Security benefits that were 13 percent lower than if he had been born in 1916, this reduction had very little effect on retirement trends. This book has shown that, over time, income has exerted less and less of an effect on the retirement decision. If this insensitivity to income arises from social norms, perhaps established by Social Security, then a reversal is certainly possible. But I have shown that this insensitivity arises in part from the relatively high wealth levels of today's retirees and the affordability of mass tourism and mass entertainment, both of which enable the elderly to pursue the good life. If incomes continue to rise, and if leisure-time activities continue to be relatively inexpensive and enticing, then the rise of retirement is unlikely to reverse.

Nor is the rise of retirement likely to reverse because of the improving health of the elderly. Retirement rates have been rising in spite of improving health, and health is becoming less and less important to the retirement decision. A temporary reversal is possible if, in the tight labor markets likely to prevail when the baby-bust generation reaches prime working ages, jobs become available that not only are part-time but also permit time off for extended periods of travel. A reversal is also possible if the early age of retirement for Social Security were changed unexpectedly or if benefits were sharply and unexpectedly reduced so that households who depend primarily on Social Security for their retirement income found themselves facing a shortfall in savings. These households would either have to postpone retirement and extend their working life, accept transfers from their children, or experience a large decline in retirement consumption.

Rather than postpone retirement when faced with unexpected benefit cuts, the elderly may choose to reduce their consumption. In the case of men who involuntarily retired sooner than expected, Hausman and Paquette (1987) observed declines in consumption. The elderly could reduce their consumption by living with their children. But I showed that the effect of changes in income on the coresidence decision has become smaller since the turn of the century. Independent living may be not only relatively inexpensive but also much more highly valued than it was in the past. Migration may permit the elderly to cope with income declines while still maintaining their standard of living. Improvements in transport have made the elderly more mobile than they were in the past. Graves and Knapp (1988) argue that, because the elderly have incomes that are independent of their residential locations, they move where the value of amenities, such as climate, is reflected in labor rather than in land markets. By forming communities at the fringes of such areas the elderly rapidly gain the political clout to use tax monies for the purchase of the goods that they want, substituting senior centers and golf courses for playgrounds and public schools. They can thus both lower the price of recreation and increase the variety of recreational goods. In fact, as this book points out, both the increased public provision of recreational facilities and technological change have made income a less important component of recreation and retirement extremely attractive. Even the elderly with low incomes who cannot afford mass tourism can afford mass entertainment such as television. Provided that the elderly have enough income to live independently of their children and to enjoy low-cost recreational activities, they are likely to feel more time rather than income constrained. Under these circumstances a reversal in retirement rates is unlikely.

Notes

1. In 1970 life expectancy was seventy-one at birth and fifteen at age sixty-five. In 1991 the respective life expectancies were seventy-six and seventeen (National Center for Health Statistics 1995).

2. See tables 14, 25, and 37 in *Health Care Financing Review: Medicare and Medicaid Statistical Supplement* (1996).

Appendix A: Union Army Pensions and Civil War Records

Real data is messy.

Tom Stoppard, *Arcadia*

The scope of the Union army pension program, run for the benefit of veterans and their dependent children and widows, came to be enormous. What had begun as a program to provide for severely wounded veterans became the first general disability and old-age pension program in the United States. The program was generous both in the level of benefits and in its coverage. The average pension paid to Union army veterans from 1866 to 1912 replaced about 30 percent of the income of an unskilled laborer, making the Union army pension program as generous as Social Security retirement benefits today. The total number of beneficiaries collecting a pension was slightly more than 100,000 in 1866 but reached a peak of almost 1 million in 1902. By 1900 21 percent of all white males age fifty-five or older were on the pension rolls, and the program that had consumed a mere 3 percent of all federal government expenditures in 1866 consumed almost 30 percent.

Running the pension program was an enormous undertaking. Pensioners' claims had to be validated by checking old military service records and sending special examiners to interview men and women who had known the claimant. Guidelines for medical examinations needed to be established, and medical examinations had to be arranged. Finally, the Pension Bureau had to determine what size pension the claimant was entitled to. This entire process generated copious records. Much of the life history of an individual can be reconstructed from the pension records. Additional information can be gathered by linking pension records to military records while in the service and to census records. This appendix describes the records and the pension program that generated them.

Civil War Pensions

Origins

The Civil War affected an entire generation. Forty-one percent of all northern white men born between 1822 and 1845, 60 percent of those born between 1837 and 1845, and 81 percent of those born in 1843 served in the Union army during the Civil War. Union soldiers constituted a fairly representative cross section of their generation. Compared to the general population, recruits came from households that were neither disproportionately rich nor disproportionately poor in 1860 (Fogel 1993). Ninety-five percent of them were volunteers. Because death in the army had come to both rich and poor alike, survivors of the war remained a representative cross section of their generation. Those who survived the war to reach their fifties had life expectancies similar to those of the general population and died of the same causes (Fogel 1993). The soldiers who survived the war were unique in one respect. At a time when private pensions were rare and state old-age pensions had not yet been established, they came to qualify for a Union army pension. Because Union army veterans remained a large fraction of the population, by 1900 35 percent of all white males aged fifty-five to fifty-nine were collecting a Union army pension, 21 percent of all white males aged sixty to sixty-four, 14 percent of all white males aged sixty-five to sixty-nine, and 9 percent of all white males aged seventy and over.

Congress established the Union army pension program on 14 July 1862. In passing this act, Congress founded what later became known as the General Law pension system. This system of pension laws was the only one in force until 1890. It provided pensions for soldiers who had incurred permanent bodily injury or disability while in the service of the Union army after 4 March 1861 and provided for the dependents of soldiers who had died from causes that could be traced directly to injuries received or diseases contracted while in Union army service. The dollar amount that was received depended on the degree of disability, where *total disability* meant "a total disability for the performance of manual labor requiring severe and continuous exertion" and provided enlisted men with a pension of $8.00 per month, an amount equivalent to 30 percent of the earnings of an unskilled laborer. If the claimant had lesser disabilities, he received an amount proportionate to the degree of his disabilities. A board of surgeons appointed by the Pension Bureau rated applicants' disabilities, following guidelines established by the bureau. The Pension Bureau compiled lists of physical wounds, pensionable diseases, and allowed ratings.

Inability to perform manual labor remained the standard in this and all subsequent pension laws, regardless of the wealth of the individual, his ability to earn a living by other than manual means, his labor force participation, or his employment in manual labor. The manual labor standard was soon liberalized.

In 1866 Congress raised the pension for total disability for "any manual labor" from $8.00 per month to $20.00 and in 1872 to $24.00, a sum that replaced 76 percent of the monthly earnings of an unskilled laborer. The Pension Bureau construed the words *any manual labor* to include also "the lighter kinds of labor which require education and skill" (1874 *Report of the Commissioner of Pensions,* quoted in Glasson 1918a, 131).

In addition to the rates enumerated in the act of 14 July 1862, Congress passed acts establishing pension rates for specific disabilities that could be traced to wartime service. By 1872 the statutory rates covered the loss of both hands, both feet, the sight in both eyes, the sight in one eye, and one hand, foot, arm, or leg; total disability in hands, feet, arms, or legs; a disability equivalent to the loss of a hand or foot; requirements of regular aid and attendance; and total deafness. Inconsistency between these separate acts and the General Law led to the passage of the Consolidation Act of 1873. This act established various grades of disabilities. A first-grade disability, providing a pension of $31.25 per month, was a permanent disability requiring the regular aid and attendance of another person. A second-grade disability, warranting a monthly pension of $24.00, was a permanent disability that incapacitated the claimant for the performance of any manual labor. Permanent disabilities equivalent to the loss of a hand or foot were third grade and were pensionable at $18.00 per month. In addition to the grade rates, veterans could receive a proportion of the third-grade rate ($18.00 per month) for any degree of disability that was not provided for in the Consolidation Act.

The Consolidation Act gave the commissioner of pensions the power to fix rates for disabilities not specified by law. The bureau established a series of rates below $18.00 per month for specific conditions. Among the rates were $6.00 per month for the loss of the great toe, $8.00 per month for anchylosis of the wrist, and $12.00 per month for the loss of the sight in one eye. These were not only dollar rates but also the rating used by the examining surgeons and were employed as standards of comparison. Thus, a disability equivalent, according to the examining surgeons, to anchylosis of the wrist was rated at $8.00. In the case of multiple disabilities each disability was rated separately in fractions of eighteen, and the total degree of disability was also rated. Rating disabilities in terms of eighteenths remained standard procedure even after the grade rates were increased between 1878 and 1883 to $24.00 per month for a third-grade disability, $30.00 per month for a second-grade disability, and $72.00 per month for a first-grade disability. When the new second rate was established, it almost completely replaced the income of a laborer. In addition to ratings in terms of eighteenths, Congress established ratings in thirtieths for partial deafness in 1888 when it authorized a $30.00 per month rate for total deafness and proportional payments for partial deafness.

Congressional exertion on behalf of veterans and their dependents was not limited to the construction of statute law. Congress showered its generosity on meritorious individuals who did not fall within the provisions of the laws by passing private pension acts, often inserted in omnibus bills. The majority of these acts increased existing rates for claimants in reduced financial circumstances. The number of pensions granted by special acts rose from twelve during the tenure of the Thirty-seventh Congress (1861–63) to a high of 9,649 during the Sixty-first Congress (1909–11), still a mere 1 percent of all pensions.

A Disability and Old-Age Pension Program

The act of 27 June 1890 marked the beginning of a universal disability and old-age pension program. Proof of at least ninety days service in the Union army, an honorable discharge, and disability not due to "vicious habits" that prohibited the veteran from the performance of manual labor qualified him for the receipt of a pension ranging from $6.00 to $12.00 per month. Dependents of a veteran who had died from any cause qualified for a pension. The veteran's disability did not need to be related to military service. However, veterans who could trace their disability to their wartime service received far more for the same disability than those who could not. In 1900 a pensioner who could trace his disability to the war was entitled to a monthly sum of $30.00 for incapacity to perform any manual labor, $24.00 for a disability equivalent to the loss of a hand or foot, $17.00 for the loss of one eye, and $6.00–$10.00 for a single hernia. His counterpart who could not trace his disability to the war received $12.00, $10.00, $6.00, and $6.00, respectively, for these ailments. Veterans who could trace their disabilities to the war received up to $100 per month, almost three times the monthly income of a laborer in 1900, for the loss of both hands, feet, or eyes. However, a veteran blinded in an industrial accident received at most $12.00 per month, a sum equivalent to one-third the monthly income of an unskilled laborer (U.S. Bureau of Pensions 1899 *Report of the Commissioner of Pensions*).

Table A.1 illustrates average differences in pension amounts according to whether a veteran could trace his disability to the war and thus fell under the 1862 law rather than the 1890 law. Even though men who successfully claimed war-related disabilities were in worse health, on average, than those who could not, pension amounts were still higher among men who could trace their disabilities to the war than among those who could not. Among all men the median pension amount was $12.00 in 1900, and among men whose disabilities resulted from their wartime service and who were very disabled 84 percent were receiving more than $12.00 per month. All men whose disabilities did not result from wartime service were collecting $12.00 a month or less. Among all men on the rolls under either cause, 56 percent of the very disabled were receiving pensions of over $12.00 and 42 percent pensions of $12.00 or less.

With the passage of the act of 1890 the number of pensioners on the rolls almost doubled between 1889 and 1892. Slightly more than half of all veterans on the rolls were collecting a pension under the 1890 law. The Pension Bureau granted the maximum rate to those seventy-five years of age or older on the

Table A.1   Monthly Pension Means and Percentile by Health Status and Law, 1900 ($)

	Mean	Percentile				
		10	25	50	75	90
All veterans	12.9	6	8	12	14	24
General Law	17.6	8	12	14.5	24	30
1890 law	9.4	6	8	10	12	12
Health:						
Good	9.8	6	8	8	12	12
Fair	11.4	8	8	12	12	16
Poor	17.5	10	12	15	24	30
General Law and:						
Health good	14.3	8	8	12	15	18
Health fair	14.1	10	12	12	16	17
Health poor	20.1	12	15	17	24	30
1890 law and:						
Health good	8.6	6	6	8	12	12
Health fair	9.6	6	8	10	12	12
Health poor	10.9	8	10	12	12	12

Note: Calculated from the data used in the estimation. The health variable used is based on the ratings of the examining surgeons.

grounds of "senility alone" and the minimum rate to those at least sixty-five years of age, "unless the evidence discloses an unusual vigor and ability for the performance of manual labor on one of that age" (U.S. Bureau of Pensions 1899 *Report of the Commissioner of Pensions*). In the words of the formidable lobby for the privileges of veterans and their dependents, the Grand Army of the Republic, this act was designed to place on the rolls "all survivors of the war whose conditions of health are not practically perfect" (quoted in Glasson 1918a, 233).

After 1900 old-age pension provisions grew even more generous. In 1904, President Roosevelt issued Executive Order 78, which authorized the Pension Bureau to grant pensions on the basis of age. The bureau decreed that, at age sixty-two, an applicant was half disabled in the ability to perform manual labor and entitled to a rating of $6.00 per month and that, at ages sixty-five, sixty-eight, and seventy, he was entitled to $8.00, $10.00, and $12.00 per month, respectively. Congress officially recognized age as sufficient cause to qualify for a pension with the act of 6 February 1907, also called the Service and Age Pension. Provided that the conditions of the 1890 law were met, veterans aged sixty-two to sixty-nine received $12.00 per month, those aged seventy to seventy-four $15.00 per month, and those seventy-five years and older $20.00 per month. This act did not increase the total number of pensioners but led a significant number of pensioners to switch from the 1890 law to the 1907 law. Soon the Service and Age pension system overshadowed the General Law and

1890 systems in number of pensioners. In 1910 64 percent of all veterans were collecting a pension under the 1907 law, 22 percent under the General Law, and 14 percent under the 1890 law (U.S. Bureau of Pensions 1910 *Report of the Commissioner of Pensions*). Pension amount effectively became a function of age and of whether a veteran could trace his disabilities to the war (see table A.2).

The next major pension law was the act of 11 May 1912. According to the new schedule, rates rose with both age and length of service, regardless of disabilities incurred during that service. Most of the veterans receiving pensions under the 1907 law were transferred to the rolls under the 1912 law. Legislation after 1912 consisted mainly of automatic increases in pension ratings for age and service.

Civil War Records

Union army records are being collected as part of a project to study early indicators of later work levels, disease, and death. Information on the enlisted men in a random sample of 331 Union army infantry companies has been gathered from regimental records. These men are being linked to the 1850, 1860, 1900, and 1910 censuses, military service records, army medical records, pen-

Table A.2　　**Monthly Pension Means and Percentiles by Age, Health Status, and Law, 1910 ($)**

	Mean	Percentile				
		10	25	50	75	90
All veterans	16.5	12	12	15	20	24
General Law	22.3	17	17	24	24	30
1890 law	11.7	12	12	12	12	12
1907 law	14.5	12	12	12	15	20
Good health	16.6	12	12	15	20	24
Poor health	18.0	12	12	15	20	30
Age < 70	15.0	12	12	12	17	24
Age ≥ 70	18.8	15	15	17	20	30
Age < 70 and:						
General Law	21.3	14	17	17	24	30
1890 law	11.7	12	12	12	12	12
1907 law	12.2	12	12	12	12	12
Age ≥ 70 and:						
General Law	23.9	17	17	24	30	30
1890 law	11.5	10	12	12	12	12
1907 law	16.9	15	15	15	20	20

Note: Calculated from the data later used in estimation. The health variable used was based on the ratings of the examining surgeons.

sion records, and the successive medical reports of the examining surgeons of the Pension Bureau.

The first step in this procedure is to link men to their military service and army medical records. The military service records contain information about the individual's enlistment and discharge and where the soldier was during each roll call. Thus, the records might indicate that he was absent because he was in the hospital, ill, on furlough, or with another company or had deserted. Army medical records are generated whenever a soldier spent time in a hospital. They contain a terse description of the condition (e.g., typhoid fever), a description of the type of treatment the soldier underwent, and dates of admission and release.

Once soldiers have been linked to their records while in the army, they are then linked to their pension records, which include the reports of examining surgeons. Eighty-five percent of all soldiers who survived the war have a pension record because either the veteran or his dependents applied for a pension. Desertion, and hence ineligibility for a pension, was the primary nonrandom factor explaining linkage failure.

A single pension file contains many pension records. A new pension record is generated each time a veteran applied for an increase either because the law had changed, his health had worsened, or he had reached an age that entitled him to a pension increase. The typical veteran filed approximately twelve complaints prior to 1900 and fourteen prior to 1910. Application for a pension was made through a lawyer. Although Glasson (1918a, 150) reports that the advertisements of pension attorneys "represented the advertisors as in the enjoyment of special and peculiar facilities for the successful prosecution of claims," the records themselves provide no evidence that either the ratings of the surgeons or the total pension amount depended on the lawyer that the claimant used.

In order to file for a pension a veteran would fill out a form entitled *declaration for pension* (see fig. A.1). In this form he would indicate his name, age, place of birth, address, and current occupation and, for verification purposes, when and in what company or companies he had served and his height, complexion, hair color, and occupation at enlistment. If he was claiming to be disabled by disease or injuries, he had to specify the diseases or injuries and, if they were war related, how and when they were incurred. Philip Herbold, who served in Company K of the Twenty-first New York Infantry, wrote in 1900 that he was unfit for manual labor because of "his left foot and ankle being diseased by being hurt on the 4th Day of March 1900 and Blood Poisoning Setting in and Stiffening his ankle and cords of his left leg" (certificate 1,149,873). Charles Johnson of Company G of the 196th Ohio Infantry applied for a pension in 1890 at age forty-three because he "contracted chronic diarrhoea caused by exposure and hardships incident to the service" (certificate 748,705). Applicants might submit claims under both the General Law and the 1890 law. In subsequent pension filings Charles Johnson claimed "pension un-

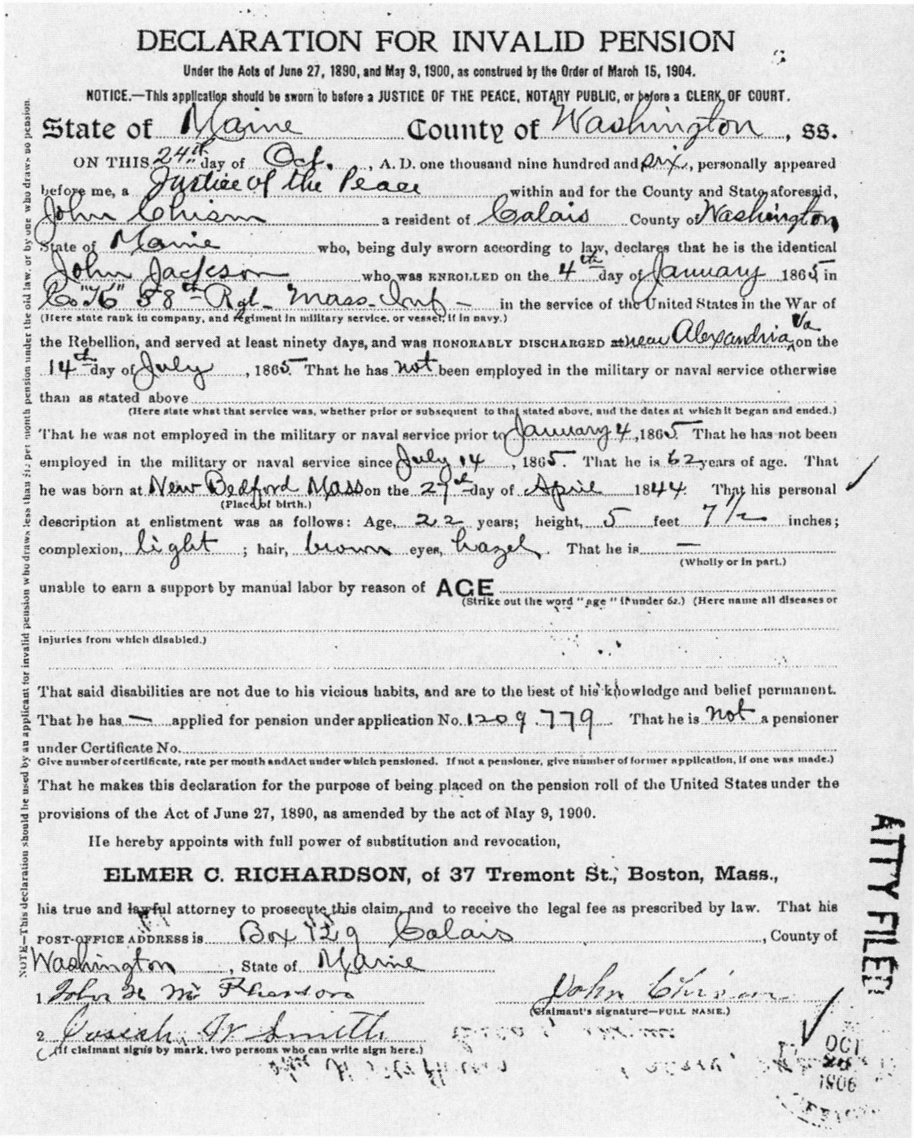

DECLARATION FOR INVALID PENSION

Under the Acts of June 27, 1890, and May 9, 1900, as construed by the Order of March 15, 1904.

NOTICE.—This application should be sworn to before a JUSTICE OF THE PEACE, NOTARY PUBLIC, or before a CLERK OF COURT.

State of _Maine_ County of _Washington_, ss.

ON THIS _24th_ day of _Oct._, A. D. one thousand nine hundred and _six_, personally appeared before me, a _Justice of the Peace_ within and for the County and State aforesaid, _John Chism_ a resident of _Calais_ County of _Washington_ State of _Maine_ who, being duly sworn according to law, declares that he is the identical _John Jackson_ who was ENROLLED on the _4th_ day of _January_ 1865 in _Co. "K" 58th Regt. Mass. Inf._ in the service of the United States in the War of

(Here state rank in company, and regiment in military service, or vessel, if in navy.)

the Rebellion, and served at least ninety days, and was HONORABLY DISCHARGED at _near Alexandria Va_ on the _14th_ day of _July_, 1865. That he has _not_ been employed in the military or naval service otherwise than as stated above.

(Here state what that service was, whether prior or subsequent to that stated above, and the dates at which it began and ended.)

That he was not employed in the military or naval service prior to _January 4, 1865._ That he has not been employed in the military or naval service since _July 14_, 1865. That he is _62_ years of age. That he was born at _New Bedford Mass_ on the _29th_ day of _April_ 1844. That his personal

(Place of birth.)

description at enlistment was as follows: Age, _22_ years; height, _5_ feet _7½_ inches; complexion, _light_; hair, _brown_ eyes, _hazel_. That he is _____

(Wholly or in part.)

unable to earn a support by manual labor by reason of ACE

(Strike out the word "age" if under 62.) (Here name all diseases or injuries from which disabled.)

That said disabilities are not due to his vicious habits, and are to the best of his knowledge and belief permanent. That he has ___ applied for pension under application No. _1209 779_ That he is _not_ a pensioner under Certificate No. ____

Give number of certificate, rate per month and Act under which pensioned. If not a pensioner, give number of former application, if one was made.

That he makes this declaration for the purpose of being placed on the pension roll of the United States under the provisions of the Act of June 27, 1890, as amended by the act of May 9, 1900.

He hereby appoints with full power of substitution and revocation,

ELMER C. RICHARDSON, of 37 Tremont St., Boston, Mass.,

his true and lawful attorney to prosecute this claim, and to receive the legal fee as prescribed by law. That his POST-OFFICE ADDRESS is _Box 129 Calais_, County of _Washington_, State of _Maine_

1 _John De Mc Pherson_   _John Chism_
(Claimant's signature—FULL NAME.)
2 _Josiah H Smith_

(If claimant signs by mark, two persons who can write sign here.)

ATTY FILED

OCT 25 1906

Fig. A.1 Declaration for pension

Note: Pension of John Chism, Company K, Fifty-eighth Massachusetts Infantry, certificate 1128382.

der the general law for chronic diarrhea" and "pension under the new law on account of piles [hemorrhoids] and rheumatism."

When he filed for an increase in his pension, a veteran had to provide accompanying information. The records thus contain affidavits or signed statements from the claimant, neighbors, employers, doctors, and men who served in the same company (see fig. A.2). In the case of Charles Johnson, a fellow soldier, Israel Cook, testified that, in 1865, Charles Johnson "contracted chronic diarrhea and it reduced him to such an extent that he became wholly unable for duty." Neighbors and doctors would recount how long they had known the claimant and how long they had known him to be suffering from either a specific or an ill-defined illness. One neighbor wrote that he had known Charles Wheeler of Company I of the Fifty-fifth Ohio Infantry for forty years and that Charles Wheeler "when drafted into the Army was a sound and hardy man, while from the time of his arrival to his home, following his discharge, he was getting weaker from year to year" (certificate 559,045). Other affidavits might be testimonials to the claimants' morals.

Men who applied on the basis of age needed to provide proof of their age. The Pension Bureau demanded a copy, verified by a magistrate, of either a public record of birth, a baptismal record, or a family record, that is, a record written in a family Bible. In the case of John Dressender of Company B of the 195th Ohio Infantry, proof consisted of a record of birth in an 1853 Bible that Dressender "placed in the Bible himself given him by a minister of the gospel before he left Germany." A notary public wrote of this record in Dressender's Bible, "It appears to be all the same writing know [*sic*] marks of erasure or alteration and from the appearance of the writing he believes the entries to have been made about the same date" (certificate 577,545).

The Pension Bureau would carefully examine the claims of individuals. They would send examiners to interview the claimant, neighbors, doctors, and men who had served in the same company. Claimants would describe in detail how they had contracted their disabilities. Charles Johnson recounted,

> We were out in grand review about a mile or a mile and a half from our quarters. The general kept us out until it began to rain. Then he dismissed us and we started on a run for our quarters like a lot of sheep. I was all wet with sweat and very warm from drilling. It rained very hard and the wind blew hard and before I got to camp I was chilled. There on the way to quarters I stopped at a spring and drank a good deal of water as I was very thirsty. In a few days after this the diarrhoea commenced on me. . . . I had the diarrhoea so bad that I had no control of my bowels at all. Finally I got it so bad that I was clear down and could not walk. I weighed one hundred and sixty-nine pounds when I enlisted and after I had recovered some from the diarrhoea I weighed but a hundred pounds. I was sick with it all the balance of my service and came home sick with it after I was discharged.

Charles Johnson's account was supported by an interview with a man who had served in the same company who testified, "He got very warm the day we

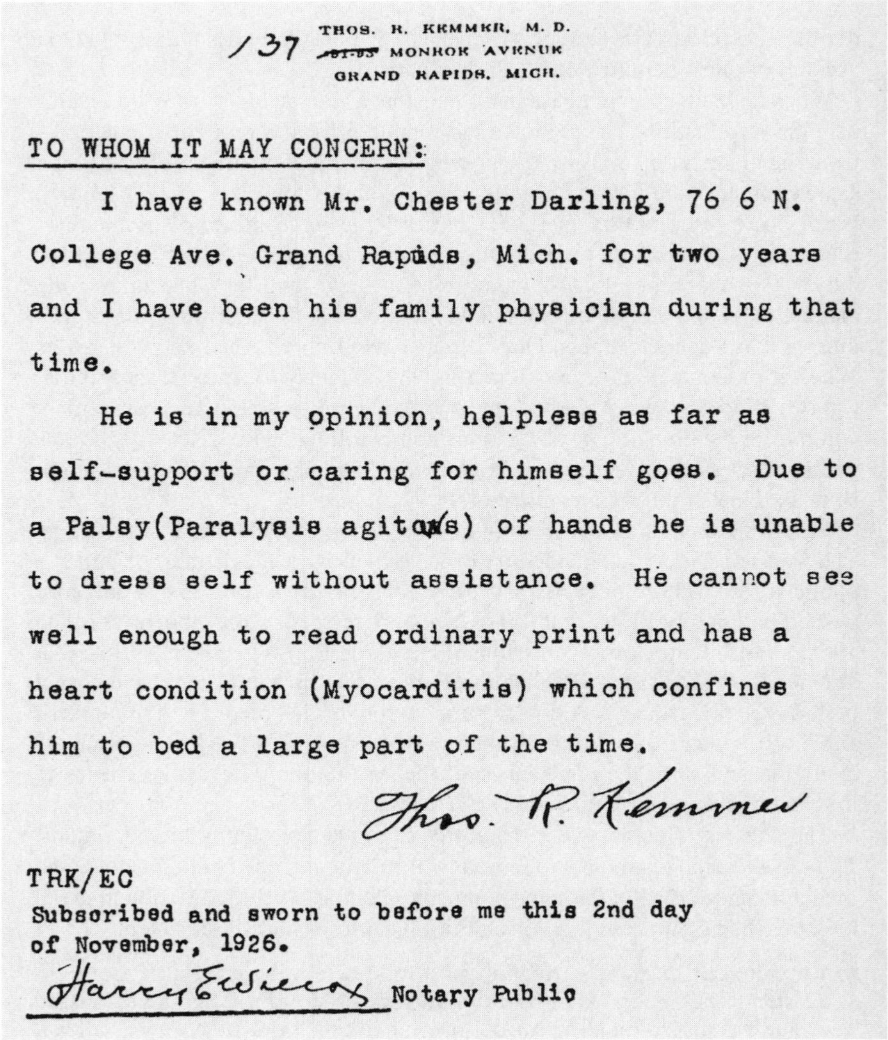

/37

THOS. R. KEMMER, M. D.
~~801-85~~ MONROE AVENUE
GRAND RAPIDS, MICH.

TO WHOM IT MAY CONCERN:

I have known Mr. Chester Darling, 76 6 N. College Ave. Grand Rapids, Mich. for two years and I have been his family physician during that time.

He is in my opinion, helpless as far as self-support or caring for himself goes. Due to a Palsy(Paralysis agitans) of hands he is unable to dress self without assistance. He cannot see well enough to read ordinary print and has a heart condition (Myocarditis) which confines him to bed a large part of the time.

Thos. R. Kemmer

TRK/EC
Subscribed and sworn to before me this 2nd day of November, 1926.

Harry E Wilcox Notary Public

Fig. A.2   Pension affidavit
Note: Pension of Chester Darling, Company I, Tenth Michigan Infantry, certificate 775726.

drilled and when the storm came up he got very wet, and it is reasonable to suppose that this caused the diarrhoea." Not everyone who knew a claimant provided favorable testimony. In 1911 one of the bureau's special examiners wrote to the Pension Commissioner,

I have the honor to report that I have recently been informed by Edgar W. Steele, of Mooers Forks, Clinton Co., N.Y., a Civil War soldier of excellent reputation, that another ex-soldier of the Civil War at that place, named Peter Facto, of Co. G, 153rd N.Y. Vol. Inf., and a pensioner under Ctf. # 374,285 is in bad shape physically because of too much drinking of bad whiskey and has gone to Plattsburg Hospital. In case the disabilities for which he is pensioned would ordinarily be aggravated by excessive liquor drinking his habits in this respect should be considered or investigated before any increase is made in his pension if any increase claim is pending.

The Pension Bureau's subsequent inquiries proved that Peter Facto had been a heavy drinker ten years ago, and the bureau asked examining surgeons to ascertain whether Peter Facto showed any signs of delirium tremens.

The Pension Bureau examined war records to check the veteran's age, whether he had any of the alleged conditions while in the army, and whether his enlistment records indicated that he had any of the conditions prior to entering the service. The Pension Bureau rejected the claim of Israel Cook of Company G of the 196th Ohio Infantry for a pension increase on the grounds that he was age sixty-nine, not seventy (certificate 497,484). The file of Frank Soverain (Company G, 195th Ohio Infantry) contains a letter from the War Department stating that his wartime hospital records showed that he was treated for diarrhea (certificate 885,848). An example of a pension ruling is given in figure A.3. By 1900, of the average of twelve complaints that had been filed, about two were rejected. Complaints might be rejected because there was no evidence of a disability or of an increase in disability or because the disability was judged to be unrelated to the war. Often the grounds for rejection are not known. By 1900 the most common ground for rejection (in 24 percent of cases) was because a veteran's disabilities were judged to be unrelated to the war.

The Pension Bureau required a medical examination by a board of three examining surgeons. The surgeons were to investigate whether a condition existed and how severe it was. The examination report contains the statement of the claimant concerning his disabilities, birthplace, age, height, weight, complexion, hair color, occupation, permanent marks or scars, pulse rate, respiration, and temperature and detailed descriptions of each condition and a rating of each. Since many men claimed various disabilities, and since the Pension Bureau would often instruct the examining surgeons to check if related conditions were present, many conditions are described. In the case of John Meitzler of Company B of the 195th Ohio Infantry, a man who was in particularly bad health in 1899 at age sixty-five, the examining surgeons wrote,

> Fracture of left clavicle. His tongue is coated, his teeth are nearly all gone, applicant is debilitated, had the appearnce [*sic*] of a man in very poor health, he walks with difficulty, cannot walk without the aid of a cane, his hands are tremulous, his muscles are flabby. Six eighteenths for disability.
>
> He suffers from an intense chronic naso-pharyngeal catarrh, the tonsils are atrophied, the posterior and anterior nares are inflamed. $^6/_{30}$.
>
> The membrana of tympani of either ear is depressed and thickened, slight

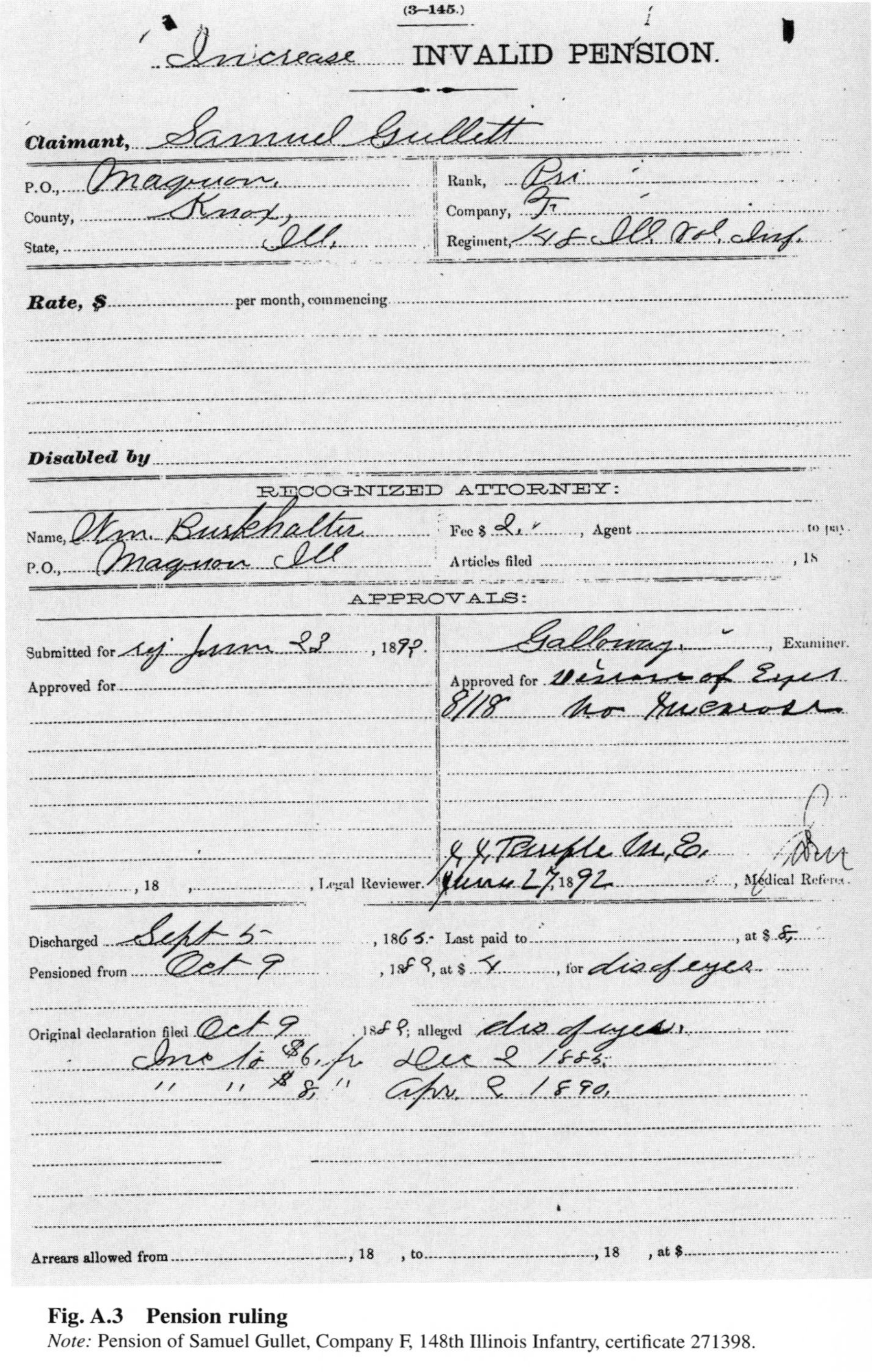

(3—145.)

Increase INVALID PENSION.

Claimant, *Samuel Gullett*

P.O., *Maquon*   Rank, *Pri*

County, *Knox*   Company, *F*

State, *Ill*   Regiment, *48 Ill Vol Inf*

Rate, $ .... per month, commencing ....

Disabled by ....

RECOGNIZED ATTORNEY:

Name, *Wm. Burkhalter*   Fee $ *2.*, Agent .... to pay

P.O., *Maquon Ill*   Articles filed .... , 18

APPROVALS:

Submitted for *rej June 22*, 1879.   *Galloway*, Examiner.

Approved for ....   Approved for *vision of eyes*
                                8/18   no increase

.... , 18 , ..., Legal Reviewer. *J. J. Temple M.E.* *June 27,* 1892 ...., Medical Referee.

Discharged *Sept 5*, 186 *5*. Last paid to ...., at $ *8*.

Pensioned from *Oct 9*, 18 *9*, at $ *4*, for *dis of eyes*

Original declaration filed *Oct 9*, 188 *9*; alleged *dis of eyes*
Inc to $6. p. Dec 2 1885.
"   " # 8. " Apr 2 1890.

Arrears allowed from ...., 18 , to ...., 18 , at $ ....

Fig. A.3   Pension ruling
Note: Pension of Samuel Gullet, Company F, 148th Illinois Infantry, certificate 271398.

deafness of right ear, can not hear ordinary conversation at 6 feet, can hear loud conversation at 3 feet, slight deafness of left ear, can not hear ordinary conversation at 6 feet, can hear loud conversation at 3 feet. $\frac{6}{30}$.

Applicant suffers from rheumatism in both shoulder- and knee-joints and lumbago, the shoulder joints are stiff, crepitant and impaired in motion, he is not able to bring his arms to a level with the shoulder-joints, the knee-joints are stiff, crepitant and impaired in motion about $\frac{1}{2}$, bending backward and forward causes severe pain, no swelling or enlargement of joints at the present time. Ten eighteenths.

The action of his heart is very irregular, the first sound is prolonged into a slight blowing murmur, apex heart beat is $2\frac{1}{2}$ inches below and 1 inch internal to left nipple, cardiac dulness [*sic*] extends from $1\frac{1}{2}$ inch above left nipple to the left border of the sternum, he suffers from intense dysponoea, no signs of oedema or cyanosis, pulse-rate sitting 30, standing 96, after exercise 118. Six eighteenths.

Right eye, arcus senilis is well marked, the lens is cloudy, vision 20/100, left eye, arcus senilis is well marked, lens is cloudy. Vision 20/100. Four eighteenths.

We find callus as evidence of a former fracture of left clavicla at the junction of inner and middle third, motion of left shoulder joint is impaired about $\frac{1}{2}$, he is not able to bring his arm to a level with the shoulder-joint. Four eighteenths.

Applicant suffers from left hemiplegia, the tongue, when protuded, deflects toward the left side, the articulation of words is somewhat indistinct, the naso-labial fold is less marked, than on the right side, the upper lip is less arched and the angle of the mouth droops somewhat on the left side, grip of left hand is very much impaired, in walking he drags the toes on left side, there is some impairment of cutaneous sensibility on left side. This claimant is so disabled from left hemiplegia, rheumatism and disease of heart, as to be incapacitated for performing any manual labor and is entitled to $30 a month. (certificate 24,375)

Another example of a surgeons' certificate is given in figure A.4.

The surgeons' certificates illustrate just how few tools the nineteenth-century doctor had at his disposal. He was limited to what he could see, hear, feel, or smell. Cancers would go undetected. Recurring conditions, such as chronic diarrhea, might also go undetected. Charles Johnson, who was judged to have chronic diarrhea in 1890, 1897, 1900, and 1903, was not found to have chronic diarrhea in 1893 after the examining surgeons wrote, "Diarrhoea probably has existed but no evidence now except an ulcerated condition of the rectum." Average health in the veteran population was therefore probably much worse than the surgeons' certificates would indicate. But it is unlikely that the examining surgeons attributed poor health to individuals on the basis of characteristics other than health. Within the veteran sample the degree of disability can be measured by the rating assigned by the examining surgeons. These ratings are related to health measures such as pulse rate and weight adjusted for height. There is no evidence that the characteristics of the pen-

Attention is invited to the outlines of the human skeleton and figure upon the back of this certificate, and they should be used whenever it is possible to indicate precisely the location of a disease or injury, the entrance and exit of a missile, an amputation, &c.

The absence of a member from a session of a board and the reason therefor, if known, and the name of the absentee, must be indorsed upon each certificate.

Insert character and number of claim.
Increase .... Pension Claim No. _24,375._
[State above whether for original, increase, or restoration.]

Name and rank of claimant.
John H. Meitzler ...., Rank, _Pri_
Company _C_, _49_ Reg't _Ohio Inf._ | _Fostoria. O._ State,
[Post office address of the Board.]

Claimant's post-office address.
Tiffin. O. | _Feb'y 3_ , 189_2_
[Date of examination.]

We hereby certify that in compliance with the requirements of the law we have carefully examined this applicant, who states that he is suffering from the following disability, incurred

Cause of disability.
in the service, viz: _fracture of left clavicle, disability of left side of chest affecting left shoulder & left leg and rheu. & resulting irritable heart & impaired vision_

If a pensioner, fill in the amount; if not, erase the whole line.
and that he receives a pension of _twelve_ dollars per month.

He makes the following statement upon which he bases his claim for _inc. pension._
[Original, increase, restoration, etc.]

Here give the claimant's statement as briefly and as compactly as possible.
Present rating too low. Disabilities for which pensioned have increased. Has more pain in left shoulder & the heart's action is more rapid than when present rating was granted. Has rheu. pain in left shoulder & side. Vision has been bad about ten years. Cant see to read without glasses. Has been a carpenter. Cant do any labor.

Upon examination we find the following objective conditions: Pulse rate, _106. 120. 126._ respiration, _20_ ; temperature, _100°_; height, _5_ feet _10½_ inches; weight, _143_ pounds; age, _58_ years.

Here give a full description of the disabilities, in accordance with Book of Instructions.

_1_ _Left Clavicle – There has been fracture of the left clavicle in three parts which have not united. The injury to the bone was at the middle third & the fragments are displaced & the bone now presents this shape – See fig. The left shoulder droops 1" lower than the right & there is slight stiffness in the movements of the left shoulder joint. We think he should be rated ten eighteenths for injury to left clavicle._

_2_ _Chest: Flat 35" at rest. 36½" Ins. 34" Ex. No dullness on percussion. No rales. Lungs normal in every respect._

_3_ _Left leg. No disability except varicose veins –_

_4_ _Rheu. Complains of rheu. pain in left shoulder & in all parts of the body. As stated above there is slight stiffness in the left shoulder. No enlarged joints, no contracted tendons or stiff muscles except as above stated. Think he has rheu. Four eighteenths._

_5_ _Heart. The apex beat is found by auscultation between the 6th & 7th ribs 4½" from median line of the sternum. Dullness on percussion 1" beyond the normal limits over the cardiac region. Action rapid. Pulse_

He is, in our opinion, entitled to a _ten eighteenths_

Rate for EACH cause of disability.
rating for the disability caused by _fractured left clavicle, four eighteenths_ for that caused by _rheu._ and _twelve eighteenths_ for that caused by _disease of the heart & six eighteenths for varicose veins._

sioner or of his region of residence predict the ratings of the examining surgeon. The ratings are also internally consistent. Conditions worsen with age.

The job of the examining surgeons was purely descriptive. They could not determine whether a condition was related to wartime service. Sometimes the surgeons clearly stated this. In the case of John Dressender, who claimed a war-related pension because he had dislocated his knee when thrown by a blind horse, the surgeons wrote, "It is possible that the cartileges have been injuried [*sic*], but the exact cause of the disability is not clearly apparent to us, yet there is evidently a disability." The decision as to whether a condition was related to wartime service rested with the Pension Bureau and was based on the veteran's war record and on the medical theories of the time. Examining surgeons could, however, determine whether a condition was due to "vicious habits" and hence not pensionable. In the case of Andrew Benell of Company F of the 148th Illinois Infantry, the examining surgeons wrote, "We do not find any objective signs of syphilis and we believe paralysis due to cerebral hemorrhages" (certificate 935,336).

Approximately 88 percent of the men found in the pension records have surgeons' certificates. Those who did not consist of two types: those who applied on the grounds of age alone and those who were so severely disabled during the war that a medical exam was not required to establish ill health. By 1900 men without a surgeons' record were, on average, more likely to be collecting a higher pension, to have been discharged for disability, to have entered the pension rolls earlier, and to be out of the labor force. The sample of men without a surgeons' certificate may, therefore, be slightly healthier than those without, but inferences based only on the sample of men with a surgeons' certificate are still likely to be valid since the findings remain unaffected even when those known to be unhealthy were deleted from the sample.

Once the Pension Bureau was in possession of all the necessary information, it ruled on the pension amount. This ruling generated a form containing the name of the claimant's pension attorney, what the claimant was approved for, any rejections and the reasons for the rejections, and the total dollar amount. Occasionally, information, including pension amount, is missing. These slips appear to have been random lapses on the part of the bureaucracy.

Additional information on the life history of a veteran was generated incidental to the pension process. The claimant's financial status is sometimes described in the claimant's or neighbors' affidavits or in the claimant's cover letter to the Pension Bureau. Therefore, we learn that Horace Stephens of Company I of the Twenty-third Michigan Infantry "had a helpless family of children dependent upon him for support, not one of them able to assist him or support themselves that he is dependent upon Charity partially of Hancock Post GAR and partially upon Clare County" (certificate 384,261). Information of this sort is extremely rare. There was no gain to pleading poverty. Those who did were not statistically more likely to have a higher pension. Further information on financial status comes from the claims of the veteran's widow. To qualify for a pension a widow needed to prove that she was dependent on her husband's earnings for support. Therefore, we learn that George Smith of Company H of the 137th New York Infantry left real estate worth $320, three horses worth $35.00, five cattle worth $59.00, and farm implements and furniture worth $11.00 (certificate 521,276). At other times we learn that the veteran was very well off when he died. Families of impoverished veterans would ask the Pension Bureau to pay for the veterans' burial costs. Faced in 1912 with doctor and burial expenses of $39.00, and left an estate consisting of "nothing but a few heirlooms and some clothing," the family of Samuel Gullet of Company F of the 148th Illinois Infantry made just such a request (certificate 271,398). The poverty of these men had not helped them when they were still alive to gain a larger pension.

Other information can be found in the pension records as well. To facilitate later filings by dependents, the Pension Bureau asked veterans to fill out a form listing their wives' and their children's names and birth dates and their marriage dates. When the pensioner's wife applied for a pension, her affidavit sometimes contained information on her husband's life history since the date of his marriage. Widows often provided copies of their marriage certificates and of their husbands' death certificates, thus providing information on cause of death and on occupation at time of death.

Individuals are linked from the pension records to the manuscript censuses. Searches in the 1900 and 1910 censuses were limited to men found in the pension records because address information is required for linkage and this information is available only from the pension records. Also, restricting the sample to men in the pension records limits searches to men who did not die before the census dates because the pension records provide death dates. Seventy-three percent of men at risk to be linked to the 1900 census were linked. Somewhat fewer (65 percent) were linked to the 1910 census because this census is only partially indexed.

The censuses provide information on occupation, family structure, and home ownership. Although some of the same information appears in the pension records, the census records provide information for every veteran at the same point in time. The census information can also be easily compared with the public-use samples to determine how the Union army veteran sample differs from a random sample of the elderly population. In both 1900 and 1910, the Union army veteran sample resembles a national sample of the northern-born Civil War cohort in terms of marital status, property ownership, and illiteracy. The sample contains a larger proportion of men who are rural, native born, and farmers, but there is enough variation in the sample to control for the effect of these characteristics. Union army veterans were more likely to be retired and were more likely to head their own households, suggesting that being a Union army veteran affected economic decisions.

References

Abbott, Michael, and Orley Ashenfelter. 1976. Labour supply, commodity demand and the allocation of time. *Review of Economic Studies* 43, no. 3: 389–411.

Achenbaum, Andrew W. 1978. *Old age in the new land: The American experience since 1790.* Baltimore: Johns Hopkins University Press.

———. 1983. *Shades of gray: Old age, American values, and federal policies since 1920.* Boston: Little, Brown.

———. 1986. *Social Security: Visions and revisions.* Cambridge: Cambridge University Press.

Anderson, Patricia M., Alan L. Gustman, and Thomas L. Steinmeier. 1997. The trend to earlier retirement among males. Working Paper no. 6028. Cambridge, Mass.: National Bureau of Economic Research.

Atack, Jeremy, and Fred Bateman. 1990. How long was the workday in 1880? *Journal of Economic History* 52, no. 1 (March): 129–60.

Barker, D. J. P. 1992. *Fetal and infant origins of adult disease.* London: British Medical Journal.

———, ed. 1994. *Mothers, babies, and disease in later life.* London: British Medical Journal.

Bartel, Ann, and Paul Taubman. 1979. Health and labor market success: The role of various diseases. *Review of Economics and Statistics* 61, no. 1:1–8.

Bauder, Ward W., and Jon A. Doerflinger. 1967. Work roles among the rural aged. In *Older rural Americans,* ed. E. Grant Youmans. Lexington: University of Kentucky Press.

Becker, Gary. 1965. A theory of the allocation of time. *Economic Journal* 75 (September): 493–517.

Beller, Daniel J., and Helen H. Lawrence. 1992. Trends in private pension plan coverage. In *Trends in pensions,* ed. John A. Turner and Daniel J. Beller. Washington, D.C.: U.S. Government Printing Office.

Belous, Richard S. 1990. Flexible employment: The employer's point of view. In *Bridges to retirement: Older workers in a changing labor market,* ed. Peter Doeringer. Ithaca, N.Y.: ILR Press.

Berkowitz, Edward D. 1991. *America's welfare state: From Roosevelt to Reagan.* Baltimore: Johns Hopkins University Press.

Bernheim, B. Douglas. 1995. Do households appreciate their financial vulnerabilities? An analysis of actions, perceptions, and public policy. In *Tax Policy and Economic Growth,* ed. C. Walker, M. Bloomfield, and M. Thorning. Washington, D.C.: American Council for Capital Formation.

213

Bernheim, B. Douglas, and J. Karl Scholz. 1993. Private savings and public policy. *Tax Policy and the Economy* 7:73–110.

Bevans, George Estradas. 1913. How workingmen spend their spare time. Ph.D. diss., Columbia University.

Bogue, Allan G. 1971. Financing the prairie farmer. In *The re-interpretation of American economic history,* ed. Robert W. Fogel and Stanley L. Engerman. New York: Harper & Row.

Börsch-Supan, Axel, Vassilis Hajivassiliou, Laurence J. Kotlikoff, and John N. Morris. 1992. Health, children, and elderly living arrangements: A multiperiod-multinomial model with unobserved heterogeneity and autocorrelated errors. In *Topics in the economics of aging,* ed. David A. Wise. Chicago: University of Chicago Press.

Boskin, Michael J., and John B. Shoven. 1987. Concepts and measures of earnings replacement during retirement. In *Issues in pension economics,* ed. Zvi Bodie, John B. Shoven, and David A. Wise. Chicago: University of Chicago Press.

Bound, John. 1989. The health and earnings of rejected disability insurance applicants. *American Economic Review* 79, no. 3:482–503.

Bound, John, and Timothy Waidmann. 1992. Disability transfers and the labor force attachment of older men: Evidence from the historical record. *Quarterly Journal of Economics* 107, no. 4:1393–1419.

Bowen, William G., and T. Aldrich Finegan. 1969. *The economics of labor force participation.* Princeton, N.J.: Princeton University Press.

Braden, Donna R. 1988. *Leisure and entertainment in America.* Dearborn, Mich.: Henry Ford Museum and Greenfield Village.

Britten, Rollo H. 1941. Blindness, as recorded in the National Health Survey—amount, causes and relation to certain social factors. *U.S. Public Health Service Public Health Reports* 56, no. 46 (14 November): 2191–2215.

Buck, C., and H. Simpson. 1982. Infant diarrhoea and subsequent mortality from heart disease and cancer. *Journal of Epidemiology and Community Health* 36, no. 1:27–30.

Burkhauser, Richard V., J. S. Butler, Jean M. Mitchell, and Theodore Pincus. 1986. Effects of arthritis on wage earnings. *Journal of Gerontology* 41, no. 2:277–81.

Burkhauser, Richard V., and Joseph F. Quinn. 1983. The effect of pension plans on the pattern of life cycle compensation. In *The measurement of labor cost,* ed. J. E. Triplett. Chicago: University of Chicago Press.

Burtless, Gary. 1986. Social Security, unanticipated benefit increases, and the timing of retirement. *Review of Economic Studies* 53, no. 5:781–805.

Cantor, Richard, and Andrew Yuengert. 1994. The baby boom generation and aggregate savings. *Federal Reserve Bank of New York Quarterly Review* 19, no. 2:76–91.

Carter, Susan B., and Richard Sutch. 1996. Myth of the industrial scrap heap: A revisionist view of turn-of-the-century American retirement. *Journal of Economic History* 56, no. 1:5–38.

Caselli, Graziella, and Riccardo Capocaccia. 1989. Age, period, cohort and early mortality: An analysis of adult mortality in Italy. *Population Studies* 43, no. 1:133–53.

Center for Human Resource Research. 1985. *National Longitudinal Surveys of Labor Market Experience.* ICPSR 7610. Ann Arbor, Mich.: Inter-University Consortium for Political and Social Research.

Coleman, Mary T., and John Pencavel. 1993. Changes in work hours of male employees, 1940–1988. *Industrial and Labor Relations Review* 46, no. 2:262–83.

Collins, Selwyn. 1935. Age incidence of specific causes of illness. *U.S. Public Health Service Public Health Reports* 50, no. 41 (11 October): 1401–27.

Congressional Budget Office. 1993. *Baby boomers in retirement: An early perspective.* Washington, D.C.: September.

Conrad, Christoph. 1990. La naissance de la retraite moderne: L'Allemagne dans une comparison internationale (1850–1960). *Population* 45, no. 3:531–64.

Converse, Philip E., and John P. Robinson. 1980. *Americans' use of time, 1965–1966.* ICPSR 7254. Ann Arbor, Mich.: Inter-University Consortium for Political and Social Research.

Conzen, Kathleen. 1985. Peasant pioneers. In *The countryside in the age of capitalist transformation,* ed. Steven Hahn and Jonathan Prude. Chapel Hill, N.C.: University of North Carolina Press.

Costa, Dora L. 1993. Health, income, and retirement: Evidence from nineteenth century America. Ph.D. diss., University of Chicago.

———. 1995a. Agricultural decline and the secular rise in male retirement rates. *Explorations in Economic History* 32, no. 4:540–52.

———. 1995b. Pensions and retirement: Evidence from Union army veterans. *Quarterly Journal of Economics* 110, no. 2:297–320.

———. 1996. Health and labor force participation of older men, 1900–1991. *Journal of Economic History* 56, no. 1:62–89.

———. In press. Displacing the family: Union army pensions and elderly living arrangements. *Journal of Political Economy.*

Costa, Dora L., and Richard H. Steckel. 1997. Long-term trends in health, welfare, and economic growth in the United States. In *Health and welfare during industrialization,* ed. Richard H. Steckel and Roderick Floud. Chicago: University of Chicago Press.

Cragg, Michael, and Matthew E. Kahn. 1997. Climate consumption and climate pricing from 1940 to 1990. Columbia University. Typescript.

Day, Jennifer Cheeseman. 1993. *Population projections of the United States, by age, sex, race, and Hispanic origin: 1993–2050.* U.S. Bureau of the Census, Current Population Reports, P25–1104. Washington, D.C.: U.S. Government Printing Office.

Deolaliker, A. B. 1988. Nutrition and labor productivity in agriculture: Estimates for rural South India. *Review of Economics and Statistics* 70, no. 2:406–13.

Dewhurst, J. Frederic, et al. 1955. *America's needs and resources.* New York: Twentieth Century Fund.

Diamond, Peter A. 1996. Proposals to restructure Social Security. *Journal of Economic Perspectives* 10, no. 3:67–88.

Diamond, Peter A., and Jerry A. Hausman. 1984. The retirement and unemployment behavior of older men. In *Retirement and economic behavior,* ed. Henry J. Aaron and Gary Burtless. Washington, D.C.: Brookings.

Dorfman, Robert. 1954. The labor force status of persons aged sixty-five and over. *American Economic Review* 44, no. 2:634–44.

Dulles, Foster Rhea. 1965. *A history of recreation: America learns to play.* New York: Appleton-Century-Crofts.

Durand, John D. 1948. *The labor force in the United States, 1890–1960.* New York: Social Science Research Council.

Easterlin, Richard A., Christine M. Schaeffer, and Diane J. Macunovich. 1993. Will the baby boomers be less well off than their parents? Income, wealth, and family circumstances over the life cycle in the United States. *Population and Development Review* 19, no. 3:497–522.

Elo, Irma T., and Samuel H. Preston. 1992. Effects of early-life conditions on adult mortality: A review. *Population Index* 58, no. 2:186–212.

Employees need to save more for retirement: Survey. 1994. *Employee Benefit Plan Review* 12 (June): 47–50.

Epstein, Abraham. 1922. *Facing old age dependency in the United States and old age pensions.* New York: Knopf.

———. 1928. *The challenge of the aged.* New York: Vanguard.

Eveleth, Phyllis B., and James C. Tanner. 1990. *Worldwide variation in human growth.* 2d ed. Cambridge: Cambridge University Press.

Feldstein, Martin. 1996. The missing piece in policy analysis: Social Security reform. *American Economic Review* 86, no. 2:1–14.

Fischer, David Hackett. 1977. *Growing old in America.* New York: Oxford University Press.

Fogel, Robert W. 1986. Nutrition and the decline in mortality since 1700: Some preliminary findings. In *Long-term factors in American economic growth,* ed. Stanley L. Engerman and Robert E. Gallman. Chicago: University of Chicago Press.

———. 1989. *Without consent or contract: The rise and fall of American slavery.* New York: Norton.

———. 1993. New sources and new techniques for the study of secular trends in nutritional status, health, mortality, and the process of aging. *Historical Methods* 26, no. 1:1–44.

———. 1994. Economic growth, population theory, and physiology: The bearing of long-term processes on the making of economic policy. *American Economic Review* 84, no. 3: 369–95.

Foster, Andrew D., and Mark R. Rosenzweig. 1992. Information flows and discrimination in rural areas in developing countries. In *Proceedings of the World Bank Annual Conference on Development Economics.* Washington, D.C.: World Bank.

Friedberg, Leora F. 1996. The effect of government programs on the labor supply of the elderly. Ph.D. diss., Massachusetts Institute of Technology.

Friedberger, Mark W. 1983. The farm family and the inheritance process: Evidence from the Corn Belt. *Agricultural History* 57, no. 1:1–13.

Fries, James F. 1980. Aging, natural death, and the compression of morbidity. *New England Journal of Medicine* 303, no. 3:130–35.

———. 1989. The compression of morbidity: Near or far? *Milbank Quarterly* 67, no. 2:208–32.

Fuchs, Victor R. 1982. Self-employment and labor force participation of older males. *Journal of Human Resources* 17, no. 3:339–57.

Glasson, William H. 1918a. *Federal military pensions in the United States.* New York: Oxford University Press.

———. 1918b. The South's pension and relief provisions for soldiers of the Confederacy. In *Proceedings of the Eighteenth Annual Session of the State Literacy and Historical Association of North Carolina,* Bulletin no. 23. Raleigh, NC: North Carolina Historical Commission.

Gokhale, Jagadeesh, Laurence J. Kotlikoff, and John Sabelhaus. 1996. Understanding the postwar decline in U.S. savings: A cohort analysis. *Brookings Papers on Economic Activity,* no. 1: 315–90.

Goldin, Claudia. 1990. *Understanding the gender gap: An economic history of American women.* Oxford: Oxford University Press.

Goldin, Claudia, and Lawrence F. Katz. 1995. The decline of non-competing groups: Changes in the premium to education, 1890–1940. Working Paper no. 5202. Cambridge, Mass.: National Bureau of Economic Research.

Gordon, Robert. 1990. *The measurement of durable goods prices.* Chicago: University of Chicago Press.

Gorman, W. M. 1981. Some engel curves. In *Essays in the theory and measurement of consumer behavior in honor of Richard Stone,* ed. Angus Deaton. Cambridge: Cambridge University Press.

Graebner, William. 1980. *A history of retirement: The meaning and function of an American institution.* New Haven, Conn.: Yale University Press.

Gratton, Brian. 1986. *Urban elders: Family, work, and welfare among Boston's aged, 1890–1950.* Philadelphia: Temple University Press.

———. 1996. The poverty of impoverishment theory: The economic well-being of the elderly, 1890–1913. *Journal of Economic History* 56, no. 1:39–61.

Gratton, Brian, and Frances M. Rotondo. 1991. Industrialization, the family economy, and the economic status of the American elderly. *Social Science History* 15, no. 3:337–62.

Graves, Phillip E., and Thomas A. Knapp. 1988. Mobility behavior of the elderly. *Journal of Urban Economics* 24, no. 1:1–8.

Haber, Carole, and Brian Gratton. 1994. *Old age and the search for security: An American social history.* Bloomington: Indiana University Press.

Haddad, Lawrence J., and Howarth E. Bouis. 1991. The impact of nutritional status on agricultural productivity: Wage evidence from the Philippines. *Oxford Bulletin of Economics and Statistics* 53, no. 1:45–68.

Haines, Michael R., and Allen C. Goodman. 1992. Housing demand in the late nineteenth century: Evidence from the Commissioner of Labor Survey, 1889/90. *Journal of Urban Economics* 31, no. 1:99–122.

Hausman, Jerry A. 1997. Valuation of new goods under perfect and imperfect competition. In *The economics of new goods,* ed. Timothy F. Bresnahan and Robert J. Gordon. Chicago: University of Chicago Press.

Hausman, J. A., W. K. Newey, and J. L. Powell. 1995. Nonlinear errors in variables: Estimation of some Engel curves. *Journal of Econometrics* 65, no. 1:205–33.

Hausman, Jerry A., and Lynn Paquette. 1987. Involuntary early retirement and consumption. In *Work, health, and income among the elderly* (Studies in Social Economics Series), ed. Gary Burtless. Washington, D.C.: Brookings.

Hausman, Jerry A., and David A. Wise. 1985. Social Security, health status, and retirement. In *Pensions, labor, and individual choice,* ed. David A. Wise. Chicago: University of Chicago Press.

Haveman, Robert H., and Barbara L. Wolfe. 1984a. The decline in male labor force participation. *Journal of Political Economy* 92, no. 3:532–41.

———. 1984b. Disability transfers and early retirement: A causal relationship? *Journal of Public Economics* 24, no. 1:47–66.

Health Care Financing Review: Medicare and Medicaid Statistical Supplement. 1996. Baltimore: U.S. Department of Health and Human Services, Health Care Financing Administration, Office of Research and Demonstrations, Superintendent of Documents.

Henderson, Charles Richmond. 1909. *Industrial insurance in the United States.* Chicago: University of Chicago Press.

Hoffmans, M. D. A. F., D. Kromhout, and C. de Lezenne Coulander. 1989. Body mass index at the age of 18 and its effects on 32-year-mortality from coronary heart disease and cancer. *Journal of Clinical Epidemiology* 42, no. 6:513–20.

Hurd, Michael D. 1994. The economic status of the elderly in the United States. In *Aging in the United States and Japan: Economic trends,* ed. Yukio Noguchi and David A. Wise. Chicago: University of Chicago Press.

Hurd, Michael D., and Michael J. Boskin. 1984. The effect of Social Security on retirement in the early 1970s. *Quarterly Journal of Economics* 99, no. 4:767–90.

Hurd, Michael, and Kathleen McGarry. 1993. The relationship between job characteristics and retirement. Working Paper no. 4558. Cambridge, Mass.: National Bureau of Economic Research.

Hurd, Michael, and John B. Shoven. 1982. Real income and wealth of the elderly. *American Economic Review* 72, no. 2 (May): 314–18.

Ippolito, Richard A. 1986. *Pensions, economics, and public policy.* Homewood, Ill.: Dow Jones–Irwin for the Pension Research Council, Wharton School, University of Pennsylvania.

Jacobs, Klaus, Martin Kohli, and Martin Rein. 1991. The evolution of early exit: A comparative analysis of labor force participation patterns. In *Time for retirement: Comparative studies of early exit from the labor force,* ed. Martin Kohli, Martin Rein,

Anne-Marie Guillemard, and Herman van Gunsteren. Cambridge: Cambridge University Press.

James, John A., Michael G. Palumbo, and Mark Thomas. 1997. Have working-class Americans always been low savers? Savings and accumulation before the advent of social insurance: The United States, 1885–1910. University of Virginia. Typescript.

Johnson, Paul, and Jane Falkingham. 1992. *Ageing and economic welfare.* Newbury Park, Calif.: Sage.

Jondrow, Jim, Frank Brechling, and Alan J. Marcus. 1987. Older workers in the market for part-time employment. In *The problem isn't age: Work and older Americans,* ed. Steven H. Sandell. New York: Praeger.

Kannisto, Väinö. 1994. *Development of oldest-old mortality, 1950–1990: Evidence from 28 developed countries.* Odense: Odense University Press.

Kaplan, Max. 1960. *Leisure in America: A social inquiry.* New York: Wiley.

Kasson, John F. 1978. *Amusing the millions: Coney Island at the turn of the century.* New York: Hill & Wang.

Kennedy, Kim. 1980. *Part-time employment desires of older workers: The findings of a survey of persons aged 55 and over.* Boston: Policy and Evaluation Division, Massachusetts Department of Manpower Development.

Kermack, W. O., A. G. McKendrick, and P. L. McKinlay. 1934a. Death rates in Great Britain and Sweden: Some regularities and their significance. *Lancet* 1 (31 March): 698–703.

———. 1934b. Death rates in Great Britain and Sweden: Expression of specific mortality rates as products of two factors, and some consequences thereof. *Journal of Hygiene* 34 (December): 433–57.

Keyssar, Alexander. 1986. *Out of work: The first century of unemployment in Massachusetts.* New York: Cambridge University Press.

Killingsworth, Mark R. 1983. *Labor supply.* Cambridge: Cambridge University Press.

Kim, John M. 1996. The economics of nutrition, body build and health: Waaler surfaces and physical human capital. Ph.D. diss., University of Chicago.

Kohn, R. R. 1982. Causes of death in very old people. *Journal of the American Medical Association* 247, no. 20:2793–2979.

Kotlikoff, Laurence J. 1988. The relationship of productivity to age. In *Issues in contemporary retirement,* ed. Rita Ricardo-Campbell and Edward P. Lazear. Stanford, Calif.: Hoover Institution Press.

———. 1996. Simulating the privatization of Social Security in general equilibrium. Boston University. Typescript.

Kotlikoff, Laurence J., and David A. Wise. 1987. The incentive effects of private pension plans. In *Issues in pension economics,* ed. Zvi Bodie, John B. Shoven, and David A. Wise. Chicago: University of Chicago Press.

Krueger, Alan B., and Jörn-Steffen Pischke. 1992. The effect of Social Security on labor supply: A cohort analysis of the notch generation. *Journal of Labor Economics* 10, no. 4:412–37.

Kurian, George Thomas. 1994. *Datapedia of the United States, 1790–2000: America year by year.* Lanham, Md.: Bernan.

Lamale, Helen Humes. 1959. *Study of consumer expenditures, incomes and savings: Methodology of the Survey of Consumer Expenditures in 1950.* Philadelphia: University of Pennsylvania.

Lazear, Edward P. 1979. Why is there mandatory retirement? *Journal of Political Economy* 87, no. 6:1261–84.

Lebergott, Stanley. 1964. *Manpower in economic growth: The American record since 1800.* New York: McGraw-Hill.

———. 1993. *Pursuing happiness: American consumers in the twentieth century.* Princeton, N.J.: Princeton University Press.

Lee, Chulhee. 1996. Essays on retirement and wealth accumulation in the United States, 1850–1990. Ph.D. diss., University of Chicago.

Lee, I-Min, JoAnn E. Manson, Charles H. Hennekens, and Ralph S. Paffenbarger. 1993. Body weight and mortality: A 27-year follow-up of middle-aged men. *Journal of the American Medical Association* 270, no. 23:2823–28.

Lee, Lung-Fei. 1979. Identification and estimation in binary choice models with limited (censored) dependent variables. *Econometrica* 47, no. 4:977–96.

Leonard, Jonathan S. 1979. The Social Security disability program and labor force participation. Working Paper no. 392. Cambridge, Mass.: National Bureau of Economic Research.

Leonard, Thomas C. 1995. *News for all: America's coming of age with the press.* Oxford: Oxford University Press.

Leser, C. E. V. 1963. Forms of Engel functions. *Econometrica* 31 (October): 694–703.

Levine, Phillip B., and Olivia S. Mitchell. 1991. Expected changes in the workforce and implications for labor markets. Working Paper no. 3743. *Cambridge, Mass.: National Bureau of Economic Research.*

Levy, Frank, and Richard J. Murnane. 1992. U.S. earnings levels and earnings inequality: A review of recent trends and proposed explanations. *Journal of Economic Literature* 30, no. 3:1333–81.

Lillard, Lee A., and Robert J. Willis. 1997. Motives for intergenerational transfers: Evidence from Malaysia. *Demography* 34 (February): 115–34.

Linder, Staffan Burenstam. 1970. *The harried leisure class.* New York: Columbia University Press.

Lindert, Peter H. 1994. The rise of social spending, 1880–1930. *Explorations in Economic History* 31, no. 1:1–37.

Logue, Larry M. 1992. Union veterans and their government: The effects of public policies on private lives. *Journal of Interdisciplinary History* 22 (Winter): 411–34.

Longino, Charles F., Jr. 1990. Geographical distribution and migration. In *Handbook of aging and the social sciences,* ed. Robert H. Binstock and Linda K. George. San Diego: Academic.

Lubove, Roy. 1968. *The struggle for Social Security, 1900–1935.* Cambridge, Mass.: Harvard University Press.

Lumsdaine, Robin L., James H. Stock, and David A. Wise. 1996. Why are retirement rates so high at age 65? In *Advances in the economics of aging,* ed. David A. Wise. Chicago: University of Chicago Press.

Lumsdaine, Robin L., and David A. Wise. 1994. Aging and labor force participation: A review of trends and explanations. In *Aging in the United States and Japan: Economic trends,* ed. Yukio Noguchi and David A. Wise. Chicago: University of Chicago Press.

Lynd, Robert Staughton, and Helen Merrell Lynd. 1929. *Middletown: A study in contemporary American culture.* New York: Harcourt, Brace.

Makela, M., M. Heliovaara, K. Sievers, O. Impivaara, P. Knekt, and A. Aromaa. 1991. Prevalence, determinants, and consequences of chronic neck pain in Finland. *American Journal of Epidemiology* 134, no. 11:1356–67.

Manton, Kenneth G., Larry S. Corder, and Eric Stallard. 1993. Estimates of change in chronic disability and institutional incidence and prevalence rates in the U.S. elderly population from the 1982, 1984, and 1989 National Long Term Care Survey. *Journal of Gerontology: Social Sciences* 48, no. 4:S153–S166.

Manton, Kenneth G., and James W. Vaupel. 1995. Survival after the age of 80 in the United States, Sweden, France, England, and Japan. *New England Journal of Medicine* 333, no. 18:1232–35.

Marchand, Olivier. 1991. *Deux siecles de travail en France: Population active et structure sociale, duree et productivite de travail.* Paris: INSEE.

Margo, Robert A. 1990. Unemployment in 1910: Some preliminary findings. In *Unemployment and underemployment in historical perspective: Session B-9: Proceedings, Tenth International Economic History Conference, Leuven, August 1990.* Leuven: Leuven University Press.

————. 1993. The labor force participation of older Americans in 1900: Further results. *Explorations in Economic History* 30, no. 4:409–23.

Margo, Robert A., and Richard H. Steckel. 1982. The heights of American slaves: New evidence on slave nutrition and health. *Social Science History* 6, no. 4:516–38.

Massachusetts Commission on Old Age Pensions, Annuities, and Insurance. 1910. *Report of the Commission on Old Age Pensions, January, 1910*. Boston: Wright & Potter.

Matthews, R. C. O., C. H. Feinstein, and J. C. Odling-Smee. 1982. *British economic growth, 1856–1973*. Stanford, Calif.: Stanford University Press.

McGarry, Kathleen, and Robert F. Schoeni. 1995. Transfer behavior in the health and retirement study: Measurement and the redistribution of resources within the family. *Journal of Human Resources* 30:S184–S226.

Merriam, Ida C., and Alfred M. Skolnik. 1968. *Social welfare expenditures under public programs in the United States, 1929–66*. United States Department of Health, Education, and Welfare, Social Security Administration, Office of Research and Statistics, Research Report no. 25. Washington, D.C.: U.S. Government Printing Office.

Meyer, Bruce D. 1990. Unemployment insurance and unemployment spells. *Econometrica* 58, no. 4:757–82.

Michael, Robert T., Victor R. Fuchs, and Sharon R. Scott. 1980. Changes in the propensity to live alone, 1950–1976. *Demography* 17, no. 1:39–56.

Miron, Jeffrey A., and David N. Weil. 1998. The genesis and evolution of Social Security. In *The defining moment: The Great Depression and the American economy in the twentieth century,* ed. Michael D. Bordo, Claudia Goldin, and Eugene N. White. Chicago: University of Chicago Press.

Modell, J., and Tamara K. Hareven. 1973. Urbanization and the malleable household: An examination of boarding and lodging in American families. *Journal of Marriage and the Family* 35 (August): 467–79.

Moen, Jon Roger. 1987. Essays on the labor force and labor force participation rates: The United States from 1860 through 1950. Ph.D. diss., University of Chicago.

————. 1994. Rural nonfarm households: Leaving the farm and the retirement of older men, 1860–1980. *Social Science History* 18, no. 1:55–76.

Moffitt, Robert A. 1987. Life-cycle labor supply and Social Security: A time series analysis. In *Work, health, and income among the elderly,* ed. G. Burtless. Washington, D.C.: Brookings.

More, Louise Bolard. 1907. *Wage-earners' budgets: A study of standards and costs of living in New York City.* New York: H. Holt.

Morse, Dean W., and Susan H. Gray. 1980. *Early retirement—boon or bane? A study of three large corporations.* Montclair, N.J.: Allanheld, Osmun.

Mushkin, S. J., and Alan Berman. 1947. Factors influencing trends in employment of the aged. *Social Security Bulletin* 10 (August): 18–23.

Myers, Robert J. 1993. *Social Security.* 4th ed. Philadelphia: Pension Research Council, Wharton School of the University of Pennsylvania, and University of Pennsylvania Press.

National Center for Health Statistics. 1995. *Vital statistics of the United States, 1991.* Vol. 2, sec. 6, *Life tables.* Washington, D.C.: Public Health Service.

National Conference on Social Welfare. 1985. *The report of the Committee on Economic Security of 1935 and other basic documents relating to the development of the Social Security Act.* Washington, D.C.

Negri, E., R. Pagano, A. Decarli, and C. La Vecchia. 1988. Body weight and the prevalence of chronic neck pain. *Journal of Epidemiology and Community Health* 42, no. 1:24–29.

New York State Commission on Old Age Security. 1930. *Old age security: Report of the New York State Commission: Transmitted to the Legislature, February 17, 1930.* Albany, N.Y.: J. B. Lyon.

New York State Factory Investigating Commission. 1915. *Fourth report of the Factory Investigating Commission, 1915: Transmitted to the Legislature, February 15, 1915.* Vol. 4. S. Doc. 43. Albany, N.Y.: J. B. Lyon.

Ohio Health and Old Age Insurance Commission. 1919. *Health, health insurance, old age pensions: Summary of findings, recommendations and dissenting opinions.* Columbus, Ohio: F. J. Heer.

Owen, John D. 1969. *The price of leisure: An economic analysis of the demand for leisure time.* Rotterdam: Rotterdam University Press.

Palmore, Erdman. 1964. Retirement patterns among aged men: Findings of the 1963 Survey of the Aged. *Social Security Bulletin* 27, no. 8:3–10.

Parsons, Donald O. 1980. The decline in male labor force participation. *Journal of Political Economy* 88, no. 1:117–34.

———. 1991. Male retirement behavior in the United States, 1930–1950. *Journal of Economic History* 51, no. 3:657–74.

Parsons, Kenneth H., and Eliot O. Waples. 1945. Keeping the farm in the family: A study of ownership processes in a low tenancy area of eastern Wisconsin. *Wisconsin Agricultural Experiment Station Research Bulletin,* no. 157.

Pederson, Harold. 1950. A cultural evaluation of the family farm concept. *Land Economics* 26, no. 1:52–64.

Peiss, Kathy. 1986. *Cheap amusements: Working women and leisure in turn-of-the-century New York.* Philadelphia: Temple University Press.

Pennsylvania Old Age Pension Commission. 1919. *Report of the Pennsylvania Commission on Old Age Pensions.* Harrisburg, Pa.: J. L. L. Kuhn.

Pincus, Theodore, Jean M. Mitchell, and Richard V. Burkhauser. 1989. Substantial work disability and earnings losses in individuals less than age 65 with osteoarthritis: Comparisons with rheumatoid arthritis. *Journal of Clinical Epidemiology* 42, no. 5:449–57.

Poterba, James M. 1996. Demographic structure and the political economy of public education. Working Paper no. 5677. Cambridge, Mass.: National Bureau of Economic Research.

Poterba, James M., Steven F. Venti, and David A. Wise. 1994. Targeted savings and the net worth of elderly Americans. *American Economic Review* 84, no. 2:180–85.

Pratt, Henry J. 1976. *The gray lobby.* Chicago: University of Chicago Press.

Preston, Samuel H. 1993. Demographic change in the United States, 1970–2050. In *Forecasting the health of elderly populations,* ed. Kenneth G. Manton, Burton H. Singer, and Richard M. Suzman. New York: Springer.

Preston, Samuel H., and Michael R. Haines. 1991. *Fatal years: Child mortality in late nineteenth century America.* Princeton, N.J.: Princeton University Press.

Preston, Samuel H., and Etienne van de Walle. 1978. Urban French mortality in the nineteenth century. *Population Studies* 32, no. 2:275–97.

Putnam, Jackson. 1970. *Old age politics in California: From Richardson to Reagan.* Stanford, Calif.: Stanford University Press.

Quadagno, Jill S. 1988. *The transformation of old age security: Class and politics in the American welfare state.* Chicago: University of Chicago Press.

Quinn, Joseph F., and Richard V. Burkhauser. 1990. Work and retirement. In *Handbook of aging and the social sciences,* ed. Robert H. Binstock and Linda K. George. San Diego, Calif.: Academic.

Ransom, Roger L., and Richard Sutch. 1986. The labor of older Americans: Retirement of men on and off the job, 1870–1937. *Journal of Economic History* 46, no. 1:1–30.

Reno, Virginia P., and Susan Grad. 1985. Economic security, 1935–85. *Social Security Bulletin* 48, no. 12:5–20.

Riley, James C. 1989. *Sickness, recovery, and death: A history and forecast of ill health.* Houndmills: Macmillan.

Rivers, Douglas, and Quang H. Vuong. 1988. Limited information estimators and exogeneity tests for simultaneous probit models. *Journal of Econometrics* 39, no. 3:347–66.

Robinson, John. 1993. *Americans' use of time, 1985.* ICPSR 9875. Ann Arbor, Mich.: Inter-University Consortium for Political and Social Research.

Roman Diaz, M. 1992. Prevalencia de obesidad y condiciones associadas en un centro de medicina de familia. *Boletin-Asociacion Medica de Puerto Rico* 84, no. 11:302–4.

Rosen, Sherwin. 1981. The economics of superstars. *American Economic Review* 71, no. 5:845–58.

Rosenzweig, Roy. 1983. *Eight hours for what we will: Workers and leisure in an industrial city, 1870–1920.* Cambridge: Cambridge University Press.

Rubinow, Isaac. 1916. *Social insurance: With special reference to American conditions.* New York: H. Holt.

Rubinow, Isaac. 1934. *The quest for security.* New York: H. Holt.

Ruggles, Steven. 1987. *Prolonged connections: The rise of the extended family in nineteenth century England and America.* Madison: University of Wisconsin Press.

Ruggles, Steven, and Matthew Sobek. 1995. *Integrated public use microdata series, IPUMS-95, Version 1.0.* Social History Research Laboratory, Department of History, University of Minnesota, Minneapolis.

Ruhm, Christopher J. 1990. Career jobs, bridge employment, and retirement. In *Bridges to retirement: Older workers in a changing labor market,* ed. Peter Doeringer. Ithaca, N.Y.: ILR Press.

Rust, John. 1990. Behavior of male workers at the end of the life cycle: An empirical analysis of states and controls. In *Issues in the economics of aging,* ed. David A. Wise. Chicago: University of Chicago Press.

Salamon, Sonya. 1992. *Prairie patrimony: Family, farming, and community in the Midwest.* Chapel Hill: University of North Carolina Press.

Sauer, Howard M., Ward W. Bauder, and Jeanne C. Biggar. 1964. Retirement plans, concepts and attitudes of farm operators in three eastern South Dakota counties. *U.S. Department of Agriculture Bulletin,* no. 515.

Schor, Juliet B. 1991. *The overworked American: The unexpected decline of leisure.* New York: Basic.

Schorr, Alvin L. 1960. *Filial responsibility in the modern American family: An evaluation of current practice of filial responsibility in the United States and the relationship to it of Social Security programs.* Washington, D.C.: U.S. Department of Health, Education, and Welfare, Social Security Administration, Division of Program Research.

Schultz, T. W. 1945. *Agriculture in an unstable economy.* New York: McGraw-Hill.

Schwartz, Saul, Sheldon Danziger, and Eugene Smolensky. 1984. The choice of living arrangements by the elderly. In *Retirement and economic behavior,* ed. Henry J. Aaron and Gary Burtless. Washington, D.C.: Brookings.

Scitovsky, Tibor. 1976. *The joyless economy: An inquiry into human satisfaction and consumer dissatisfaction.* New York: Oxford University Press.

Shearon, Marjorie. 1938. Economic status of the aged. *Social Security Bulletin* 1, no. 3 (March): 5–16.

Sherman, Sally R. 1974. Labor force status of nonmarried women on the threshold of retirement. *Social Security Bulletin* 37, no. 9 (September): 3–15.

———. 1985. Reported reasons retired workers left their last job: Findings from the New Beneficiary Survey. *Social Security Bulletin* 48, no. 3:22–25.

———. 1989. *Fast facts and figures about Social Security.* U.S. Department of Health and Human Services, Social Security Administration, Office of Policy, Office of Research Statistics. Washington, D.C.: U.S. Government Printing Office.

Skocpol, Theda. 1992. *Protecting soldiers and mothers: The political origins of social policy in the United States.* Cambridge, Mass.: Harvard University Press, Belknap Press.

Slichter, Sumner H. 1919. *The turnover of factory labor.* New York: D. Appleton.

Smigel, Erwin Orson. 1963. *Work and leisure: A contemporary social problem.* New Haven, Conn.: College and University Press.

Smith, Daniel Scott. 1979. Life course, norms, and the family system of older Americans in 1900. *Journal of Family History* 4, no. 3:285–98.

Social Security Bulletin: Annual Statistical Supplement. 1994. Washington, D.C.: U.S. Government Printing Office.

Starr, Paul. 1982. *The social transformation of American medicine: The rise of a sovereign profession and the making of a vast industry.* New York: Basic.

Stecker, M. L. 1955. Why beneficiaries retire: Who among them return to work? *Social Security Bulletin* 18, no. 5:3–12, 35–36.

Steiner, J. F. 1933. Recreation and leisure time activities. In *Recent social trends in the United States,* by the U.S. President's Research Committee on Social Trends. New York: McGraw-Hill.

Stock, James H., and David A. Wise. 1990. The pension inducement to retire: An option value analysis. In *Issues in the economics of aging,* ed. David A. Wise. Chicago: University of Chicago Press.

Strauss, John, and Duncan Thomas. 1996. Human resources: Empirical modeling of household and family decisions. In *Handbook of development economics,* vol. 3A, ed. Jere R. Berhman and T. N. Srinivasan. Amsterdam: Elsevier.

Sum, Andrew M., and W. Neal Fogg. 1990. Profile of the labor market for older workers. In *Bridges to retirement: Older workers in a changing labor market,* ed. Peter Doeringer. Ithaca, N.Y.: ILR Press.

Taietz, P., G. F. Streib, and M. L. Barron. 1956. Adjustment to retirement in rural New York State. *Cornell Experiment Station Bulletin,* no. 919.

Tverdal, A. 1988. Height, weight, and incidence of tuberculosis. *Bulletin of the International Union against Tuberculosis and Lung Disease* 63, no. 2:16–18.

U.S. Board of Trustees of the Federal Hospital Insurance Trust Fund. 1996. *Annual report of the Board of Trustees of the Federal Hospital Insurance Trust Fund.* Washington, D.C.: U.S. Government Printing Office.

U.S. Board of Trustees of the Federal Old-Age and Survivors Insurance and Disability Insurance Trust Funds. 1996. *Annual report of the Board of Trustees of the Federal Old-Age and Survivors Insurance and Disability Insurance Trust Funds.* Washington, D.C.: U.S. Government Printing Office.

U.S. Bureau of the Census. 1975. *Historical statistics of the United States, colonial times to 1970.* Washington, D.C.: U.S. Government Printing Office.

———. 1991. *Statistical abstract of the United States: 1991.* Washington, D.C.: U.S. Government Printing Office.

———. 1993. *Statistical abstract of the United States: 1993.* Washington, D.C.: U.S. Government Printing Office.

———. Annual. *Government finances in.* . . . Washington, D.C.: U.S. Government Printing Office.

U.S. Bureau of Economic Analysis. 1986. *Fixed reproducible tangible wealth in the United States.* Washington, D.C.: U.S. Government Printing Office.

U.S. Bureau of Labor Statistics. 1956. *Study of Consumer Expenditures, Incomes, and Savings: Statistical tables: Urban U.S.—1950.* Philadelphia: University of Pennsylvania.

U.S. Bureau of Pensions. Annual. *Report of the commissioner of pensions.* Washington, D.C.: U.S. Government Printing Office.

U.S. Committee on Economic Security. 1935. *Report to the president of the Committee on Economic Security.* Washington, D.C.: U.S. Government Printing Office.

U.S. Department of Commerce. Bureau of Economic Analysis. National Income and Wealth Division. 1995. Unpublished national income and product accounts estimates: 1959–93. Washington, D.C. [Computer file.]

U.S. Department of Commerce. Office of Business Economics. 1966. *The national income and product accounts of the United States: Statistical tables.* Washington, D.C.: U.S. Government Printing Office.

U.S. Department of Labor. 1959. *How American buying habits change.* Washington, D.C.: U.S. Government Printing Office.

———. 1986. *Cost of living of industrial workers in the United States and Europe, 1888–1890.* ICPSR 7711. Ann Arbor, Mich.: Inter-University Consortium for Political and Social Research.

———. 1992. *Consumer expenditures in 1991.* Bureau of Labor Statistics Report no. 835. Washington, D.C.: U.S. Government Printing Office.

U.S. Department of Labor. Bureau of Labor Statistics. 1986. *Cost of living in the United States, 1917–1919.* ICPSR 8299. Ann Arbor, Mich.: Inter-University Consortium for Political and Social Research.

———. 1987. *Survey of Consumer Expenditures, 1972–1973.* ICPSR 9034. Ann Arbor, Mich.: Inter-University Consortium for Political and Social Research.

———. 1991. Consumer Expenditure Survey, interview survey public use tape, 1991. Washington, D.C.

U.S. Department of Labor. Bureau of Labor Statistics. Works Progress Administration. 1941. *Family expenditures in selected cities, 1935–35. Vol. 7, Recreation, reading, formal education, tobacco, contributions, and personal taxes.* Bulletin no. 648. Washington, D.C.: U.S. Government Printing Office.

U.S. Public Health Service. 1938. *The National Health Survey, 1935–36: Accidents as a cause of disability.* Preliminary Reports of the National Health Survey, Sickness and Medical Series, Bulletin no. 3. Washington, D.C.

University of Michigan Survey Research Center. 1962. *Income and welfare in the United states: A study [by] James N. Morgan [and others] with the assistance of Norma Meyers and Barbara Baldwin.* New York: McGraw-Hill.

Vaupel, James W. 1991. The impact of population aging on health and health care costs: Uncertainties and new evidence about life expectancy. Center for Health and Social Policy, Odense University. Typescript.

Veblen, Thorstein. 1994. *The theory of the leisure class* (1899). Reprint. New York: Dover.

Verbrugge, L. 1984. Longer life but worsening health? Trends in health and mortality of middle-aged and older persons. *Milbank Memorial Fund Quarterly* 62:475–519.

Vinovskis, Maris A. 1990. Have social historians lost the Civil War? Some preliminary demographic speculations. In *Toward a social history of the American Civil War,* ed. Maris A. Vinovskis. Cambridge: Cambridge University Press.

Waaler, H. T. 1984. Height, weight, and mortality: The Norwegian experience. *Acta Medica Scandinavica* 679:S1–S56.

Weaver, Carolyn. 1982. *The crisis in Social Security: Economic and political origins.* Durham, N.C.: Duke University Press.

Wentworth, Edna C. 1945. Why beneficiaries retire. *Social Security Bulletin* 8, no. 1:16–20.

————. 1950. Income of old-age and survivors insurance beneficiaries, 1941 and 1949. *Social Security Bulletin* 13, no. 5 (May): 3–14.

Whaples, Robert. 1990. The shortening of America's work week: An economic and historical analysis of its context, causes, and consequences. Ph.D. diss., University of Pennsylvania.

Wiatrowski, William J. 1994. Employee benefits for union and nonunion workers. *Monthly Labor Review* 117, no. 2:33–44.

Wilensky, Harold L. 1963. The impact of economic growth on free time. In *Work and leisure: A contemporary social problem,* ed. E. O. Smigel. New Haven, Conn.: College and University Press.

Williams, Faith M. 1941. *Money disbursements of wage earners and clerical workers, 1934–1936: Summary volume.* Bureau of Labor Statistics Bulletin no. 638. Washington, D.C.: U.S. Government Printing Office.

Wolf, Douglas A. 1990. Household patterns of older women: Some international comparisons. *Research on Aging* 12, no. 4:463–86.

————. 1994. The elderly and their kin: Patterns of availability and access. In *Demography of aging,* ed. Linda G. Martin and Samuel H. Preston. Washington, D.C.: National Academy Press.

Working, H. 1943. Statistical laws of family expenditure. *Journal of the American Statistical Association* 38, no. 221:43–56.

The WPA Life Histories Collection. American Memory. Library of Congress. Washington, D.C. http://lcweb2.loc.gov/ammem/amhome.html.

Name Index

Subject Index

Age: Age Discrimination Act (1978), 24; as determinant of Union army pension, 37; population distribution and projected distribution by, 188–92; retirement age under Social Security, 10–14. *See also* Elderly; Old age

Aging of population: baby-boom generation, 189–93; perception in early twentieth century of, 11; as public issue, 4; in United States, 188–93

Agriculture: decline in importance, 99; labor force decrease, 99–100. *See also* Farmers

Altruism model: in determining living arrangement of Union army veteran, 117–21

Arrears Act (1879), 161–62

Baby-boom generation: described, 189–93; saving of, 195

Baby bust, 189

Bargaining model: in predicting living arrangement of Union army veterans, 116–21

Beneficiaries: under Union army pension program, 161

Birthrate: baby-boom increase (1946–64), 189

Body Mass Index (BMI): correlation with ill health, 68–69; defined, 67; interpreting, 78–81; of men born in nineteenth century, 71; modern American men (ages fifty to sixty-four), 67–78; relation to labor force participation, 71–78; Union army veterans, 71

Chronic conditions: Union army and U.S. World War II veterans, 61–62; U.S. population (1928–31, 1992), 63–65, 83n2

Chronic disease: declining rates among elderly, 194; elderly in United States (1900–1950), 81; people born in nineteenth century, 81; Union army veterans, 81; U.S. population (1928–31, 1992), 63–65, 83n2

Committee on Economic Security, 4, 11

Consolidation Act (1873), 199

Data sources: Union army chronic health conditions, 61; Union army veterans' pensions, 32–33, 197–212

Disability: under Consolidation Act (1873), 199; as determinant of Union army pension, 33, 36–37, 40–42, 44–45; pension rates for specific Union army–incurred, 199; under Union army pension program, 161, 198–99; of Union veteran under 1890 pension system act, 161, 200. *See also* Health

1890 act pension system: Union army veterans' benefits under, 36–37, 161, 200–201

Elderly: chronic diseases of (1900–1950), 81; government promotion of labor force participation, 194; during Great Depression, 168; improved health of, 106; income through Social Security system, 18; increase in population of, 188–93; as inter-

231

Author photo by L. Barry Hetherington

Dora L. Costa is the Ford Career Development Associate Professor of Economics at the Massachusetts Institute of Technology and a faculty research fellow of the National Bureau of Economic Research.

....

National Bureau of Economic Research Series on Long-term Factors in Economic Development

For information on books of related interest or for a catalog of new publications, please write:

> Marketing Department
> The University of Chicago Press
> 5801 South Ellis Avenue
> Chicago, Illinois 60637
> U.S.A.
> www.press.uchicago.edu

Printed in U.S.A.

Jacket illustrations: *top*, photograph by Ted Lacey; *bottom*, photographer's parents, by William Henry Jackson, ca. 1890, courtesy of the Library of Congress, Prints and Photographs Division, Detroit Publishing Company Photograph Collection, reproduction number LC-D419-166 DLC.